GETTING TO THE RULE OF LAW

NOMOS

L

NOMOS

Harvard University Press
I   *Authority* 1958, reissued in 1982 by Greenwood Press

The Liberal Arts Press
II   *Community* 1959
III   *Responsibility* 1960

Atherton Press
IV   *Liberty* 1962
V   *The Public Interest* 1962
VI   *Justice* 1963, reissued in 1974
VII   *Rational Decision* 1964
VIII   *Revolution* 1966
IX   *Equality* 1967
X   *Representation* 1968
XI   *Voluntary Associations* 1969
XII   *Political and Legal Obligation* 1970
XIII   *Privacy* 1971

Aldine-Atherton Press
XIV   *Coercion* 1972

Lieber-Atherton Press
XV   *The Limits of Law* 1974
XVI   *Participation in Politics* 1975

New York University Press
XVII   *Human Nature in Politics* 1977
XVIII   *Due Process* 1977
XIX   *Anarchism* 1978
XX   *Constitutionalism* 1979
XXI   *Compromise in Ethics, Law, and Politics* 1979
XXII   *Property* 1980
XXIII   *Human Rights* 1981
XXIV   *Ethics, Economics, and the Law* 1982
XXVI   *Marxism* 1983
XXVII   *Criminal Justice* 1985

NOMOS L

Yearbook of the American Society for Political and Legal Philosophy

GETTING TO THE RULE OF LAW

Edited by

James E. Fleming

NEW YORK UNIVERSITY PRESS • *New York and London*

NEW YORK UNIVERSITY PRESS
New York and London
www.nyupress.org

References to Internet websites (URLs) were accurate at the time of writing.
Neither the author nor New York University Press is responsible for URLs
that may have expired or changed since the manuscript was prepared.

Library of Congress Cataloging-in-Publication Data
Getting to the rule of law / edited by James E. Fleming.
p.   cm. — (Nomos)
Includes bibliographical references and index.
ISBN 978-0-8147-2843-7 (cl : alk. paper)
 ISBN 978-0-8147-2844-4 (e-book : alk. paper)
1. Rule of law—Philosophy. 2. Procedure (Law)—Philosophy. 3. Due
process of law. 4. Intervention (International law) 5. Law—Political
aspects.   I. Fleming, James E.
K3171.G48 2011
340'.11—dc22   2011012528

New York University Press books are printed on acid-free paper,
and their binding materials are chosen for strength and durability.
We strive to use environmentally responsible suppliers and materials
to the greatest extent possible in publishing our books.

Manufactured in the United States of America

10 9 8 7 6 5 4 3 2 1

16087611

CONTENTS

PREFACE

This volume of NOMOS—the fiftieth in the series—emerged from papers and commentaries given at the annual meeting of the American Society for Political and Legal Philosophy (ASPLP) in New Orleans on January 6, 2010, held in conjunction with the annual meeting of the Association of American Law Schools. Our topic, "Getting to the Rule of Law," was selected by the Society's membership.

The conference consisted of three panels: (1) "Getting to the Concept of the Rule of Law"; (2) "Maintaining or Restoring the Rule of Law after September 11, 2001"; and (3) "Building the Rule of Law after Military Interventions." This volume includes revised versions of the principal papers delivered at that conference by Jeremy Waldron, Benjamin A. Kleinerman, and Jane E. Stromseth. It also includes essays that developed out of the original commentaries on those papers by Curtis A. Bradley, Corey Brettschneider, Tom Ginsburg, Larry May, Lionel K. McPherson, and Robin West. The volume includes three additional essays (one related to each panel), by Martin Krygier, Sotirios A. Barber and me, and Richard W. Miller. I am grateful to all of these authors for the thoughtfulness of their contributions and for their expeditiousness in bringing this volume to press.

Thanks are also due to the editors and production team at New York University Press, particularly to Ilene Kalish, Despina Papazoglou Gimbel, and Aiden Amos. On my own behalf and on behalf of the Society, I wish to express deep gratitude for the Press's ongoing support for the series and the tradition of interdisciplinary scholarship that it represents.

Finally, thanks to Natalie Logan and Eric Lee, my excellent research assistants at Boston University, and Danielle Amber Papa, my highly capable and extraordinarily efficient and resourceful secretary, for providing critical assistance during the editorial and production phases of the volume.

JAMES E. FLEMING
Boston, August 2010

CONTRIBUTORS

SOTIRIOS A. BARBER
Professor of Political Science, University of Notre Dame

CURTIS A. BRADLEY
Richard A. Horvitz Professor of Law and Professor of Public Policy Studies, Duke Law School

COREY BRETTSCHNEIDER
Associate Professor of Political Science, Brown University

JAMES E. FLEMING
Professor of Law, The Honorable Frank R. Kenison Distinguished Scholar in Law, and Associate Dean for Research, Boston University School of Law

TOM GINSBURG
Professor of Law, University of Chicago Law School

BENJAMIN A. KLEINERMAN
Assistant Professor of Constitutional Democracy, Michigan State University

MARTIN KRYGIER
Gordon Samuels Professor of Law and Social Theory and Co-Director, Centre for Interdisciplinary Studies of Law, University of New South Wales

LARRY MAY
W. Alton Jones Professor of Philosophy and Professor of Law, Vanderbilt University; Professorial Fellow, Centre for Applied Philosophy and Public Ethics, Charles Sturt and Australian National Universities

LIONEL K. MCPHERSON
Associate Professor of Philosophy, Tufts University

RICHARD W. MILLER
Professor of Philosophy, Cornell University

JANE E. STROMSETH
Professor of Law, Georgetown University Law Center

JEREMY WALDRON
University Professor, New York University, and Chichele Professor of Social and Political Theory, University of Oxford

ROBIN WEST
Frederick J. Haas Professor of Law and Philosophy, Georgetown University Law Center

PART I

GETTING TO THE CONCEPT OF THE RULE OF LAW

1

THE RULE OF LAW AND THE
IMPORTANCE OF PROCEDURE

JEREMY WALDRON

1. GETTING TO THE RULE OF LAW

The Rule of Law is one star in a constellation of ideals that domi-
nate our political morality: the others are democracy, human
rights, and economic freedom. We want societies to be democratic;
we want them to respect human rights; we want them to organize
their economies around free markets and private property to the
extent that this can be done without seriously compromising social
justice; and we want them to be governed in accordance with the
Rule of Law. We want the Rule of Law for new societies—for newly
emerging democracies, for example—and old societies alike, for
national political communities and regional and international governance, and we want it to extend into all aspects of governments'
dealings with those subject to them—not just in day-to-day criminal law, or commercial law, or administrative law but also in law administered at the margins, in antiterrorism law and in the exercise
of power over those who are marginalized, those who can safely be
dismissed as outsiders, and those we are tempted just to destroy as
(in John Locke's words) "wild Savage Beasts, with whom men can
have no Society or Security."[1] Getting to the Rule of Law does not
just mean paying lip service to the ideal in the ordinary security
of a prosperous modern democracy; it means extending the Rule
of Law into societies that are not necessarily familiar with it; and

3

in those societies that are familiar with it, it means extending the Rule of Law into these darker corners of governance, as well.

When I pay attention to the calls that are made for the Rule of Law around the world, I am struck by the fact that the features that people call attention to are not necessarily the features that legal philosophers have emphasized in their academic conceptions. Legal philosophers tend to emphasize formal elements of the Rule of Law, such as rule by general norms rather than particular decrees; rule by laws laid down in advance rather than by retrospective enactments; rule under a system of norms that has sufficient stability (is sufficiently resistant to change) so as to furnish for those subject to the norms a calculable basis for running their lives or their businesses; rules by norms that are made public, not hidden away in the closets of bureaucracy; rule by clear and determinate legal norms, norms whose meaning is not so obscure or contestable as to leave those who are subject to them at the mercy of official discretion. These are formal aspects of the Rule of Law, because they concern the form of the norms that are applied to our conduct: generality, prospectivity, stability, publicity, clarity, and so on. But we don't value them just for formalistic reasons. In F. A. Hayek's theory of the Rule of Law, we value these features for the contribution they make to predictability, which Hayek thinks is indispensable for liberty.[2] In Lon Fuller's theory, we value them also for the way they respect human dignity: "To judge [people's] actions by unpublished or retrospective laws . . . is to convey to [them] your indifference to [their] powers of self-determination."[3] (I shall say more about this in section 5.) In Fuller's theory, too, there is a hunch that if we respect dignity in these formal ways, we will find ourselves more inhibited against more substantive assaults on dignity and justice. That has proved very controversial, but it is further evidence of the point that the interests of those who adopt a formal conception of the Rule of Law are not just formalistic.

I have said that this formal conception is not what ordinary people have in the forefront of their minds when they clamor for the extension of the Rule of Law into settings or modes of governance where it has not been present before. Saying that is usually a prelude to a call for a more *substantive* vision of the Rule of Law. I am not as hostile as I once was to a substantive conception of this ideal.[4] I believe that there is a natural overlap between substantive and formal elements, not least because—as we have just seen—the formal elements are usually argued for on substantive grounds of dignity and liberty. I still believe that it is important not to let our enthusiasm for a substantive conception—whereby the Rule of Law is treated as an ideal that calls directly for an end to human rights abuses or as an ideal that calls directly for free markets and respect for private property rights—obscure the independent importance that the formal elements I have mentioned would have even if these other considerations were not so directly at stake.[5] But it is probably a mistake to exaggerate the distinctiveness of our several political ideals or the clarity of the boundaries between them.

Still, it is not a substantive conception that I have in mind when I say that ordinary people are urging something other than the formal elements that I have mentioned when they clamor for the Rule of Law. Instead, I have in mind elements of legal procedure and the institutions, like courts, that embody them. When people clamored recently in Pakistan for a restoration of the Rule of Law, their concern was for the independence of the judiciary and the attempt by an unelected administration to fire a whole slew of judges.[6] When people clamor for the Rule of Law in China, they are demanding impartial tribunals that can adjudicate their claims. And when advocates for the detainees in the American base at Guantanamo Bay clamor for the Rule of Law, they are clamoring for hearings on their clients' comprehensive loss of liberty in which they or their clients would have an opportunity to put their case, confront and examine the evidence against them, such as it is, and make arguments for their freedom, in accordance with what we would say were normal legal procedures.[7]

2. LAUNDRY LISTS

What sort of procedural principles do I have in mind? Theorists of the Rule of Law are fond of producing laundry lists of demands. The best known are the eight formal principles of Lon Fuller's "inner morality of law":[8]

1. Generality;
2. Publicity;

3. Prospectivity;
4. Intelligibility;
5. Consistency;
6. Practicability;
7. Stability; and
8. Congruence.

I think we need to match this list with a list of procedural characteristics that are equally indispensable. As a preliminary sketch,[9]
we might say that no one should have any penalty, stigma, or serious loss imposed upon him by government except as the upshot of
procedures that involve:

A. A hearing by an impartial tribunal that is required to act
   on the basis of evidence and argument presented formally
   before it in relation to legal norms that govern the imposition of penalty, stigma, loss, and so forth;
B. A legally trained judicial officer, whose independence of
   other agencies of government is ensured;
C. A right to representation by counsel and to the time and
   opportunity required to prepare a case;
D. A right to be present at all critical stages of the proceeding;
E. A right to confront witnesses against the detainee;
F. A right to an assurance that the evidence presented by the
   government has been gathered in a properly supervised
   way;
G. A right to present evidence in one's own behalf;
H. A right to make legal argument about the bearing of the
   evidence and about the bearing of the various legal norms
   relevant to the case;
I. A right to hear reasons from the tribunal when it reaches
   its decision that are responsive to the evidence and arguments presented before it; and
J. Some right of appeal to a higher tribunal of a similar character.

These requirements are often associated with terms such as "natural justice,"[10] and as such they are important parts of the Rule of
Law. I believe we radically sell short the idea of the Rule of Law if

we understand it to comprise a list like Fuller's list (1)–(8) without also including something like the procedural list (A)–(J) that I have just set out. We say the Rule of Law is violated when due attention is not paid to these procedural matters or when the institutions that are supposed to embody these procedures are undermined or interfered with. Equally, I think we misrepresent the debate about whether the Rule of Law has also a substantive dimension if we do not contrast a possible list of substantive items —such as:

(α) Respect for private property;
(β) Prohibitions on torture and brutality;
(γ) A presumption of liberty; and
(δ) Democratic enfranchisement

—with *both* of the lists I have set out (the formal list and the procedural list), rather than with the formal list by itself.

3. FORM AND PROCEDURE IN THE WORK OF HAYEK, FULLER, AND DICEY

It is remarkable how little attention is paid to demands of this *procedural* kind—demands like (A)–(J)—in the literature in academic legal and political philosophy devoted specifically to discussion of the Rule of Law.

The key chapter in F. A. Hayek's book, *The Constitution of Liberty*—the chapter titled "Laws, Commands, and Order"—makes no mention whatever of courts or legal procedures; it is wholly concerned with the relation between formal characteristics like abstraction and generality and individual freedom.[11] Later chapters in that book do talk a little about courts but hardly ever about their procedures.[12] The same is true of Hayek's later work on the Rule of Law, in his trilogy *Law, Legislation and Liberty*. Hayek talks a lot about the role of judges in chapter 5 of the first volume of that work. But it is all about the role of judges in generating norms of the appropriate form, rather than about the procedures that characterize courtrooms.[13]

The case of Lon Fuller is even more instructive. Fuller calls his internal morality of law—comprising (1) generality, (2) publicity,

(3) prospectivity, and so on—"procedural," but what he seems to mean is that it is not substantive. Fuller says this:

> As a convenient (though not wholly satisfactory) way of describing the distinction . . . we may speak of a procedural, as distinguished from a substantive natural law. What I have called the internal morality of law is in this sense a procedural version of natural law, though to avoid misunderstanding the word "procedural" should be assigned a special and expanded sense so that it would include, for example, a substantive accord between official action and enacted law. The term "procedural" is, however, broadly appropriate as indicating that we are concerned, not with the substantive aims of legal rules, but with the ways in which a system of rules for governing human conduct must be constructed and administered if it is to be efficacious and at the same time remain what it purports to be.[14]

In fact, *substantive* can be contrasted either with *procedural* or with *formal*; the two contrasts are quite different, and patently what Fuller has in mind is what we should call a formal/substantive contrast.[15] The features of his internal morality of law all relate to the form that legal norms take, not to either the procedure of their enactment or (more important) the procedural mode of their administration. Among his eight desiderata, only one comes close to being procedural (in the sense I am distinguishing from formal), namely the requirement of congruence between official action and law on the books—yet that is the one for which he says (in the passage quoted) "the word 'procedural' should be assigned a special and expanded sense"!

The point is that there is very little about due process or courtroom procedure in Fuller's account of law's internal morality in chapters 2 and 3 of *The Morality of Law*.[16] Much the same is true of Fuller in his earlier response to H. L. A. Hart's Holmes Lecture.[17] There, too, Fuller focuses on what we should call formal characteristics of law—generality, publicity, consistency, and so on—and his argument that they are prophylactics against injustice is based on an incompatibility between evil ends and law's forms.

> [C]oherence and goodness have more affinity than coherence and evil. Accepting this belief, I also believe that when men are compelled to explain and justify their decisions, the effect will generally

be to pull those decisions toward goodness, by whatever standards of ultimate goodness there are. . . . [E]ven in the most perverted regimes there is a certain hesitancy about writing cruelties, intolerances, and inhumanities into law.[18]

The whole of his discussion along these lines, and the whole of his excoriation of Nazi "legality," has to do with legislative form, not judicial procedure. That is the ground on which Fuller makes what we would call his "Rule of Law" argument.

I do not mean that Fuller was uninterested in procedure. Towards the end of chapter 4 of *The Morality of Law*, there is some consideration about whether the internal morality of law applies to the processes by which allocative decisions are made by government agencies in a mixed economy. Fuller says we face problems of institutional design "unprecedented in scope and importance."

It is inevitable that the legal profession will play a large role in solving these problems. The great danger is that we will unthinkingly carry over to new conditions traditional institutions and procedures that have already demonstrated their faults of design. As lawyers we have a natural inclination to "judicialize" every function of government. Adjudication is a process with which we are familiar and which enables us to show to advantage our special talents. Yet we must face the plain truth that adjudication is an ineffective instrument for economic management and for governmental participation in the allocation of economic resources.[19]

This seems to indicate an interest in procedural as well as formal aspects of the Rule of Law (and, indeed, a skepticism about their applicability across the board of all government functions).[20] But it is remarkable that the interest in the adjudicative process shown in this passage is not matched by anything in the earlier discussion in his book of the inner morality of law.

Fuller was in fact a great proceduralist, who made an immense contribution to our understanding of the judicial process.[21] Nicola Lacey has ventured the suggestion that Fuller would have been on much stronger ground in his argument with Hart had he focused on procedural and institutional as well as formal aspects of legality.[22] But he allowed Hart to set the agenda, with the crucial question "What is law and what is its relation to morality?" and did not force him to open that up, in any particular way, to "What, in terms of institutional procedures, is a legal system, and what is the relation of all that to morality?"

Fortunately, we are not bound to follow him in that. I think we can usefully pursue a procedural (and institutional) dimension of the Rule of Law, as well as a formal dimension, and distinguish both of them (separately as well as jointly) from a more substantive conception. There is certainly precedent for this elsewhere in the Rule of Law literature.

Albert Venn Dicey, for example, when he explained the Rule of Law as a distinguishing feature of the English Constitution, identi-fied it in the first instance with the following feature:

> When we say that the supremacy or the rule of law is a characteris-tic of the English constitution, we . . . mean, in the first place, that no man is punishable or can be lawfully made to suffer in body or goods except for a distinct breach of law *established in the ordinary legal manner before the ordinary Courts of the land.* In this sense the rule of law is contrasted with every system of government based on the exercise by persons in authority of wide, arbitrary, or discretionary powers of constraint.[23]

The passage I have emphasized is important. Without it, we tend to read the contrast between the rule of law and arbitrary govern-ment in terms of the application of a rule versus purely individual-ized application of punishment (without guidance by a rule). With it, however, the contrast between law and discretion has to do with institutions and procedures: a person must not be made to suffer except pursuant to a decision of a court arrived at in the ordinary manner observing ordinary legal process.

When E. P. Thompson insisted (alarming his fellow Marxists) that the Rule of Law was "an unqualified human good" and a "cul-tural achievement of universal significance,"[24] he did so by refer-ence in large part to the importance of procedure:

> [N]ot only were the rulers (indeed, the ruling class as a whole) in-hibited by their own rules of law against the exercise of direct un-mediated force (arbitrary imprisonment, the employment of troops against the crowd, torture, and those other conveniences of power with which we are all conversant), but they also believed enough in these rules, and in their accompanying ideological rhetoric, to allow, in certain limited areas, the law itself to be a genuine forum

within which certain kinds of class conflict were fought out. There were even occasions . . . when the Government itself retired from the courts defeated.[25]

As I said earlier, in recent legal philosophy the phrase "the Rule of Law" is often used to conjure up a sort of laundry list of features that a healthy legal system should have. These are mostly variations of the eight formal desiderata of Lon Fuller's "internal morality,"[26] but occasionally procedural and institutional considerations creep in. Thus, the fourth, fifth, and seventh items on Joseph Raz's list are the following: "(4) The independence of the judiciary must be guaranteed . . . (5) The principles of natural justice must be observed . . . [o]pen and fair hearing, absence of bias, and the like . . . (7) The courts should be easily accessible."[27] The justifications Raz gives often go to the issue of legal determinacy (e.g., "Since the court's judgment establishes conclusively what is the law in the case before it, the litigants can be guided by law only if the judges apply the law correctly"), but at least the procedural and institutional considerations rate a mention.

In many other discussions of the Rule of Law, however, the procedural dimension is simply ignored (or, worse, it is assumed thoughtlessly that the procedural dimension is taken care of by calling the formal dimension "procedural"). I do not mean that judges and courts are ignored. In the last *Nomos* volume devoted to this subject, there is extensive discussion of judicial authority and judicial discretion: some of it is about equitable decision by judges in hard cases (together with an intriguing account of the idea of practical wisdom as applied to the judiciary), and some of it is about the interpretive techniques that judges should use in difficult cases.[28] But, if one didn't know better, one would infer from these discussions that problems were just brought to wise individuals called judges for their decision (with or without the help of sources of law) and that the judges in question proceeded to deploy their interpretive strategies and practical wisdom to address those problems; there is no discussion in these papers of the highly proceduralized hearings in which problems are presented to a court, let alone the importance of the various procedural rights and powers possessed by individual litigants in relation to these hearings. Certainly, there is no indication by any of

the volumes' contributors that the procedures themselves and the
rights and powers associated with them are in and of themselves
part of what we value under the heading of "the Rule of Law."

4. PROCEDURE AND THE CONCEPT OF LAW

Elsewhere I have remarked on an interesting parallel between
the failure of some of our leading theorists of the Rule of Law to
highlight procedural (as opposed to formal) considerations and
the failure of our leading legal philosophers to include procedural
and institutional elements in their conception of law itself.[29]

For my part, I do not think we should regard something as a legal system absent the existence and operation of the sort of institutions we call courts. By courts, I mean institutions that apply norms
and directives established in the name of the whole society to individual cases and that settle disputes about the application of those
norms. And I mean institutions that do this through the medium
of hearings, formal events that are tightly structured procedurally
in order to enable an impartial body to determine the rights and
responsibilities of particular persons fairly and effectively after
hearing evidence and argument from both sides.[30]

It is remarkable how little there is about courts in the conceptual accounts of law presented in modern positivist jurisprudence. The leading source is H. L. A. Hart's magisterial work,
The Concept of Law. Hart conceives of law in terms of the union
of primary rules of conduct and secondary rules that govern the
way in which the primary rules are made, changed, applied, and
enforced. He certainly seems to regard *something like* courts as essential. When he introduces the concept of secondary rules, he
talks of the emergence of "rules of adjudication" in the transition
from a pre-legal to a legal society: "secondary rules empowering
individuals to make authoritative determinations of the question
of whether, on a particular occasion, a primary rule has been broken."[31] Notice, however, that this account defines the relevant institutions simply in terms of their output function—the making
of "authoritative determinations . . . of whether . . . a primary rule
has been broken." There is nothing on the distinctive process by
which this function is performed.[32] A Star Chamber proceeding
ex parte without any sort of hearing would satisfy Hart's definition;

and so would the tribunals we call in the antipodes "kangaroo courts."

Much the same is true of Joseph Raz's view about the importance of what he calls primary norm-applying institutions in *Practical Reason and Norms* and elsewhere.[33] Raz believes that norm-applying institutions are key to our understanding of legal systems (much more so than legislatures).[34] Now, there are all sorts of institutionalized ways in which norms may be applied, according to Raz, but "primary norm-applying organs" are of particular interest. Raz describes their operation as follows: "They are institutions with power to determine the normative situation of specified individuals, which are required to exercise these powers by applying existing norms, but whose decisions are binding even when wrong."[35] He tells us that "[c]ourts, tribunals and other judicial bodies are the most important example of primary organs."[36] In his abstract philosophical account, however, the operation of primary norm-applying institutions is understood solely in terms of output (and in terms of what is done with their output). Again, there is nothing about mode of operation or procedure. Secret military commissions might meet to "determine the normative situation of specified individuals . . . by applying existing norms" in the absence of the individuals in question and without affording any sort of hearing. The impression one gets from Raz's account is that a system of rule dominated by institutions like that would count as a legal system. Of course, Raz would criticize such institutions, and, as we have seen, he might use the ideal of the Rule of Law to do so.[37] But he seems to suggest that this is relevant to law only at an evaluative level, not at the conceptual level.

I think there is a considerable divergence here between what these philosophers say about the concept of law and how the term is ordinarily used. Most people, I think, would regard hearings and impartial proceedings and the safeguards that go with them as an essential, rather than a contingent, feature of the institutional arrangements we call legal systems.[38] Their absence would for most people be a disqualifying factor, just like the absence of free and fair elections in what was alleged to be a democracy.

Moreover, a procedural conception of the Rule of Law helps bring our conceptual thinking about law to life. There is a distressing tendency among academic legal philosophers to see law simply as a set of normative propositions and to pursue their task of developing an understanding of the concept of law to consist simply in understanding what sort of normative propositions these are. But law comes to life *in institutions*. An understanding of legal systems that emphasizes argument in the courtroom as much as the existence and recognition of rules provides the basis for a much richer understanding of the values and requirements that law and legality represent in modern political argument.

If it were up to me, I would bring the two concepts together— the concept of law and the concept of legality or the Rule of Law. I would suggest that the concept of law should be understood along Fullerian lines to embrace the fundamental elements of legality, but I would argue this only if the latter were understood to give pride of place to procedural and institutional elements. You may be relieved to hear that that is not the task of the present essay. However, I have attempted this elsewhere and so have one or two others.[39] But it is not the received position. According to Joseph Raz and others, you cannot understand what the Rule of Law is unless you already and independently understand what law is and the characteristic evils law is likely to give rise to.[40] I mention this further conceptual debate in order to register the points that the absence of a proper emphasis on procedural aspects on either side —in the academic account of the concept of law and in the academic account of the Rule of Law—may have a common source and may have something to do with our inability to see the connection between the two ideas.

5. PROCEDURE AND THE UNDERLYING MORAL CONCERNS

When Fuller developed his formal principles of generality, prospectivity, clarity, stability, consistency—principles whose observance is bound up with the basics of legal craftsmanship[41]—legal positivists expressed bewilderment as to why he called this set of principles a "morality."[42] He did so because he thought his eight principles had inherent moral significance. It was not only that he believed that observing them made it much more difficult to do substantive injustice, though this he did believe.[43] It was also because he thought observing the principles he identified was itself a way of respecting human dignity:

To embark on the enterprise of subjecting human conduct to rules involves . . . a commitment to the view that man is . . . a responsible agent, capable of understanding and following rules. . . . Every departure from the principles of law's inner morality is an affront to man's dignity as a responsible agent. To judge his actions by unpublished or retrospective laws, or to order him to do an act that is impossible, is to convey . . . your indifference to his powers of self-determination.[44]

I think what Fuller said about the connection between his formal principles and dignity can be said even more about the connection between procedure and dignity.

The essential idea of procedure is much more than merely functional: applying norms to individual cases. It is partly structural; it involves Martin Shapiro's idea of the triad structure:[45] a first party, a second opposing party, and, above them, a separate, impartial officer with the authority to make a determination. Most important, it is procedural: the operation of a court involves a way of proceeding that offers those who are immediately concerned in the dispute or in the application of the norm an opportunity to make submissions and present evidence (such evidence being presented in an orderly fashion according to strict rules of relevance oriented to the norms whose application is in question). The mode of presentation may vary, but the existence of such an opportunity does not. Once presented, the evidence is made available to be examined and confronted by the other party in open court. And each party has the opportunity to present arguments and submissions at the end of this process and to answer those of the other party. In the course of all of this, both sides are treated respectfully, if formalistically, but, above all, they are listened to by a tribunal that (as Lon Fuller stressed in his work "Forms and Limits of Adjudication") is bound in some manner to attend to the evidence presented and to respond to the submissions that are made in the reasons it eventually gives for its decision.[46]

These are abstract characteristics, and, of course (as I said), it would be a mistake to try to get too concrete given the variety of court-like institutions in the world. But they are not just arbitrary abstractions. They capture a deep and important sense associated foundationally with the idea of a legal system, that law is a mode of governing people that treats them with respect, as though they had a view or perspective of their own to present on the application of the norm to their conduct and situation. Applying a norm to a human individual is not like deciding what to do about a rabid animal or a dilapidated house. It involves paying attention to a point of view and respecting the personality of the entity one is dealing with. As such, it embodies a crucial dignitarian idea—respecting the dignity of those to whom the norms are applied as *beings capable of explaining themselves*. None of this is present in the dominant positivist account; all of it, I submit, should be regarded as an essential aspect of our working conception of law.

6. APPREHENSIONS ABOUT LAWLESSNESS

Think of the concerns expressed about the plight of detainees in Guantanamo Bay from 2003 to the present. When jurists worried that the detention facility there was a "black hole" so far as legality was concerned,[47] it was precisely the lack of these procedural rights that they were concerned about. What the detainees demanded, in the name of the Rule of Law, was an opportunity to appear before a proper legal tribunal, to confront and answer the evidence against them (such as it was), and to be represented so that their own side of the story concerning their detention could be explained to a tribunal that (as I said) would be required to listen and respond to the arguments that were made. That was the gist of their habeas corpus demands. No doubt the integrity of these proceedings would depend in part on the formal characteristics of the legal norms (whether laws and customs of armed conflict or other antiterrorist laws) that were supposed to govern their detention, whose application in their case they could call in question at the hearings that they demanded; no doubt the formal features stressed by Fuller, Hayek, and others would be important, because it is very difficult to make a case at a hearing if the laws governing detention are unacceptably vague, or indeterminate, or kept secret. Even so, we still miss out on a whole important dimension of the Rule of Law ideal if we do not also focus on the procedural demands themselves, which, as it were, give the formal side of the Rule of Law this purchase.[48]

These concerns are prominent not just in extreme cases like Guantanamo Bay. Among working lawyers, they have been at the forefront of concerns about the compatibility of the Rule of Law with the modern administrative state. When Dicey spoke of a "Decline in Reverence for the Rule of Law" in England at the beginning of the twentieth century, one of the things he had in mind was the transfer of authority to impose penalties or take away property or livelihood from courts to administrative entities, and the content of his concern was precisely that those entities would not act as courts acted, would not feel constrained by rules of procedure and other scruples of "natural justice" in the way that judges characteristically felt constrained.[49] True, even Dicey expressed this partly in terms of the existence of determinate rules:

> State officials must more and more undertake to manage a mass of public business. . . . But Courts are from the nature of things unsuited for the transaction of business. The primary duty of a judge is to act in accordance with the strict rules of law. He must shun, above all things, any injustice to individuals. The well-worn and often absurdly misapplied adage that "it is better that ten criminals should escape conviction than that one innocent man should without cause be found guilty of crime" does after all remind us that the first duty of a judge is not to punish crime but to punish it without doing injustice. A man of business, whether employed by a private firm or working in a public office, must make it his main object to see that the business in which he is concerned is efficiently carried out. He could not do this if tied down by the rules which rightly check the action of a judge.[50]

I guess one *could* parse this purely in terms of judges (as opposed to managers of public business) being bound by determinate rules —and then the whole thing could be brought in under Fuller's eighth principle of congruence.[51] But, again, I think that would miss a whole dimension of the matter. It is not simply that one bunch of officials are bound to apply determinate rules while another bunch of officials are not; it is that the former operate in the context of highly proceduralized institutions in which procedural rights and duties of all sorts are oriented to allowing the application of determinate rules to be established fairly and minutely with ample opportunity for contestation. If we neglect this aspect of the Rule of Law, we make much of Dicey's concern about contemporary decline in regard for that ideal quite mysterious.

Something similar may be true of our concerns about the role

of the Rule of Law in nation building. When theorists like Robert
Barro argue that it is more important to secure the Rule of Law in
a developing society than it is to secure the institutions of democracy, what they often have in mind is the elimination of corruption
and the establishment of stable legal institutions.[52] We cannot understand these concerns unless we focus on the distinctive procedural features of legal institutions and their procedural integrity
vis-à-vis the elimination of corruption, the securing of judicial independence, the guarantee of due process, and the separation of
powers.

True, it has to be said also that sometimes when commenta-
tors call for the Rule of Law to be given priority over democracy
in developing societies, what they mainly have in mind are quasi-
substantive features like the protection of property, the proper enforcement of contracts, and the protection of outside investments,
and the safeguarding of all this as against democratically enacted
social-justice or environmental or labor-rights legislation. Sometimes this is quite cynical.[53] I have argued vehemently elsewhere
against this Washington-consensus-based abuse of the idea of the
Rule of Law.[54]

7. Law, Argumentation, and Predictability

When I set out my preliminary list of procedural characteristics of
the Rule of Law at the beginning of this chapter, I mentioned the
requirement that those facing the imposition of penalty, stigma,
or serious loss at the hands of government must have the right to
make legal argument about the bearing of the evidence and about
the bearing of the various legal norms relevant to the case. I believe this is particularly important. But it also sets up an interesting
tension between the procedural requirements of the Rule of Law
and the formal requirements that relate to the determinacy of legal norms.

In the systems with which we are familiar, law presents itself as
something one can make sense of. The norms that are administered in our legal system may seem like just one damned command
after another, but lawyers and judges try to see the law as a whole;
they attempt to discern some sort of coherence or system, integrat-
ing particular items into a structure that makes intellectual sense.[55]

And ordinary people and their representatives take advantage of this aspiration to systematicity and integrity in framing their own legal arguments, by inviting the tribunal hearing their case to consider how the position they are putting forward fits generally into a coherent conception of the spirit of the law. These are not just arguments about what the law *ought to be*—made, as it were, in a sort of lobbying mode. They are arguments of reason that present competing arguments about what the law *is*. Inevitably, they are controversial: one party will say that such-and-such a proposition cannot be inferred from the law as it is; the other party will respond that it can be so inferred if only we credit the law with more coherence (or coherence among more of its elements) than people have tended to credit it with in the past. And so the determination of whether such a proposition has legal authority may often be a matter of contestation. Law, in other words, becomes a matter of argument.[56]

In this regard, too, law has a dignitarian aspect: it conceives of the people who live under it as bearers of reason and intelligence. They are thinkers who can grasp and grapple with the rationale of the way they are governed and relate it in complex but intelligible ways to their own view of the relation between *their* actions and purposes and the actions and purposes of the state. Once again, I don't think we would accept that a society was governed by the Rule of Law if its judicial procedures did not afford parties the opportunity to make arguments of this kind in complex cases where the state was bearing down on them.

But this strand of the Rule of Law, this strand of dignitarian respect, has a price: it probably brings with it a diminution in law's certainty. On my view, the procedural side of the Rule of Law requires that public institutions sponsor and facilitate reasoned argument in human affairs. But argument can be unsettling, and the procedures that we cherish often have the effect of undermining the certainty and predictability that are emphasized in the formal side of the ideal.[57] By associating the Rule of Law with the legal process rather than with the form of the determinate norms that are supposed to emerge from that process, the procedural aspect of the Rule of Law seems to place a premium on values that are somewhat different from those emphasized in the formal picture.[58] The formal picture, particularly as it is put forward by thinkers like

F. A. Hayek, emphasizes clarity, determinacy, and predictability as features of governance that make private freedom possible.[59] The procedural idea sponsors a certain conception of freedom also, but it is more like positive freedom: active engagement in the administration of public affairs, the freedom to participate actively and argumentatively in the way that one is governed. And that positive freedom may stand in some tension with private freedom in Hayek's vision of liberty, which presupposes that law is determinate enough to allow people to know in advance where they stand and to have some advance security in their understanding of the demands that law is likely to impose upon them.

The tension may also be represented as a tension between various strands of dignity associated with the Rule of Law. Fuller, we saw, associated his formal criteria with a dignitarian conception of the legal subject as an agent capable of monitoring and freely governing his own conduct. In its action-guiding aspect, law respects people as agents; the Rule of Law is sometimes represented as the conditions of such respect.[60] But how, it may be asked, can we maintain this mode of respect if law becomes contestable and uncertain as a result of argumentation? Insisting on an opportunity for argumentation respects dignity, too, but at the cost of diminishing the confidence that we can have in the dignity of law's self-application at the hands of ordinary individuals. On the other hand, it is worth remembering that law consists not only of determinate rules but also standards and that law's confidence in the possibility of self-application does not necessarily presuppose that it takes the form only of determinate rigid rules. Law's dignitarian faith in the practical reason of ordinary people may be an act of faith in their *thinking*—for example, about what is reasonable and what is not—not just in their recognition of a rule and its mechanical application. And so also it may be an act of faith not just in their ability to apply general moral predicates (such as "reasonable") to their actions but also to think about and interpret the bearing of a whole array of norms and precedents to their conduct, rather than just the mechanical application of a single norm.

So we cannot just brush the argumentative aspect of law's procedures aside so far as the Rule of Law is concerned. I believe this tension in the Rule of Law ideal is largely unavoidable, and we should own up to the fact that the Rule of Law points, as it were, in both directions. I think we find symptoms of this tension in the ambivalence of the Rule of Law ideal so far as the role of judges in society is concerned and in a similar ambivalence about the role of litigation.[61]

There is no denying that theories that place great stress on legal certainty, predictability, and settlement, on the determinacy and intelligibility of the norms that are upheld in society, and on the relatively straightforward character of their administration by the state are among the most influential conceptions of the Rule of Law.[62] According to these conceptions, the most important thing that people need from the law that governs them is certainty and predictability in the conduct of their lives and businesses. There may be no getting away from legal constraint in the circumstances of modern life, but freedom is possible nevertheless if people know in advance how the law will operate and how they have to act if they are to avoid its application. Knowing in advance how the law will operate enables one to make plans and to work around its requirements.[63] And knowing that one can count on the law's protecting certain personal property rights gives each citizen some certainty on what he can rely on in his dealings with other people and the state. Accordingly, they highlight the role of rules rather than standards, literal meanings rather than systemic inferences, direct applications rather than arguments, and *ex ante* clarity rather than labored interpretations.[64] The Rule of Law is violated, on this account, when the norms that are applied by officials do not correspond to the norms that have been made public to the citizens or when officials act on the basis of their own discretion rather than according to norms laid down in advance. If action of this sort becomes endemic, then not only are people's expectations disappointed, but increasingly they will find themselves unable to *form* expectations on which they can rely, and the horizons of their planning and their economic activity will shrink accordingly. So it is natural to think that the Rule of Law must condemn the uncertainty that arises out of law's argumentative character.

But the contrary considerations embodied in the procedural side of the Rule of Law will not easily give way. As the late and lamented Neil MacCormick has pointed out, law is an argumentative discipline, and no analytic theory of what law is and what distinguishes legal systems from other systems of governance can afford to ignore this aspect of our legal practice and the distinctive role it plays in a legal system's treating ordinary citizens with respect as active centers of intelligence.[65] A fallacy of modern positivism, it seems to me, is its exclusive emphasis on the command-and-control aspect of law, or the norm-and-guidance aspect of law, without any reference to the culture of argument that a legal system frames, sponsors, and institutionalizes. The institutionalized recognition of a distinctive set of norms may be an important feature. But at least as important is what we do in law with the norms that we identify. We don't just obey them or apply the sanctions that they ordain; we argue over them adversarially, we use our sense of what is at stake in their application to license a continual process of argument back and forth, and we engage in elaborate interpretive exercises about what it means to apply them faithfully as a system to the cases that come before us.

When positivists in the tradition of H. L. A. Hart pay attention to this aspect of interpretation and argument, they tend to treat it as an occasional and problematic sideline. The impression given is that, in most cases, the authoritative identification of legal norms using a rule of recognition is sufficient; once it is recognized, a legal norm can become a straightforward guide to official action. But, it is said, *occasionally* the language is unclear—because words have open texture or because our aims are indeterminate or because for some other reasons there is a hiccough in the interface between words and the facts that they apply to—and then, unfortunately, we have no choice but to argue the matter through.[66] And, usually, the positivist will add, the upshot is that the court will just have to cut through the Gordian knot and make a new rule that can be recognized and applied more readily without any attendant controversy.[67] But this account radically underestimates the point that argumentation (about what this or that provision means or about the effect of this array of precedents) is *business as usual* in law. We would be uneasy about counting a system that did not exhibit it and make routine provision for it as a legal system.

So: I don't think that a conception of law or a conception of the Rule of Law that sidelines the importance of argumentation can really do justice to the value we place on government treating ordinary citizens with respect as active centers of intelligence. The demand for clarity and predictability is commonly made in the name of individual freedom—the freedom of the Hayekian individual in charge of his own destiny who needs to know where he stands so far as social order is concerned.[68] But, with the best will in the world and the most determinate-seeming law, circumstances and interactions can be treacherous. From time to time, the free Hayekian individual will find himself charged or accused of some violation. Or his business will be subject—as he thinks, unjustly or irregularly—to some detrimental rule. Some such cases may be clear, but others may be matters of dispute. An individual who values his freedom enough to demand the sort of calculability that the Hayekian image of freedom under law is supposed to cater to is not someone whom we can imagine always tamely accepting a charge or a determination that he has done something wrong. He will have a point of view, and he will seek an opportunity to bring that to bear when it is a question of applying a rule to his case. And, when he brings his point of view to bear, we can imagine his plaintiff or his prosecutor responding with a point of view whose complexity and tendentiousness matches his own. And so it begins: legal argumentation and the facilities that law's procedures make for the formal airing of these arguments.[69] Courts, hearings, and arguments—those aspects of law are not optional extras; they are integral parts of how law works, and they are indispensable to the package of law's respect for human agency. To say that we should value aspects of governance that promote the clarity and determinacy of rules for the sake of individual freedom but not the opportunities for argumentation that a free and self-possessed individual is likely to demand, is to slice in half, to truncate, what the Rule of Law rests upon: respect for the freedom and dignity of each person as an active intelligence.

8. LEGAL PROCEDURES IN SOCIAL AND POLITICAL DECISION MAKING

Alexis de Tocqueville famously remarked that "[s]carcely any political question arises in the United States that is not resolved, sooner or later, into a judicial question."[70] Does a proceduralist account of the Rule of Law, with its emphasis on due process and the sort of argumentation that one finds in courtrooms, endorse this characteristic? Is a society governed by the Rule of Law necessarily a

society in which judicial procedures loom large in the settlement
of social and political questions?

I think that is, for the most part, an unwarranted extrapolation.
It is one thing to say that a person threatened by the government
with penalty, stigma, or serious loss must be offered an opportunity and a setting for argumentatively contesting that imposition.
It is another thing to say that the courtroom setting, with its highly
proceduralized modes of consideration, is an appropriate venue
for settling general questions of common concern in a society. We
may accept the procedural implications of the Rule of Law—along
the lines of those set out in my list (A)–(J) in section 2—without
denying that, nevertheless, in the end, the legislature, rather than
the courtroom, is the appropriate place for settling such matters.
Certainly, what happens in the courtroom in argument about particular applications may affect how the measures enacted in the
legislature are subsequently understood. That, as I have said, may
have an effect on predictability, and we should not be in the business of trying to avoid that by minimizing the impact of judicial
proceedings. Such an effect can and will accrue even in a society
in which courts do not have the power to override legislation, and
endorsing or accepting that effect by no means amounts to an endorsement of anything like judicial review of legislation.

I do not mean that the Rule of Law precludes judicial review
of legislation. I believe that, as a political ideal, it is neutral on the
issue. In a society with a constitutional Bill of Rights and a practice of strong judicial review, the Rule of Law requires us to accept
a much greater role for courts in public decision making than I
have set out here. In such a society—I am thinking particularly
of the United States—arguments made in courtrooms according
to the procedural principles that I say constitute the Rule of Law
will have a greater impact on the life of a society and a greater
impact probably on social predictability than they have in a society
with weak or no judicial review.[71] Also, the more robust the Bill of
Rights, the more it will seem that the upshot of taking the Rule of
Law seriously is substantive, not just procedural and formal. This,
I think, is the gist of Dworkin's position on the Rule of Law in *A
Matter of Principle*.[72]

Some people argue that the Rule of Law in a society is incomplete unless legislatures as much as executive agencies are bound

to act in accordance with (higher) constraining laws. I do not accept that, though I understand the position. Some even say that the crucial distinction here is between the Rule of Law and rule *by law*, and they say that a system of legislative supremacy is an example of the latter but not the former. A position like this is sometimes associated with a general denigration of legislatures— as though, in the end, the Rule of Law must amount to something other than the rule of men. The position is often associated with an almost mythic reverence for common law, not conceived necessarily as deliberately crafted by judges but understood as welling up impersonally as a sort of resultant of the activity of courts. Hayek hints at some such nonsense when he writes in *The Constitution of Liberty* that most genuine rules of law

> have never been deliberately invented but have grown through a gradual process of trial and error in which the experience of successive generations has helped to make them what they are. In most instances, therefore, nobody knows or has ever known all the reasons and considerations that have led to a rule being given a particular form.[73]

In a similar way, the suggestion that legislatures need to be constrained by law rather than regarded as ultimate sources of law often involves a strange sort of constitutionalist mythology. It sees the framing of a constitution or a Bill of Rights as some sort of transcendent event—amounting to something other than the rule of men (by law): perhaps it is supposed to have been a spontaneous effulgence of unprecedented superhuman virtue hovering around the activity of giants like James Madison and the Federalists. But I see no reason to associate the Rule of Law with any such mythology or to embody in it any denial that law is human in origin and often the product of deliberate manufacture. Even if positivists (as I have argued) give an inadequate account of it, the Rule of Law is, in the end, the rule of positive law; it is a human ideal for human institutions, not a magic that somehow absolves us from human rule.

Having said that, let me add two final points by way of qualification. First, even in systems of parliamentary supremacy, legislatures do act in ways that are constituted by rules, and procedural rules at that. (I mention this because, sometimes, when people allude to the procedural side of the Rule of Law, they have in mind the way laws are made, rather than—as I have emphasized—the way they are administered.) They are—in their own way—highly procedur- alized institutions, and people rely on their articulated procedures as indicating the points of access at which citizens can hope to in- fluence and participate in their proceedings. It is no accident that enemies of the Rule of Law, such as Carl Schmitt, sought compre- hensively to disparage the rule-governed character of parliamen- tary democracy.[74]

Second, the Rule of Law applies not only within national poli- ties but also increasingly between them. The Rule of Law as an in- ternational legal ideal remains undertheorized,[75] and I am afraid much of the work that has been done on it simply adopts uncriti- cally the perspective of those who say, at the national level, that the ideal consists in determinacy, clarity, and predictability.[76] I believe there is much more to be said on this. I have tried to say some of it in some other writings,[77] and I will try to say more. For the mo- ment, this must suffice: to the extent that we take international law seriously, it will be the case that national legislatures, like other na- tional institutions, will appropriately regard themselves as bound and constrained by law in what they do (whether or not they have a national Bill of Rights). The content of that constraint will be determined by the content of multilateral treaties (including hu- man rights conventions), by customary international law, and by *ius cogens* provisions of various kinds. The character of the con- straint will no doubt be determined, formally and procedurally (if not substantively), by the ideal of the Rule of Law, adapted to the international context. Accordingly, it is a matter of some urgency —which more or less implies these days that legal philosophers are going to neglect it—to consider what that adaptation of this ideal to the international context involves.

NOTES

1. John Locke, *Two Treatises of Government* (Cambridge: Cambridge University Press, 1988), 274 (II: section 11).
2. F. A. Hayek, *The Constitution of Liberty* (Chicago: University of Chi- cago Press, 1960), esp. chs. 9–10.

3. Lon L. Fuller, *The Morality of Law* (New Haven: Yale University Press, 1969), 162.

4. See Jeremy Waldron, "The Rule of Law in Contemporary Liberal Theory," *Ratio Juris* 2 (1989): 79. For a discussion of substantive Rule of Law ideas, see Paul Craig, "Formal and Substantive Conceptions of the Rule of Law: An Analytical Framework," *Public Law* (1997): 467.

5. See Jeremy Waldron, "Legislation and the Rule of Law," *Legisprudence* 1 (2007): 91, 115.

6. See, e.g., Editorial, "Gathering Storm," *New York Times*, November 8, 2007: "The American Bar Association, its members horrified by events in Pakistan, has written to General Musharraf and condemned his profound breach of the rule of law." See also Letter, "Pakistan's Leaders Must Respect the Rule of Law," *The Times* (London), November 14, 2007 (signed by chairs of Bar Associations in England, Scotland, Ireland, and Wales).

7. See, e.g., Editorial, "The Rule of Law in Guantánamo," *New York Times*, October 11, 2008, and Laura Dickinson, "Using Legal Process to Fight Terrorism: Detentions, Military Commissions, International Tribunals, and the Rule of Law," *Southern California Law Review* 75 (2002): 1407.

8. See also the lists in John Finnis, *Natural Law and Natural Rights* (Oxford: Clarendon Press, 1980), 270; John Rawls, *A Theory of Justice* (Cambridge MA: Harvard University Press, 1971), 236–39; and Joseph Raz, "The Rule of Law and Its Virtue," in his collection *The Authority of Law: Essays on Law and Morality* (Oxford: Clarendon Press, 1979), 214–19.

9. I have adapted this list from A. Wallace Tashima, "The War on Terror and the Rule of Law," *Asian American Law Journal* 15 (2008): 245, 264.

10. In the United Kingdom and elsewhere, the term "natural justice" is used to refer to the most elementary aspects of what Americans would call procedural due process. See, for example, Paul Jackson, *Natural Justice* (London: Sweet and Maxwell, 1979).

11. Hayek, *Constitution of Liberty*, 148–61.

12. See ibid., 218–19, for the suggestion that, apart from the formal characteristics of the Rule of Law, its procedural aspects are unimportant: "[T]hey presuppose for their effectiveness the acceptance of the rule of law as here defined and . . . , without it, all procedural safeguards would be valueless."

13. F. A. Hayek, *Rules and Order*, vol. 1 of *Law, Legislation and Liberty* (Chicago: University of Chicago Press, 1973), 94–123.

14. Fuller, *Morality of Law*, 96–97.

15. Brian Tamanaha, *On the Rule of Law: History, Politics, Theory* (New York: Cambridge University Press, 2004), gets this right by locating his discussion of Fuller in a chapter called "Formal Theories." That is then contrasted with a chapter called "Substantive Theories." Procedural theories

don't rate a mention, but at least it is not assumed by Tamanaha that everything nonsubstantive is procedural.

16. There is a reference to "due process" in Fuller, *Morality of Law*, 105–6, but that is in the technical sense of the term, and it addresses whether ex post facto laws violate due process (in that sense).

17. Lon L. Fuller, "Positivism and Fidelity to Law: A Reply to Hart," *Harvard Law Review* 71 (1959): 630.

18. Ibid., 636–37.

19. Fuller, *Morality of Law*, 176.

20. For the implications of this for Fuller's theory, see Jeremy Waldron, "The Appeal of Law: Efficacy, Freedom, or Fidelity," in *Law and Philosophy* 13 (1994): 259, 272–75.

21. See Lon L. Fuller, "The Forms and Limits of Adjudication," *Harvard Law Review* 92 (1978): 353.

22. See Nicola Lacey, "Out of the 'Witches' Cauldron?—Reinterpreting the Context and Re-assessing the Significance of the Hart-Fuller Debate," in *The Hart-Fuller Debate in the Twenty-First Century*, ed. Peter Cane (Oxford: Hart, 2010), 1.

23. A. V. Dicey, *Introduction to the Study of the Law of the Constitution*, 8th ed. (Indianapolis: Liberty Classics, 1982), 110 (my emphasis).

24. E. P. Thompson, *Whigs and Hunters: The Origin of the Black Act* (Harmondsworth: Penguin Books, 1977), 265–66.

25. Ibid., 265.

26. See, e.g., Finnis, *Natural Law and Natural Rights*, 270.

27. Raz, "The Rule of Law and Its Virtue," 216–17.

28. See the essays on equitable judgment and practical reason by Lawrence Solum, "Equity and the Rule of Law," in *Nomos XXXVI: The Rule of Law*, ed. Ian Shapiro (New York: New York University Press, 1994), 120, and Stephen Burton, "Particularism, Discretion, and the Rule of Law," ibid., 178. See also the essays on judges' interpretive strategies by Jack Knight and James Johnson, "Public Choice and the Rule of Law: Rational Choice Theories of Statutory Interpretation," ibid., 244, and William Eskridge and John Ferejohn, "Politics, Interpretation, and the Rule of Law," ibid., 265.

29. See Jeremy Waldron, "The Concept and the Rule of Law," *Georgia Law Review* 43 (2008): 1.

30. See Martin Shapiro, *Courts, A Comparative and Political Analysis* (Chicago: University of Chicago Press, 1981), 1–2, and Fuller, "The Forms and Limits of Adjudication," passim.

31. H. L. A. Hart, *The Concept of Law*, 2nd ed. (Oxford: Clarendon Press, 1994), 96.

32. Hart acknowledges that, of course, secondary rules will have to

define processes for these institutions (ibid., 97). But he seems to think that this can vary from society to society and that nothing in the concept of law constrains that definition.

33. Joseph Raz, *Practical Reason and Norms*, new ed. (Oxford: Oxford University Press, 1999), 134–37.

34. Ibid., 132–33.

35. Ibid., 136.

36. Ibid.

37. Raz, "The Rule of Law and Its Virtue," 217.

38. See, e.g., Jamil Anderlini, "Rewards and Risks of Chinese Legal Career," *Financial Times*, July 24, 2008, where a dissident Chinese lawyer, commenting on abuses of the "court" system in China, observes: "Actually, there is no real legal system in the western sense in China."

39. See Waldron, "The Concept and the Rule of Law," and see also Nigel Simmonds, *Law as a Moral Idea* (Oxford: Oxford University Press, 2008).

40. Raz, "The Rule of Law and Its Virtue," 224.

41. Fuller, *The Morality of Law*, esp. chapter 2.

42. See, e.g., H.L.A. Hart, "Book Review of Lon L. Fuller, *The Morality of Law*," *Harvard Law Review* 78 (1965): 1281, at 1284. For a characterization of Hart's bewilderment as disingenuous, see Jeremy Waldron, "Positivism and Legality: Hart's Equivocal Response to Fuller," *NYU Law Review* 83 (2008): 1135, esp. 1154–56.

43. Fuller, "Positivism and Fidelity to Law," 636–37.

44. Fuller, *Morality of Law*, 162.

45. Shapiro, *Courts*, 1–2.

46. Fuller, "The Forms and Limits of Adjudication," 366–67.

47. See, e.g., Johan Steyn, "Guantanamo Bay: The Legal Black Hole," Twenty-Seventh F. A. Mann Lecture, November 25, 2003, http://www .statewatch.org/news/2003/nov/guantanamo.pdf.

48. It is also worth noting that the demand for a clear rule to apply to and to regulate the detention is not only a demand for something that the potential detainees can use *ex ante* to guide their conduct—as though terrorists most wanted to know (and guide their action by) what they were forbidden to do! The demand for the formal aspects of the Rule of Law is often just a way of getting to the procedural aspects of the Rule of Law, which is what the detainees really care about.

49. See Dicey's "Introduction" to the 8th edition of *Introduction to the Study of the Law of the Constitution*, lv–lvii.

50. Ibid., lvii.

51. Fuller, *The Morality of Law*, 39 and 81–91.

52. Robert Barro, "Democracy and the Rule of Law," in *Governing for Prosperity*, ed. B. Bueno de Mesquita and H. Root (New Haven: Yale

University Press, 2000). See also R. D. Cooter, "The Rule of State Law versus the Rule of Law State: Economic Analysis of the Legal Foundations of Development," in *The Law and Economics of Development*, ed. E. Buscaglia, W. Ratliff, and R. Cooter (Greenwich, CT: JAI Press, 1997), 101.

53. For examples, see the World Bank ideal of Rule of Law as described by Frank Upham, "Mythmaking in the Rule of Law Orthodoxy," http://www.carnegieendowment.org/files/wp30.pdf. See also the discussion in Waldron, "Legislation and the Rule of Law," 118 ff.

54. Waldron, "Legislation and the Rule of Law," passim.

55. See also the discussion in Jeremy Waldron, "Transcendental Nonsense and System in the Law," *Columbia Law Review* 100 (2000): 16, 30–40.

56. The legal philosopher who has done the most to develop this theme is, of course, Ronald Dworkin, particularly in *Law's Empire* (Cambridge, MA: Harvard University Press, 1986).

57. See the discussion of the relation between civil disobedience and disputes about which laws are valid in Ronald Dworkin, *Taking Rights Seriously* (Cambridge, MA: Harvard University Press, 1977), 184–205. I have discussed this argumentative aspect of Dworkin's conception of the Rule of Law in Jeremy Waldron, "The Rule of Law as a Theater of Debate," *Dworkin and his Critics*, ed. Justine Burley (Oxford: Blackwell, 2004), 319.

58. See Richard Fallon, "The Rule of Law as a Concept in Constitutional Discourse," *Columbia Law Review* 97 (1997): 1, 6.

59. See, e.g., Hayek, *The Constitution of Liberty*, 152–57.

60. Raz, "The Rule of Law and Its Virtue, 214: "This is the basic intuition from which the doctrine of the rule of law derives: the law must be capable of guiding the behaviour of its subjects."

61. See the discussion in Jeremy Waldron, "Is the Rule of Law an Essentially Contested Concept (in Florida)?" *Law and Philosophy* 21 (2002): 137.

62. See also T. Carothers, "The Rule of Law Revival," *Foreign Affairs* 77 (1998): 95, and Jeffrey Kahn, "The Search for the Rule of Law in Russia," *Georgetown Journal of International Law* 37 (2006): 353, 359–61.

63. See, especially, Hayek, *The Constitution of Liberty*, 153 and 156–57.

64. See also James R. Maxeiner, "Legal Indeterminacy Made in America: U.S. Legal Methods and the Rule of Law," *Valparaiso University Law Review* 41 (2006): 517, and Antonin Scalia, "The Rule of Law as a Law of Rules," *University of Chicago Law Review* 56 (1989): 1175.

65. Neil MacCormick, *Rhetoric and the Rule of Law: A Theory of Legal Reasoning* (Oxford: Oxford University Press, 2005), 14–15 and 26–28. I am greatly indebted to MacCormick's account.

66. Hart, *The Concept of Law*, 124–36.

67. Ibid., 135–36.

68. See, e.g., Hayek, *The Constitution of Liberty*, 148–61.

69. There is a fine account of this in MacCormick, *Rhetoric and the Rule of Law*, 12–31.

70. Alexis de Tocqueville, *Democracy in America* (New York: Knopf, 1994), 1:280.

71. For the contrast between strong and weak judicial review, see Jeremy Waldron, "The Core of the Case against Judicial Review," *Yale Law Journal* 115 (2006): 1346.

72. Ronald Dworkin, "Political Judges and the Rule of Law," in his collection *A Matter of Principle* (Cambridge, MA: Harvard University Press, 1985), 9

73. Hayek, *Constitution of Liberty*, 157. This line of thought is even more pronounced in Hayek's later work; see Hayek, *Rules and Order*, 72 ff.

74. See, e.g., Carl Schmitt, *The Crisis of Parliamentary Democracy* (Cambridge, MA: MIT Press, 1988).

75. The papers that I have found most helpful include James Crawford, "International Law and the Rule of Law," *Adelaide Law Review* 24 (2003): 3, and Mattias Kumm, "International Law in National Courts: The International Rule of Law and the Limits of the Internationalist Model," *Virginia Journal of International Law* 44 (2003): 19.

76. See Simon Chesterman, *The UN Security Council and the Rule of Law: The Role of the Security Council in Strengthening a Rules-Based International System* (Final Report and Recommendations from the Austrian Initiative, 2004–2008), also published by the Institute for International Law and Justice, New York University School of Law, http://ssrn.com/abstract=1279849.

77. See Jeremy Waldron, "The Rule of International Law," *Harvard Journal of Law and Public Policy* 30 (2006): 15, and "Are Sovereigns Entitled to the Benefit of the International Rule of Law?" New York University School of Law, Public Law and Legal Theory Research Paper Series, Working Paper no 09-01 (2009), http://ssrn.com/abstract=1323383.

2

THE LIMITS OF PROCESS

ROBIN WEST

Jeremy Waldron's claim, as I understand it, is that the "Rule of Law" requires not only that the various laws that govern us consist of general, knowable rules with which we can all comply—the so-called formal requirements of the Rule of Law often identified with Lon Fuller's notorious King Rex and his eight ways to fail to make law[1]—but also that those laws be applied in a way that acknowledges our intelligence, respects our dignity, and broadly treats each of us as a worthy equal when it imposes its censorial and punitive will upon us.[2] Waldron wants to think of these latter ideals as the "procedural" requirements of the Rule of Law, which, he claims, are not reducible to Fuller's requirements and may on occasion conflict with them.[3] So, he distinguishes the "formal" from the "procedural" requirements of the Rule of Law. The formal, Fullerian Rule of Law requires that, whatever their content, laws must have a certain form, while the procedural, Waldronian Rule of Law requires that, however formally virtuous they may be, those rules must be applied in a way that is procedurally just.[4] The state may not, consistent with the Rule of Law thus understood, expose any of us to the risk of state-imposed punishment, liability, censure, or stigma without ensuring that the laws that have this consequence are applied against us in a fair way that respects our dignity.[5] And what does that fairness require? Minimally, that we have the opportunity, should we be so targeted by the state, to participate intelligently in the legal system that has brought

32

down its sword upon us.[6] Our rules of procedure should all be interpreted and applied toward that end. So, the procedural Rule of Law requires, for example, that we be granted a fair trial, that we be assured, at that trial, of the assistance of an attorney, and that, through decent procedures, we have a chance to tell our side of the story, and to do so in accordance with rules of evidence that guarantee that only relevant information will be garnered by the state to secure a conviction or verdict against us, rather than any old piece of defamatory nonsense the state might feel free to unleash.

More generally, the procedural Rule of Law requires that we be treated as an intelligent participatory member of law's empire, even when the state seeks to use law's sword to punish, stigmatize, or penalize us. The formal requirements broadly associated with Lon Fuller's work protect our interest in law's certainty and predictability and hence maximize our liberty and to some degree our dignity—they respect, for example, our agentic capacity to *decide* to be law abiding. Such a choice is available to us only if the laws we are being asked to abide by are in accordance more or less with Fuller's eight formal requirements. This is not, however, sufficient, Waldron argues, for a Rule of Law regime. Such a regime must also be procedurally just. Again, these are not the same thing, nor do they stem from the same core values. The procedural Rule of Law respects not so much our liberty or our agentic capacity to choose for or against law abidance but rather our intelligence and our individual perspective: decent procedure should grant us an opportunity to participate as an equal and intelligent citizen in the system of law that inflicts its will upon us, and to do so in a way that allows our elaboration of our own perspective on both the rules being applied against us and our own story about the events that triggered the law's hand. Finally, both contrast with a substantive understanding of the Rule of Law, argued by legal and political philosophers as requiring a state that protects property and contract rights and actively seeks to impose this understanding in emerging democracies interested in embracing a rule of law. Against such substantive and formal understandings, Waldron offers his procedural interpretation as a necessary complement. That's the argument as I understand it.

It would be churlish to object too strenuously to this humane

proposal to expand the Rule of Law of our imaginings to include a
procedural dimension, particularly given contemporary national,
global, and political realities. We are indeed suffering a deficit
of procedural fairness in our various courts of criminal justice,
from the military commissions in Guantanamo Bay,[7] to the district
courts of Baltimore City,[8] to various points abroad. And, a growing
body of Rule of Law scholarship that is proving influential in those
countries with systems seeking to emulate our own identifies the
Rule of Law almost exclusively with the certainty and predictability
in economic life that are so beneficial to those with property: a limited and generally regressive conception of legalism that protects
market-based liberties but little else.[9] Complementing that prop-
erty-centered Rule of Law ideology with something that centers on
people rather than profit can't hurt. We are also facing, although
this may be low on the list of world problems, a badly demoralized domestic law school environment. The economic pressures
on our graduates, who are facing a very poor job market; declining
or lost faith, and for good reason, among constitutional academic
lawyers that the Supreme Court will use its powers to move us toward a more just society and a lost faith in the adjudicative process
that for many in the academy provided the raison d'être of law
itself, of academic legal scholarship, and of their own participation in it; a growing malaise afflicting faculty and students caused
by a lack of any shared sense of law's moral purpose or point to
replace that declining faith;[10] despair among ethics professors and
constitutional lawyers over the use of law's forms—"legal memoranda," "justice departments," "offices of legal counsel," and the
like—in the George W. Bush administration to promote the seemingly lawless ends of the most powerful leviathan on Earth[11] cou-
pled with the failure of the Obama administration to do anything
about it; increased calls from the academy to the academy to stop
doing "merely" normative, or "advocacy," or "doctrinal" scholarship, thus calling into question the point and even the existence of
what has been for almost a century the bread and butter of good
legal scholarship—because of all these factors, law school facul-
ties, and therefore their students, find themselves in a profound
crisis of identity, all stemming from a sense that both the academy
and the profession it serves have been demoralized: they both self-
avowedly lack a moral point. Briefly put, it's not clear anymore

that this perhaps not-very-remunerative-after-all profession for which we train our students and which for some time now has not been very much fun, either, is actually good for anything anymore, or whether it ever was, or whether it really is, as some skeptics have been saying for a long time, nothing but a legitimating mask of an increasingly insane and psychopathic sovereign beast. A little bit of Rule of Law idealism—whether formal, procedural, or substantive—can't hurt, in such a climate, and it might help. It might help make the case for robust procedural protections for our prisoners of our wars on terror abroad and on drugs here, it might help us temper, or at least complement, the Rule of Law interpretations that center profit with one that centers individual dignity and intelligence, and it might help us reclaim a sense of law's ennobling purpose in the contemporary legal academy. All of that would be terrific. I have no quarrel with the basic thrust of this project.

I do, though, have some objections—four of them—which I'll move through quickly and which I hope, if addressed, will strengthen the project. All are in the nature of suggested friendly amendments. My fifth and major comment—not an objection quite—goes to some of the features of all three paradigms of Rule of Law scholarship that Waldron has usefully identified and distinguished: formal, procedural, and substantive. All three identify the Rule of Law with a legalist impulse that might be used in a way to blunt or counter the pernicious abuse of power by a too-fierce state besotted by its own political will. This is not, I want to suggest, an exhaustive account of our hopes for Law, in mediating the relationship between the individual and the state, nor should it be. All three accounts, I will argue, ignore the ways in which the law expresses the will of the state to protect weaker parties harmed not by the state but by stronger private entities—employers, landlords, union bosses, private criminal gangs, oppressive church authorities, abusive parents or spouses, too-powerful private associations, and the like. This, too, should be a part of our theorizing over the Rule of Law if that theorizing is intended to capture our ideals of law, but it is almost routinely slighted in Rule of Law writing. And, it is not addressed here, so I will urge, at the end of these comments, that we do so.

Let me start, though, with my objections. First, I'm confused by Waldron's claim that there is no literature that expounds a procedural conception of the Rule of Law as it is presented here. Owen Fiss, at Yale Law School, has devoted the better part of his extremely fruitful career to doing just that. His highly regarded leading casebook on civil procedure,[12] coauthored with Judith Resnick, makes the two-thousand-page case for the moral value of decent procedure, its centrality to the Rule of Law, and the role of procedure in furthering the deeply foundational purpose Waldron identifies here—giving voice to each individual participant in a way that treats him or her respectfully as an intelligent human being with a perspective that is worthy of attention and that must be heard. Fiss has also defended precisely this understanding of the Rule of Law in an extensive body of writings stressing the moral superiority of adjudication over alternative dispute resolution (ADR) methods.[13] The virtue of traditional adjudication, Fiss has argued, in contrast with ADR, is that it meets the imperative of justice that the law must, through procedure, give litigants full participation, an opportunity to voice their perspectives and views, and a panoply of procedural and evidentiary rules designed to protect that voice and participation. In fact, for Fiss, these procedural virtues are *so* central and so overriding—the opportunities for intelligent participation presented by the procedural aspects of adjudication so plentiful and profound—that they apparently obviate the need for civil disobedience and even external moral critique of law: there's virtually no claim, Fiss has asserted in his most extreme version of this position, that can't be voiced in a legal register and aired in a court of law, so there is literally never a basis for the anarchical claim that law can be reformed only from outside, rather than from inside the system itself.[14] These procedural values, furthermore, Fiss goes on to argue, constitute the long-sought bridge between the *ought* and the *is* and thus undercut legal positivism; to the extent that a legal system honors them, so says Fiss, the system has real and not just moral authority.[15] It is the source of a functional legal system's moral authority. This is an extreme version of the proceduralism Waldron wants us to recognize here, and it is certainly not required by the proceduralism urged here, but, nevertheless, even if overstated, Fissian jurisprudence is a counterexample to Waldron's claim that law scholars have overlooked the important of procedural justice when thinking through law's basic values.

But it's not just the Yale proceduralists who get overlooked in Waldron's claim that we've somehow neglected procedural values in our thinking about the Rule of Law. Led by the Warren Court, an entire generation of constitutional lawyers and thinkers, as well as large swaths of legal scholarship, underwent a so-called due process revolution in the 1960s and 1970s, itself fueled by a near-religious faith in—at least a romance with—the purifying powers of decent procedure. In a nutshell, that revolution was premised on exactly the understanding of the Rule of Law expounded by Waldron here: justice, the Fourteenth Amendment, and the due process clause, we all learned in those decades, all demand intelligent participation by individuals in the systems of law that impose stigma, harm, liability, or punishment. The due process revolution was real, not a dream—this is exactly what Gideon's trumpet was trumpeting—and, although it is easy to fault it for giving poor people an awful lot of procedure and very little substance—plenty of rights, but no means to enjoy any of them; all sorts of venues to voice complaints to a system unwilling to rectify the injustices that prompted them—it did nevertheless rest on precisely the values and even the vision that Waldron is calling for: a recognition that human dignity requires that we be treated respectfully as intelligent participants in the machinations of government, particularly when they are threatening us with stigma, harm, loss, liability, or punishment. That revolution bore fruit. As a result of it, for example, although we have no right to welfare, we have a right not to have our welfare benefits cut or taken from us without a decent hearing.[16] We may not have a right to various social security benefits, but we have a (limited) right to a hearing that determines what benefits we'll get or lose.[17] We may not have a right to various government jobs, but we have a right to a hearing before being sacked,[18] and, most famous, of course, pursuant to *Gideon v. Wainwright*,[19] lionized in Anthony Lewis's *Gideon's Trumpet*,[20] a loving history of the case that was read for years by every entering law student in "orientation weeks" of law school, we have a right to a lawyer before being punished for violating the state's criminal code. In almost a dozen cases, not just one or two, the Supreme Court held during the heyday of this due process movement that, while we may not have a right to some specified set of benefits, we nevertheless have a right not to have them taken away without

our having an opportunity to be heard.[21] It was that procedural
revolution, in fact, at least as much as *Brown v. Board* or *Roe v.
Wade*, that fueled an entire generation's outsize faith in the restorative
abilities of adjudicative law and the arguably disproportionate allocation of progressive resources given over to adjudicative constitutionalism—a development that Waldron has in other contexts,
along with others, deplored.[22] But my point here is solely descriptive. Waldron's call to law professors that we need to attend to the
procedural rather than to the formal or substantive values of the
Rule of Law is a bit like raising the flag on the Fourth of July and
exhorting the assembled crowd to attend to the neglected value
of patriotism. (Not entirely: it may well be that the professional
philosophical literature has neglected this dimension of the Rule
of Law, and it is of course that literature that is Waldron's target.
But almost.) Legal scholars of a certain generation, process jocks
all, most assuredly have not.

The second problem I want to highlight echoes the familiar contrast, in legal realist writings, of the difference between law on the
books and law on the streets. Waldron's piece is a contribution to
our legal ideals—an exploration of the values that we *should* hold
and that *should* attend our legal system. As such, these legal ideals
are twice removed from the law on the streets: they are the ideals
that we should hold—not necessarily those we *do* hold, much less
put into practice in legal life. Nevertheless, they are not unrelated
to our extant ideals and find at least a dim echo in the practices of
the juvenile court judge and state prosecutor. Our ideals for law
must be derived at least in some way from our practice. Rule of
Law literature in particular attempts to articulate values that are
to some degree already imperfectly embedded in legal practice, as
well as values that ought to be. The same is true here: the ideal that
Waldron describes is by no means foreign to either our generally
held ideals or our practices. So, as is often the case with scholarship that explores values that partly emerge from practice but then
seeks to cleanly articulate them in order to both criticize and better guide that practice, Waldron's argument risks sugarcoating our
current practices. If we accept his argument, in other words, that
our Rule of Law scholarship is deficient in the way he suggests, because it doesn't reflect ideals embedded in practice, we might too
readily accept the claim that we respect these procedural values in

practice far more than we actually do. After all, all we need to fix to satisfy Waldron, so to speak, is the Rule of Law scholarship that describes our practices, rather than the practices themselves. Then we run the danger of just baldly refusing to see how far we have moved from these ideals, whether stated or not. If we accept these ideals as ideals we should hold, then we run the risk, in a word, of hypocrisy—we don't do as we say we should do, even though what we say we should do is based in part on what we claim to do. In fact, the extent of that hypocrisy, particularly with respect to the touted ideal of procedural justice in the criminal justice system in this country, borders on the absurd.

In our scholarship and in popular culture—television shows and the like—we extol as evidence of our appreciation of the procedural virtues Waldron champions our insistence that every criminal defendant in this country has a right to a lawyer, a right to a day in court, and a right to a jury of his or her peers. That defendant further enjoys a presumption of innocence, an extremely favorable burden of proof, and, in general, a panoply of procedural and evidentiary rules that are so vividly stacked in his or her favor that we can say, and often do with real pride, that in *this* country at least, we prefer to risk the possibility that a hundred guilty criminals will go free than risk the wrongful incarceration of even one innocent. These values are so central, Waldron wants to further claim, that they must be present in a legal system for that system to claim the mantle of the Rule of Law.[23] And surely *we* have a Rule of Law. We often use the phrase "Rule of Law" precisely to describe the virtues of our system. But—if we have a Rule of Law and if the Rule of Law protects precisely these values, then why are the prisons so full? You'd think we'd have criminals roaming the streets and relatively empty prisons. Yet, we have a massive crisis in this country of *over*-incarceration.[24] *Something* must have gone very badly wrong. More than 70 percent of the inmates in our federal prisons got there without benefit of a trial.[25] They may have had a *right* to a trial and a jury of their peers and a presumption of innocence and a stacked deck burden of proof in their favor, but something must have been lost in translation: the vast majority of defendants never see a jury. Rather, their cases are "plea bargained," meaning that, at most, the real rather than hypothetical inmates in our prisons have had the opportunity to intelligently present their

own story to their own lawyer in a quick fifteen-minute interview
prior to the recording of the bargain their lawyer recommends.
We should be very clear about this, as we tout the necessity of procedural virtues that require intelligent participation by all prior to
incarceration or other forms of stigma. We do not, in this country, accord those whom we arrest and incarcerate an opportunity
to intelligently participate in the process that led to their arrest,
conviction, or incarceration. We now have such massive overincar-
ceration and absurdly high penalties, particularly for nonviolent
offenses, that were we to switch course—were we to provide a trial
and an opportunity to participate to each of these defendants we
threaten to incarcerate—the entire criminal justice system would
crash. At the so-called back-end, as well, we see the same pattern.
Limits on appeals and habeas petitions[26] and the ever-expanding
universe of immunities of state actors,[27] from prosecutors and law-
makers down to the cops on the street, limit the opportunity to
air perspectives on the constitutionality of law enforcement in an
intelligent way in a court of law governed by fair procedures, quite
literally down to the vanishing point. We need to be careful not
to ground the insistence that the Rule of Law rests on procedural
values on our own practices when our own practices are so profoundly deficient, unless we are happy to say forthrightly that our
own legal system does not abide by the Rule of Law. Arguing that
the Rule of Law requires procedural niceties without acknowledg-
ing those deficiencies, I believe, is an embarrassment, albeit an entirely avoidable one.

Third, we should acknowledge, before championing too loudly
the cause of proceduralism, that excessively precious procedures
in the face of grotesque substantive law from which there is truly
no exit, even with all the procedure in the world, can be a massive insult to dignity. So much so, that even the "winners lose," to
quote from one particularly poignant recent article document-
ing this phenomenon.[28] First of all, even the most just procedure
might simply be pointless. Guantanamo detainees, according
to one of their lawyers, don't much value a visit with a lawyer if
given the choice: visits with lawyers just lead to trouble, and even
their (substantial) procedural victories are often empty. The detainees know they aren't getting out no matter how welcome and
fair-minded the judicial rhetoric granting them all sorts of rights.[29]

Alternatively, and I think more pervasively, a litigant might well be treated with the utmost procedural fairness, but the underlying law might be so profoundly unjust that even just procedure becomes a mockery or worse! One way to put the worry, perhaps, is that it isn't clear that all that good procedure adds more in justice than it costs in the legitimation it lends to the unjust regime or law. American antebellum courts in southern slave states decided, in open court hearings that observed decent procedures, whether litigants before them had enough drops of Negro blood before applying their slave laws and depriving the pleaders before them of their children, freedom, and husbands or wives.[30] Under these laws, and no doubt in part because of just procedure, some individuals were found not to be slaves and won some measure of freedom, but how do we weigh the value of that just procedure? Courts in Vichy France, Richard Weisberg has shown, acted with exquisitely just procedures when determining whether a litigant had a Jewish ancestor of sufficiently close sanguinity to justify depriving him of his livelihood or life under the Vichy "race laws."[31] Do we applaud their fidelity to principles of procedural justice? Israeli courts in the 1950s, according to Raif Zeik, exhibited an outsize respect for procedural justice when determining, with the utmost rectitude, whether a small number of Palestinians had returned to their life-long homes during "Freedom week"—a one-week period between judicial orders when for legalistic reasons Palestinians actually enjoyed a right of return to one particular town—or whether their return had occurred one moment before the designated week began or after it ended before deciding how or whether to apply the Law of Exclusion. As the court said in one such case, "there's a *way* to evict these people," and that way was in accordance with procedural justice.[32] Defendants sentenced to life without the possibility of parole under three-strikes laws for relatively petty and nonviolent offenses might find the justice of the procedural rules under which they are convicted to be quite generous—but they might find that very generosity to be disorienting, a mighty distraction, or worse.[33] In Hell, as Grant Gilmore observed, there will be perfect procedural justice.[34]

Now, it seems on first blush arithmetically or trivially true that application of these unjust laws under just procedures *must* lead to less injustice than the same laws imposed under unjust procedural laws. Surely hell would be even more hellish if its unjust punishments were doled out in a procedurally unjust manner. But that first blush might be misleading. The very procedural justice of the trial, with its measured fairness, its appearance of rationality, its veneer of civility, its modulated dialogue, its exquisitely tortured rules of evidence, the apparent equality and equal regard with which participants are treated, all lend a sense of legitimacy as well as finality to the entire proceeding. The procedural justice itself sends a message of fairness as well as of the futility of resistance. In an unjust regime—Vichy France's race laws, South Africa's apartheid, the South's slave laws, California's three-strikes laws—the very fairness and sense of rationality that Waldron applauds also cleanses, to some degree, the injustice of the underlying law in the eyes of observers, while underscoring, in a sense, perversely but still underscoring, the totalizing violence of the law being enforced against its victims. We can do this to you—and we can even do it to you *fairly*, in a way that everyone will agree is *just*. Procedural justice is both a luxury of and a precondition of a confident legal system—it evidences as well as effectuates a system that is beyond challenge because it is beyond reproach. A fair system, after all, ought not be challenged, and a strong enough system to risk the victories against the state that are the inevitable byproduct of the fairness—some defendants, after all, will flunk the one-drop rule, some won't have a Jewish relative of sufficiently close sanguinity, some Palestinians will be granted a right to return, and some black South Africans will have their passes ruled intact, if these procedures are truly fair—is all the more likely to be a system that won't be challenged, at least from within. Procedural justice, in other words, can be *demoralizing*. After all, you had your day in court, so what's to complain of? The procedural justice, then, strengthens the system by legitimating it, all the more so in an unjust regime. If that effect—the legitimizing effect, for short—is substantial, then the procedural justice of a trial in an unjust regime may perversely increase the overall injustice of the regime, making it all the more invulnerable to change, whether through politics, revolution, or subterfuge. A legal system that abides by the Rule of Law, where the latter is defined by reference to procedural criteria, is not necessarily thereby more just. When it isn't, it's not clear where the value of all that procedure lies, other than in the fodder it provides modernist writers.

Fourth: justice, for a range of additional reasons that have long been cited by the ADR movement[35] but have also been noted in some way ever since Bentham's broadsides,[36] may sometimes be frustrated rather than furthered by an excess of procedure: when procedures are overly technical; where they impose costs that might outweigh their value, at least to individuals; when they require skilled players; where they strengthen the monopoly power of lawyers and judges. Procedure can mask and then amplify, rather than address, the power of judges and lawyers over lay people's lives. Today, it's worth noting that when all that procedural justice is generously extended to corporations—rendered "persons" by a compliant Supreme Court—it strengthens corporate power, as well, although perhaps by this point redundantly so. All of these are reasons to treat procedural advances gingerly. The first procedural justice revolution at the beginning of the twentieth century—the creation of the federal rules of civil procedure, the invention of pretrial discovery, the innovations represented by interrogatories, depositions, and so forth—may have been in part motivated by the desire to lend transparency to a trial process that otherwise resembled a Dorothy Sayers mystery more than an attempt to find the factual truth of the matter, but it has devolved into something very different. It has become a means by which monied corporate litigants and their lawyers can defeat individual claimants through a barrage of costly motions. Privileges and immunities intended to shield the communications between embattled individual defendants and their lawyers in criminal courts of law have become means by which corporate malfeasance is rendered all the more immune from state and, therefore, public control.[37] These are not isolated examples; they represent a systemic problem. Procedures intended for the protection of beleaguered and relatively powerless individuals threatened by an all-powerful state, once generalized, become protections for the most powerful corporate actors against individuals who rightly seek the protection of the state or of state prosecutors seeking to restrain corporate power. Waldron's celebration of a procedural Rule of Law makes no mention of any of this. The story is rather of a ferocious

powerful state bent on exacting its will through punishment, censure, and the like, against a beleaguered individual, who seeks out
the protections of the Rule of Law. Litigants and defendants, however, can be more or less powerful, as can states, as can those interests on whose behalf states act.

Last: Waldron's procedural Rule of Law, like Fuller's formal
one and the libertarian's substantive one, presupposes a relation
between the individual and the state and a metaphorical narrative about that relation, which is just incomplete. On all three
accounts, substantive, formal, and procedural, the Rule of Law is
obviously a very good thing. It is law's humane face, sought by the
individual seeking protection against an act of power taken by a
potentially dangerous and overreaching state. The Rule of Law,
if we put these three models together, respects individual intelligence, perspective, dignity, liberty, and agency, as well as entrepre-
neurial and cooperative projects. The state, and the state's action,
by contrast, is fraught with evil, unrestrained power, witlessness,
and violence. The state, after all, punishes, penalizes, renders liable, censures, stigmatizes, or harms, while the Rule of Law respects, frees, supports, and so on. The harmed individual in this
picture has dignitary and liberty interests that are first endangered
by the punishing state and then protected by law. The state, in this
scenario, is at best a necessary evil but at worst, when unrestrained
by law, an unrelenting nightmare. It is far more powerful than the
individual, and it has a license to inflict harm, stigma, punishment,
and liability. The Rule of Law, on all three accounts, is further a
very good thing because it can conceivably limit this unrestrained
power—on Waldron's view, through decent procedure that requires that the state protect the individual's intelligence; on Fuller's, through formal rules that require that the state protect the
individual's liberty; and on the libertarian's substantive account,
through rules of property and contract that require that the state
protect the individual's particular projects and investments. The
unrestrained state, the power of a witless public in a functioning
democracy, is the problem solved by the Rule of Law: the political
state acts, and the Rule of Law protects the individual, his dignity
and his intelligence, against that pernicious state action by requiring that the state invite the individual's intelligent participation in
whatever proceeding the state contemplates in exacting its pound

of flesh. The individual in this story has every reason to be fearful of the state. The individual likewise has every reason to welcome the intervention of Law so as to protect him from that state's power.

There are familiar problems with this scenario. It overstates the rationality and possibly the good will of courts and of law, as the Critical Legal Studies movement argued a couple of decades back, and it understates the capacity for public-minded and reasonable deliberation by the lawmaking branches, as Jeremy Waldron has argued now for several years. There is, though, a further limitation with this understanding of the Rule of Law: it presupposes that the problem of power to which law is the solution is that of the beleaguered individual pressing up against an overbearing sovereign state. But this is not the only problem of power to which law is or ought to be the solution. Rather, law is, and I would suggest the Rule of Law is, perhaps quintessentially, the solution to the problem of private power. Without a state that monopolizes the weapons of force, any individual is vulnerable to the private violent power of any other, as Hobbes witnessed, and with decreasing public control of guns in this country we increasingly witness likewise. Without a state that regulates, somewhat, against the vagaries of fate and intergenerational family loyalty, an individual is vulnerable to the outsized economic power of another, whether that power is itself a function of genetic luck, social history, or inheritance. Without a state that guards against and compensates, through its law, fraud, bad faith, duress, negligence, breach of contracts, breach of fiduciary duties, and so on, an individual is buttressed by the tendency, not of states but of private actors, to stigmatize, inflict harm, punish, and the like. It's worth noting that this power of law—the power to intervene into the undue exercise of private power—serves a foundationally progressive function.

But there is nothing of this function of law and nothing of this in the articulation of law's ideals in most Rule of Law scholarship, including Jeremy Waldron's latest intervention. This is, I think, mightily odd. This is, after all, the Rule of *Law* we're talking about, and a lot of our laws are about protecting individuals against the undue aggressions of other individuals or corporations, not only through the criminal law but through much of private law as well. This purpose, in other words, is right at the heart of law's point.

But this understanding of law's point is somehow invisible in contemporary Rule of Law scholarship. Rather, the kind of law that is regarded as the point of the "law" that is referenced in the phrase "Rule of Law" is not our ordinary criminal law, tort law, and the rest of it that so clearly serve something like this function. Rather, it is a higher law—a constitutional law for some, a procedural law for others, a law of process maybe, a law of laws—that acts as a constraint, rhetorically, on the *state* and on pernicious state actors, as well as on the low-level law (criminal, contract, tort, and so on) that is the product of state action. That low-level law, apparently, is guided not by any deals we might have that are embraced imperfectly or not by our "Rule of Law" scholarship but rather by political whim. The higher law that constrains the state and ordinary law is what embodies the ideals expressed in Rule of Law scholarship.

The consequence of this division of labor is that a good bit of both our ideals for law and our practice is left out of the procedural, formal, and substantive ideal. First, and most striking, plaintiffs are left out. Waldron's procedural Rule of Law protects criminal and civil defendants—persons who find themselves ensnared in legal process against their will and against their wishes—against the tendency of the state to sanction, punish, impose liability, and so on. It does not protect plaintiffs—those who seek out legal process and legal protection, those who quite willfully attempt to invoke the powers of the state to protect them against the tendency of private actors—would-be defendants—to breach contracts, commit torts, or kill people, and the tendency, sometimes, of states to be complicit in those acts through a selectively willful failure to facilitate legal action against those private actors. Consequently, Waldron's procedural Rule of Law does not protect plaintiffs in court, against, for example, the immunities of various actors—not only prosecutors and police officers but also church officials or spouses or parents or charities—from liability or against rules of evidence designed to protect various "privileges" that drastically limit the liability of entire classes of defendants. His procedural Rule of Law does not protect would-be plaintiffs against various limiting doctrines, such as preemption, or limits imposed on entire classes of damages, such as pain and suffering awards, that place the public venue of the courtroom out of reach for the articulation of various sorts of injuries. Rather, it seemingly presupposes a body of private law and criminal law that either perfectly protects or overly protects victims of crime and would-be plaintiffs against private wrong and then enforces these regimes in an unjustifiably heavy-handed manner against beleaguered defendants. Plaintiffs, in this imagining, are aligned with the state—the private attorneys general, so to speak—and become part of the state machinery in need of restraint by the idealized procedures of the Rule of Law.

More fundamental, Waldron's idealized Rule of Law, like the idealized rules of law that he is criticizing, does not contain even a hint of a reference to law's protective function. Law does a lot of things but one of its core functions is to protect individuals against what would otherwise be undeterred privations against them—not by overreaching state officials but rather by undeterred private individuals, corporations, or entities. Law does, as Waldron says, stigmatize, punish, impose liability, and so on. Law also, though, compensates individuals for private wrongs and protects them at least much of the time against private violence. Sometimes it does this well, and sometimes it does it only sporadically or not at all. In my view, a society that claims to regulate conduct under the ideal of the Rule of Law—as opposed to the rule of the stronger, or the rule of the more mendacious, or the rule of the more richly endowed, or the rule of the more vindictive, or the more manipulative, or the more fraudulent, or the more violent and so forth—should, seemingly, require that law do as much. Rule of Law scholarship, then, one would think, should reflect these ideals.

But it doesn't, and it's worth asking why not? The phrase "rule of law" is obviously a metaphor—it is intended to reference the ideals we hold and should hold for actual legal systems. Presumably, an ideal legal system will target private wrongs as a problem of power that law should address. Yet, Rule of Law scholarship routinely fails to do so. One reason for this neglect may be that Rule of Law scholars share a two-step background narrative about both the state's and law's metaphoric beginnings. Individuals first create a state with a monopoly over violence to protect them from one another. The state then fashions criminal law, tort law, and the like in order to do so. That's step one. The state, however, then becomes dangerously powerful and itself must be constrained. So, we then create higher law—procedural law, constitutional law, and so on—to protect us against the state. That's step two. The

"Rule of Law" then becomes a metaphoric reference to the ideals we hold for those higher forms of law. The work of the state, then, is to control private conduct and private abuse of power through ordinary law. The work of the Rule of Law, by contrast, is to restrain the state from undue enforcement of the lower laws that are in turn intended to restrain individuals. The state constrains individuals through ordinary law. The Rule of Law constrains the state. Some other mechanism—maybe democratic accountability, maybe just conscience—prompts the promulgation of those laws intended to restrain private conduct, including prompting their creation where the state can't really be bothered.

The metaphor, however, is just that, and the narrative bears no relation to the actual creation of states, laws, higher laws, constitutions, or codes of procedure. If we scrap metaphor and narrative and simply ask what sorts of ideals our legal systems should strive to meet, I believe we get a richer and more complete picture than the metaphor and narrative implicit in Rule of Law scholarship yield. Minimally, such a picture would include, as current Rule of Law scholarship does not, acknowledgement of what we aim to do with law, not only what we aim to prohibit law from doing. And a part of what we aim to do with law, at least some of the time, is to prohibit abuses of private power or to provide a means by which conflicts over private power can be aired. This requires not only prohibiting the state from "stigmatizing, harming, punishing or imposing liability" without fair process. It also requires the state to compensate, deter, and retribute where need be and to monopolize the use of force. We want, from a liberal state that abides by the Rule of Law, not only a legal system that won't impose its will against us without respecting our intelligence and seeking out our participation. We also want, from a liberal state that abides by the Rule of Law, some measure of safety in our homes and neighborhoods against private violence, some measure of fairness in our commercial dealings, and some measure of wellbeing in our private lives, free of the privations of more powerful private actors.

This is an omission that matters. The stigma, punishment, harm, and so on that threaten the enjoyment of the lives of many people, all of which Waldron identifies as coming from state power, at least on occasion come not from states but from powerful nonstate entities. Part of the point of law is to do something about that. It has been recognized by liberal theorists of the state from Hobbes to Rawls that the state, far from being nothing but a ferocious evil in people's lives that needs constraining, can also be a force for domestic peace, for equality, and for a generally high level of social wellbeing, precisely by virtue of ensuring, through lawful process, that the state successfully monopolize the use of force and by being a generally equalizing participant in the battle over the allocation of private power. We should, I believe, construct our ideals for law—which is what I take Rule of Law scholarship as attempting to do—in a way that incorporates these realities and these hopes for Law's reach. Doing so, I think, calls not for modification of any of the three paradigms, all of which can be read conjunctively, but for the construction of a fourth. It is not incompatible with Jeremy Waldron's proceduralism, just as his proceduralism is not at bottom inconsistent with Fuller's formalism and just as Fuller's formalism is not inconsistent with substantive accounts of the Rule of Law that prioritize the protection of private property. It may, however, be in tension, at points, with all of them. So, I would just issue this plea for a more robust understanding of our legalist ideals. If we are going to talk about our ideals for legalism through the metaphor of the Rule of Law, we should expand that conversation so that it includes our ideals regarding not only what the state may not do without decent procedure but also what it must do with its law if we are to enjoy the intelligence and perspectives that we all possess and that Waldron's procedural Rule of Law, to its credit, aims to protect.

NOTES

1. Lon L. Fuller, *The Morality of Law* (New Haven: Yale University Press, 1969), 33–39.
2. Jeremy Waldron, "The Rule of Law and the Importance of Procedure," in this volume, 14–16.
3. Ibid., 5–7, 16–17.
4. Ibid., 19–20.
5. Ibid., 5, 14–16.
6. Ibid., 23.
7. *But see* Joseph Landau, "Muscular Procedure: Conditional Deference in the Executive Detention Cases," *Wash. L. Rev.* 84 (2009): 661.

8. *See* James Forman, "Exporting Harshness: How the War on Crime Helped Make the War on Terror Possible," *N.Y.U. Rev. L. and Soc. Change* 33 (2009): 331–74.

9. Waldron, "The Rule of Law and the Importance of Procedure," 18.

10. *See generally Constitution in 2020*, ed. Jack M. Balkin and Reva B. Siegel (Oxford: Oxford University Press, 2009).

11. *See* David Luban, *Legal Ethics and Human Dignity* (New York: Cambridge University Press, 2007), 162–205.

12. Owen M. Fiss and Judith Resnik, *Procedure* (New York: Foundation Press, 1988).

13. *See* Owen Fiss, "Against Settlement," *Yale L.J.* 93 (1984): 1073, 1075; Owen Fiss, "Out of Eden," *Yale L.J.* 94 (1985): 1669; Owen Fiss, *The Law as It Could Be* (New York: New York University Press, 2003).

14. *See* Owen Fiss, "Interpretation and Objectivity," *Stan. L. Rev.* 34 (1982): 739, 749.

15. Ibid., 753.

16. *See Goldberg v. Kelly*, 397 U.S. 254, 266 (1970) (right to hearing prior to termination of welfare payments).

17. *Contra Matthews v. Eldridge*, 424 U.S. 319 (1976) (right to a hearing prior to termination of social security payments). *See generally* Henry Monaghan, *"Of 'Liberty' and 'Property,'"* *Cornell L. Rev.* 62 (1977): 405, 409, and Charles Reich, "The New Property," *Yale L.J.* 73 (1964): 733, 738.

18. *See, e.g., Cleveland Bd. of Educ. v. Loudermill*, 470 U.S. 532 (1985) (right to pretermination hearing for public employees who can be discharged only for cause). *Cf. Board of Regents v. Roth*, 408 U.S. 564, 587–89 (1972) (J. Marshall dissenting) (arguing, against the majority, that pretermination hearings should be required for public employees even when renewal of their employment is not express or implied).

19. 372 U.S. 335 (1963).

20. *See* Anthony Lewis, *Gideon's Trumpet* (New York: Vintage Books, 1989).

21. *See, e.g., Goldberg*, 397 U.S. 254 (1970); *Loudermill*, 470 U.S. 532 (1985).

22. Jeremy Waldron, "The Core of the Case against Judicial Review," *Yale L. Rev.* 115 (2006): 1346.

23. Waldron, "The Rule of Law and the Importance of Procedure," 5–7, 12–14.

24. For a good discussion of the moral issues this poses for liberal democracy, *see* Sharon Dolovich, "Legitimate Punishment in Liberal Democracy," *Buff. Crim. L. Rev.* 7 (2004): 307.

25. Bureau of Justice Statistics, *Compendium of Federal Justice Statistics, 1998*, at 51 (May 2000). *See generally* William J. Stuntz, "Plea Bargaining

and Criminal Law's Disappearing Shadow," *Harv. L. Rev.* 117 (2004): 2548, 2561.

26. *See, e.g.,* James E. Pfander, "The Limits of Habeus Jurisdiction and the Global War on Terror," *Cornell L. Rev.* 91 (2006): 497; Daniel J. Meltzer, "Habeus Corpus Jurisdiction, Substantive Rights, and the War on Terror," *Harv. L. Rev.* 120 (2007): 2029; Bryan A. Stevenson, "Confronting Mass Imprisonment and Restoring Fairness to Collateral Review of Criminal Cases," *Harv. C.R.-C.L. L. Rev.* 41 (2006): 339.

27. *See* Nancy Leong, "The 'Saucier' Qualified Immunity Experiment: An Empirical Analysis," *Pepp. L. Rev.* 36 (2009): 667.

28. Raef Zreik, "When Winners Lose: On Legal Language," *International Review of Victimology* (forthcoming).

29. Muneer Ahmad, "Resisting Guantanamo: Rights at the Brink of Dehumanization," *NW. U. L. Rev.* 103 (2009): 1683.

30. *See* Mark Tushnet, *American Law of Slavery, 1810–1860, The Considerations of Humanity and Interest* (Princeton: Princeton University Press, 1981).

31. Richard H. Weisberg, *The Failure of the Word* (New Haven: Yale University Press, 1984), 181.

32. Quoted by Raef Zreik, in workshop presentation of "When Winners Lose," Georgetown Law Center, Spring, 2010.

33. Cal. Penal Code § 667; *see, e.g.,* Mike Males and Dan Macallair, "Striking Out: The Failure of California's 'Three Strikes and You're Out' Law," *Stan. L. and Pol'y. Rev.* 11 (2001): 65; Michael Vitiello, "California's Three Strikes and We're Out: Was Judicial Activism California's Best Hope?," *U.C. Davis L. Rev.* 37 (2004):1025.

34. "In Heaven there will be no law, and the lion will lie down with the lamb. . . . In Hell there will be nothing but law, and due process will be meticulously observed." Grant Gilmore, *The Ages of American Law* (New Haven and London: Yale University Press, 1977), 111.

35. *See* Symposium, "Against Settlement, Twenty-Five Years Later," *Fordham L. Rev.* 78 (2009): 1117.

36. Jeremy Bentham, *An Introduction to the Principles of Morals and Legislation,* ed. J. H. Burns and H. L. A. Hart (London: Athlone Press, 1970); Jeremy Bentham, *Of Laws in General,* ed. H. L. A. Hart (London: Athlone Press, 1970).

37. Julie O'Sullivan, "The Federal Criminal 'Code' Is a Disgrace: Obstruction Statutes as Case Study," *J. Crim. L. and Criminology* 96 (2006): 643.

3

A SUBSTANTIVE CONCEPTION OF THE RULE OF LAW: NONARBITRARY TREATMENT AND THE LIMITS OF PROCEDURE

COREY BRETTSCHNEIDER

1. Introduction

In his contribution to this volume, Jeremy Waldron[1] distinguishes among three possible ways to conceive of the rule of law. First, we might think of the rule of law as defined by formal requirements. These include the requirements that laws must be public, noncontradictory, and nonretroactive, as Lon Fuller contends in *The Morality of Law*.[2] Second, Waldron claims that the rule of law requires procedural guarantees in the courtroom, such as rights to an attorney, to an impartial judge, and to a fair trial. Procedural guarantees should be respected, writes Waldron, because they protect the dignity of individuals as "active intelligences." Third, he suggests but does not dwell on the possible substantive requirements of the rule of law, which might constrain courtroom procedures and legislative enactments.

I draw here on Waldron's powerful case for the importance of procedures to develop an argument for a more substantive understanding of the rule of law. Specifically, I emphasize two ways that Waldron's argument might be expanded. I argue first that Waldron's appeal to dignity as the moral basis of procedures commits him to an account of substantive guarantees. These guarantees may limit, at times, the procedural dimensions of both law and democratic decision making. Second, I expand on Waldron's notion of dignity—itself a substantive value—as respect for "active intelligence." In particular, I argue that those subject to law are entitled to nonarbitrary treatment. When dignity is theorized in this way, we can better understand the relationship between the substantive values at the heart of the rule of law and their substantive implications. The expanded conception, which adds nonarbitrary treatment to dignity, more clearly distinguishes between the concept of the rule of law and the ideal of democratic self-rule.

2. A SUBSTANTIVE VALUE WITH PROCEDURAL AND SUBSTANTIVE IMPLICATIONS

Among the most important contributions of Waldron's essay is his challenge to the formalistic conceptions of the rule of law that have dominated discussions about this topic. These conceptions —including those based in positivism and in Fuller's moral minimalism—are overly descriptive and fail to provide any moral normative reasons for valuing the formal elements of law or even the rule of law itself. Waldron corrects this flaw when he explains that the moral basis of the rule of law should be respect for dignity. His convincing argument presents a significant advance over the formalist theories that have not fully articulated the reasons and values that underlie the formal elements of law.

Waldron rightly emphasizes early in his essay that it would be a mistake to value the formal features of the rule of law for formalistic reasons.[3] Such reasoning, which is common among positivist thinkers, would be circular. He suggests, however, that Fuller avoids the circularity problem by basing the formal elements of law on the more basic value of dignity. By highlighting Fuller's appeal to a value that is independent from and more fundamental than law's formal requirements, Waldron opens the possibility that the rule of law requires more than the merely formal elements identified by Fuller. In order to understand what is required by the rule of law, we must engage in a normative inquiry about the meaning and implications of dignity. We cannot merely posit a set of formal requirements that exclusively define the rule of law. As Waldron forcefully suggests, the rule of law is an ideal to be endorsed, and any account of the rule of law should reference the reasons for that endorsement.

Waldron interprets dignity to mean respect for the "active intelligence" of the people who are subject to law.[4] The thought is that people bound by law have a perspective or view of their own that the courts must acknowledge before reaching a decision. As Waldron writes, law "embodies a crucial dignitarian idea—respecting the dignity of those to whom the norms are applied as *beings capable of explaining themselves.*"[5] For people to be able to explain themselves, the rule of law must provide for institutional protections such as courtroom procedures. These include "a hearing by an impartial tribunal," a "right to representation by counsel," and a "right to make legal argument about the bearing of evidence and about the bearing of the various legal norms relevant to the case."[6] Courts and their procedural protections provide the way for citizens to participate actively and to explain their own perspective when they have been accused of crimes or are otherwise subject to the force of law.[7] I would add to this account that dignity should mean *equal* dignity. The procedural elements of the rule of law should be entitlements that can be claimed by all subject to coercion.

I contend that Waldron's view—in particular, his claim that a substantive moral value of dignity underlies the rule of law—commits him to a substantive dimension to the rule of law. Just as the value of dignity requires procedural guarantees that go beyond formal requirements, so too does it require substantive guarantees that go beyond procedure. Although Waldron's emphasis in his essay is on drawing out the procedural implications of the rule of law, the substantive implications stem from the substantive value of dignity that is at the heart of his ideal of the rule of law. In a brief aside, Waldron acknowledges this point: "I believe that there is a natural overlap between substantive and formal elements [of the rule of law], not least because . . . the formal elements are usually argued for on substantive grounds of dignity and liberty."[8] It is for this reason that I think Waldron's framework commits him to the view that substantive requirements should be added to the formal and procedural aspects of the rule of law.

To make this case, it is helpful to clarify the definitions of "substantive" and "procedural." In saying that the value of dignity is itself substantive, I intend to suggest that it is independent of any particular institutional or procedural guarantee. The value is not only "procedure-independent" and "institution-independent"; it is also logically and normatively prior to any of its implications. But if this procedure-independent value is normatively prior to any procedures required by the rule of law, it follows that procedures might not be sufficient to guarantee that this value is instantiated in actual policy. The logical priority given to dignity in understanding the rule of law means that any set of procedural or institutional arrangements might fail to guarantee that the value is instantiated in policy or law. Because dignity is itself procedure-independent, we should recognize that while procedures might instantiate the value of dignity, the outcomes of these procedures might violate that value. Thus, the procedure-independent value of dignity might require additional limits on procedures. I call these limits the substantive guarantees of the rule of law.

On my view, it is possible for particular policies or legislation to satisfy the formal and procedural elements of the rule of law and yet still to violate the core value that underlies the rule of law itself. Consider, for instance, a law that banned open criticism of the government. The enforcement of such a law might comply with all of Fuller's formal desiderata. It might ensure a right to a trial and all the procedural guarantees that Waldron suggests. Yet, because it denies the entitlement to be treated as an "active intelligence," it still would violate the ideal of the rule of law. Here the substantive procedure-independent value requires limits on policy that go beyond legal formality or procedures. Moreover, the ideal of dignity might also require limits on the kind of outcomes created by democratic procedures in order to respect the equal dignity of the people who are subject to law.[9] So far I have suggested why Waldron's appeal to dignity as a principle for grounding procedural guarantees of the rule of law also might ground substantive guarantees. In the next section I elaborate on how we should understand these substantive requirements and how we should understand the notion of dignity that serves as their basis.

3. DIGNITY AS NONARBITRARY TREATMENT: DISTINGUISHING THE RULE OF LAW FROM DEMOCRATIC SELF-RULE

So far, I have worked largely within Waldron's framework for the rule of law, emphasizing why it also requires substantive guarantees. I now want to suggest an addendum to his understanding of dignity. Without this expanded understanding, I believe that his conception gestures too far in the direction of self-government, despite the fact that Waldron wants to distinguish between the rule of law and democracy. I attempt to highlight how the contrast might be drawn even more clearly by reframing the notion of dignity.

The ideal of dignity concerns a kind of status that must apply to those subject to the rule of law. Waldron explains the way we should understand this value on p. 23:

> To say that we should value aspects of governance that promote the clarity and determinacy of rules for the sake of individual freedom, but not the opportunities for argumentation that a free and self possessed individual is likely to demand, is to slice in half, to truncate, what the Rule of Law rests upon: respect for the freedom and dignity of each person as an active intelligence.

In emphasizing why dignity requires a respect for the "active" part of "active intelligence," Waldron is able to show the procedural implications of dignity. The procedures central to the rule of law should protect the right of the accused to be heard and engaged throughout the legal process. The accused should not be merely acted upon; they must be consulted.

I think, however, that the emphasis here on active intelligence raises the question of whether Waldron's conception of the rule of law risks being conflated with his conception of democracy. In his seminal work on democracy, Waldron claims that it is the "capacity to decide" that underlies "the right of rights," namely participation in the democratic process.[10] His notion of dignity in the current essay is clearly distinct from that view; it does not entitle criminals to a vote on the jury, which would give them veto power over their own conviction. However, it does seem to entail some limited kind of participation. It is not enough, for instance, to have a right to testify after a verdict is rendered or to defend oneself after the court's decision has already been made. On Waldron's view of the rule of law, criminals have the right to offer and respond to arguments as part of the process that will render a decision about their fate. Although the kind of participation implicated here is not exactly the kind elaborated in his view of democracy, it is importantly a close relative. Even if it is not a right to decide, it is a right to influence a decision.

However, a question remains about the grounds, on Waldron's account, for limiting the right to participate to a right to influence. If dignity is exclusively about participation, then why would the rule of law not give rise to a full-fledged right of criminal defendants to participate as equals in *deciding* their own fate? If this were the case, then the distinction between the rule of law and democracy would become tenuous. I take it that Waldron wishes to resist this path of argument. However, to do so he would need to identify a principle that limits and counterbalances the participatory rights to which he appeals. In the remainder of this response, I propose such a limiting principle.

I want to suggest that the participatory aspect of dignity should, at minimum, be counterbalanced by nonarbitrary treatment, a substantive value that is distinct from and that might at times limit participation. I define nonarbitrary treatment as that which (1) protects the innocent from punishment and (2) provides plausible reasons for acts of coercion that are consistent with citizens' equal status. Although, in Waldron's conception of democratic self-government, participation is the "right of rights," I believe that, when it comes to the rule of law, participation should be limited by a distinct concern to protect the interests of citizens, even when doing so requires protecting them from themselves. Nonarbitrary treatment, on my view, should serve as a limit on both the participatory and the formal aspects of the rule of law.

In order to illustrate the importance of nonarbitrary treatment as a counterbalance to participatory rights, consider the right of the accused to defend himself or herself, which seems a clear implication of Waldron's conception of dignity. The right to defend oneself in court is a recognition that defendants are not to be treated as mere objects of law. They have a potential role in interpreting and advocating for their interests. But this is a right that should be counterbalanced by a concern to protect defendants regardless of their own decisions. For instance, judges rightly attempt to persuade defendants not to defend themselves without an attorney because of a concern to ensure that defendants' interests are represented well. The interests of the defendant are emphasized here over the exercise of participatory rights. In some instances, these rights might even be curtailed. For instance, the right to self-representation does not extend to the appellate process, nor does it extend in cases where the decision is made without knowledge or reflection.[11] More controversially, I think there is reason to limit the right in cases where the accused is clearly not qualified to defend himself or herself.

The current case law, in addressing whether there is a fundamental right to self- or *pro se* representation, does gesture towards Waldron's emphasis on the procedural dimensions of the rule of law and a strong role for defendants in interpreting their own interests. It concludes that defendants have a right to self-representation even when doing so might harm their interests in the most adverse way. I worry, however, with the dissenting justices in *Faretta v. California,* that such a rule might overly endanger the substantive concern central to the rule of law that the innocent not be punished.[12] At minimum, as Justice Stewart points out in his majority decision, this is a hard case because the participatory right to a *pro se* defense should be balanced against the concern to ensure a fair trial and to avoid the punishment of the innocent. Justice Stewart's acknowledgement of this challenge suggests that a substantive value must at least be balanced against procedural entitlements to participation. However, I would go a step further, agreeing with Justice Blackmun's contention in his dissent that no "amount of pro se pleading can cure the injury to society of an unjust result."[13] On my view, the ideal of the rule of law at times requires protecting defendants from the negative consequences that might come from their own participation.

This example suggests that the notion of dignity at the heart of Waldron's conception of the rule of law could benefit from reframing. I contend that the protection of individuals' dignity as "active intelligences" with procedural rights to participation and interpretation of their own interests should be balanced against, and limited by, their protection against nonarbitrary treatment. By "nonarbitrary treatment," I mean that the state must have a moral justification for its laws and judicial decisions that is consistent with the free and equal status of individuals. This does not mean that the law must be fully just, but it does guarantee against coercion that cannot be justified by reasons consistent with free and equal citizenship. This standard applies, moreover, regardless of whether procedural rights have been guaranteed.

Paramount to both the rule of law and the notion of nonarbitrary treatment is the right not to be imprisoned if one is actually innocent. Yet, this substantive entitlement cannot sufficiently be accounted for by the procedures required by the rule of law. On my view, the rule of law is violated when innocents are imprisoned, even if no procedural right has been violated. In his majority decision in *Herrera v. Collins*, Chief Justice Rehnquist gestures in the opposite direction. His decision might be read to suggest that actual innocence might not be a reason for relief, even from capital punishment.[14] Pure procedural justice of this sort, however, risks deemphasizing the substantive ideal of the rule of law, which demands that the innocent not be punished.

I have discussed how nonarbitrariness might limit the value of participation within the institution of the courtroom. However, as I suggested at the start of this response, the substance of the rule of law has implications for limiting the outcomes of democratic procedures, as well. There is not space to develop these implications here, but I will introduce one possibility. I believe that there is a possibility of defending some of the Supreme Court's rights jurisprudence by appeal to the substantive aspects of the rule of law. In particular, I have in mind the Supreme Court's rational-basis test for evaluating the constitutionality of legislation. Under the animus doctrine, the Court struck down a law that intentionally targeted minority religions (*Lukumi*) and a law banning sodomy (*Lawrence*) on the grounds that they have no "rational basis."[15] But the animus doctrine is not merely a formal or procedural test. Laws that fail the animus test might meet both formal and procedural requirements of the rule of law. Moreover, there are reasons for such laws, many of which are religious in nature. On my view, however, the Court is declaring such laws arbitrary in the sense that they are not based in reasons consistent with the free and equal status of those impacted by these laws. Of course, such claims would place the notion of the rule of law at the center of controversies far from Fuller's formal issues. But I believe that the requirement of nonarbitrary treatment arises once we recognize the substantive concept of dignity at the core of the rule of law. Robust concepts have robust implications. (It is worth noting, given Waldron's well-known opposition to judicial review, that this thick conception of the rule of law could also be invoked by legislatures limiting their own enactments.)[16]

More needs to be said to develop this admittedly wide-ranging substantive conception of nonarbitrariness, but I want to conclude by addressing one likely complaint about it. Some will contend that nonarbitrariness is too expansive a value to ground the rule of law. Critics might agree, for instance, that laws that fail to meet a rational review standard are flawed but argue that we cannot reach this conclusion by an appeal to the rule of law itself. They might contend that understanding dignity in terms of such a broad value risks conflating all that is important in a theory of political legitimacy with the ideal of the rule of law.

This kind of challenge suggests the importance of returning to the question of how we might distinguish between the rule of law and democracy. On my view, it is easier and clearer to distinguish between the rule of law and democracy when we emphasize nonarbitrariness and not simply the participatory aspects of the rule of law. A nondemocratic regime, which fails to guarantee a right to vote or to participate in democratic self-government, might still satisfy aspects of the criteria of nonarbitrariness. A monarch, for instance, might respect the sort of substantive limits I have suggested, despite violating some basic democratic rights because these substantive guarantees are meant to be entitlements that individuals enjoy distinct from their participatory rights.[17]

In contrast, the participatory focus of Waldron's notion of dignity might invite the challenge that an exclusive emphasis on participatory rights risks conflating the values of the rule of law and those of democracy. Although Waldron emphasizes a set of legal procedures here as opposed to democratic procedures, the critic could suggest that the same value of dignity as self-government underlies both. Thus, a king who denies participatory rights in the democratic process will violate the same value that is infringed when he denies participatory rights in the courts.

Waldron might point out here that the kind of participation

central to the rule of law is distinct from that of democracy. Participation under the rule of law is of a consultative kind that does not require the right to decide or to vote. But the critic might reply that consultation is a form of participation because it attempts to influence the jury. As I noted, consultation would be worthless after the verdict. Thus, the critic might suggest that what appears to be a different value is really the same value in a different guise. This kind of criticism suggests that the real problem with those who violate the rule of law is that they fail to respect the values of democracy.

I do not believe this objection is fatal to Waldron's account, but it does highlight the added value of nonarbitrariness as a counterbalance to the procedural dimensions he convincingly presented as central to the rule of law. By emphasizing protection and not participation, nonarbitrariness can be clearly distinguished from and limit participatory values.[18]

4. CONCLUSION

In these comments, I have drawn upon and in some ways expanded Waldron's important contribution to our understanding of the rule of law. First, I have emphasized why the value of dignity itself should be understood as a substantive value that requires substantive guarantees supplementing and at times constraining procedure. Second, I have suggested that to fully account for the kind of constraints on legal and democratic procedures required by the rule of law, the value of dignity should be expanded to include not only respect for active intelligence but also an ideal of nonarbitrary treatment.

NOTES

1. Jeremy Waldron, "The Rule of Law and the Importance of Procedure," in this volume.
2. Lon L. Fuller, *The Morality of Law* (New Haven: Yale University Press, 1969).
3. Waldron, "The Rule of Law and the Importance of Procedure," 4.
4. Ibid., 23.

5. Ibid., 16.

6. Ibid., 6. Waldron provides a list of ten procedural requirements.

7. Among the many advantages of this structure, I think it provides a way to understand the rule of law as a normative concept. By appealing to a value at the core of the rule of law, that of dignity, Waldron is able to explain why the rule of law is not merely a sociological phenomenon and why we should value it. Here he breaks with certain positivist thinkers who might tell us what law is but not why we should value it or what it should require.

8. Waldron, "The Rule of Law and the Importance of Procedure," 4–5.

9. I do not take this argument to cohere only with arguments for judicial review. As Waldron suggests in his discussion of the procedural implications of the rule of law, this substantive dimension might be guaranteed by legislatures, not courts.

10. Jeremy Waldron, *Law and Disagreement* (New York: Oxford University Press, 1999), 232. Fuller, too, seems to make a gesture to self-government. In Waldron's quotation of Fuller, there is an explicit reference to the notion of "self determination" (Waldron, "The Rule of Law and the Importance of Procedure," 15) at the heart of the dignitarian interest that underlies the rule of law.

11. See the Court's unanimous decision in *Martinez v. Court of Appeal of California*, 528 U.S. 152 (2000).

12. In my view, the current law gestures too far in the direction of the participatory rights of the accused. In *Faretta v. California*, 422 U.S. 806 (1975), a closely divided Court recognized a constitutional right for defendants to refuse counsel and to represent themselves in criminal proceedings.

13. As an earlier Supreme Court decision put it, although the defendant who defends himself or herself "be not guilty, he faces the danger of conviction because he does not know how to establish his innocence." *Powell v. Alabama*, 287 U.S. 45, 69 (1932). See, too, Chief Justice Burger's dissent (joined by Blackmun and Rehnquist) in *Faretta*: "The fact of the matter is that in all but an extraordinarily small number of cases an accused will lose whatever defense he may have if he undertakes to conduct the trial himself." *Faretta v. California*, 422 U.S. 806, 838 (1975) (Burger, C.J., dissenting).

14. *Herrera v. Collins*, 506 U.S. 390 (1993).

15. See *Church of the Lukumi Babalu Aye v. City of Hialeah*, 508 U.S. 520 (1993), and *Lawrence v. Texas*, 539 U.S. 558 (2003).

16. In another place, I take issue with Waldron's position on judicial review. See my *Democratic Rights: The Substance of Self-Government* (Princeton: Princeton University Press, 2007). I also take issue with his procedural conception of democracy and offer instead what I call a "value theory of

democracy," a substantive ideal of self-government. There are parallels between our disagreement about the rule of law and our disagreement about the meaning of democracy, but I attempt to limit my response to the former dispute in this short piece.

17. I view it as no accident that Fuller's "King Rex" is a monarch. Fuller rightly assumes that the rule of law does not require the full ideals of democratic self-government.

18. I have emphasized why the notion of nonarbitrariness can be realized by regimes that fall short of the standards of ideal democracy. But I do not want to make the mistaken suggestion that the rule of law has no normative connection to democracy. While it is possible to have the rule of law without democracy, the converse is not true. I do not believe we can have democracy without the rule of law. On my view, one component of an ideal democracy is a commitment to nonarbitrariness. We cannot, for instance, arbitrarily distinguish among those eligible to vote. But this is to say that nonarbitrariness and the rule of law limit what can be done in an ideal democracy. It does not suggest that the values of the rule of law require or are the same as ideal democracy.

4

FOUR PUZZLES ABOUT THE RULE OF LAW: WHY, WHAT, WHERE? AND WHO CARES?

MARTIN KRYGIER

It appears the time of the rule of law has come. In the past twenty or so years, the concept has gone from often-derided but more often ignored margins of public concerns to a somewhat hallowed, if also sometimes hollow, center of many of them. Once a quasi-technical term of interest only to lawyers and legal philosophers, it appears all over the globe these days, at ease in the company of such unassailably Good Things as democracy, equality, and justice.

Rule of law is today an international hurrah term, on the lips of every development agency, offered as a support for economic growth, democracy, human rights, and much else. Rule of Law promotion is booming. Lots of people and organizations are contracted to work on it, lots of money is spent on it, lots of academics study it. To a partisan of the rule of law, and I am one, that should be good news, and in a way it is. But only in a way. For it is hard to boast of much success in actually fostering it, let alone understanding what "it" is. Nor, given the proliferation of people wanting a slice of it, is it as clear as it once may have seemed what it might be good for. Some still doubt whether it is good for much at all.

Over some thirty years, I have struggled to reach some clarity about the rule of law and why, as I believe, it matters so. This chapter will give some account of the reasons for the quest, some of the dragons that needed to be slain along the way, the glittering but elusive prize, and why, after so long a trek, there still appear to be long tunnels at the end of the light.

Central among the many obscurities that attend the rule of law are those named in the title of this chapter. In what follows I move through this array of puzzles in the order in which they appear there. One could rearrange the order, and many do, but I suggest that is unwise. I conclude by reflecting on the extent to which where we stand in relation to the rule of law often depends on where we sit. The concept has today become so protean partly because people can have so many reasons for being interested in it. That can lead to confusion, but it also can reflect real differences in perspective. I distinguish between two such perspectives that matter over a broad range. One is that appropriate to efforts to establish the rule of law where it has not been much in evidence. The attempt, always difficult and often fruitless, is to generate it. The other occurs where the rule of law is already in place and more or less well established. People seek to analyze it and may well want to defend it or criticize or improve it. They have it,[1] however, and can draw on it. Before we say what the rule of law is, what it depends on, and what it's worth, it helps to clarify who is asking and in what circumstances.

1. WHY?

It is common to start discussions of the rule of law by saying *what* it is before going on to ask what, if anything, it might be good for and worth. The focus is on one or other set of purportedly defining characteristics of the thing itself, made up of elements of legal institutions and legal rules. Such accounts differ in many ways. Some are abstract, some are specifically tied to particular concrete incarnations, and some are checklists of legal, particularly judicial, infrastructure, thought packageable for export.

At the most abstract level, for example, legal philosophers typically identify formal aspects of laws. Thus, the most influential such account, Lon Fuller's "internal morality of law," is made up of eight formal characteristics of legal rules—that they be

1. General;
2. Public;

3. Nonretroactive;
4. Comprehensible;
5. Noncontradictory;
6. Possible to perform;
7. Relatively stable; and
8. Administered in ways congruent with the rules as announced.

A purported legal order that fails totally in any of these dimensions does not, Fuller argues, deserve the name. One that scores
well is likely to be doing well, even though other things matter, life
is complex, and perfection in any of these dimensions is neither
desirable nor possible.[2]

More concretely and parochially,[3] in his enormously influential
account of the rule of law,[4] A. V. Dicey focused on three distinctive
elements of the British institutional order—inability of authorities
to exercise "wide, arbitrary, or discretionary powers of constraint";
subjection of all citizens, whatever their "rank or condition," to the
same, ordinary, law administered by the same ordinary courts; and
constitutional principles that flowed up from court judgments in
particular cases rather than down from general written constitutional documents. Lawyers often follow Dicey's example, whether
influenced by him or not, and identify the rule of law with what
they like about their own legal orders.

Thirdly, benighted parts of the world are today likely to be visited by numerous international Rule of Law promoters, for it has
become fashionable to believe, on arguable[5] but not insubstantial
grounds, that the rule of law is a necessary means to achieve various valuable ends beyond the rule of law itself. As Charles T. Call
observes:

> Among a plethora of development and security agencies, a new
> "rule of law consensus" has emerged. This consensus consists of two
> elements: (1) the belief that the rule of law is essential to virtually
> every Western liberal foreign policy goal—human rights, democ-
> racy, economic and political stability, international security from
> terrorist and other transnational threats, and transnational free
> trade and investment; and (2) the belief that international interven-
> tions, be they through money, people, or ideas, must include a Rule
> of Law component.[6]

The rule of law in these interventions is identified with aspects of "the justice sector," particularly the judiciary and lawyers. As Tom Ginsburg has remarked, " 'Rule of law' programming has become shorthand for all interventions targeting legal institutions, a synonym for work on the 'the justice sector.' As used in contemporary practice, it is really shorthand for the rule of lawyers rather than the rule of law in the classic sense, though of course the two projects can overlap."[7] This agenda and style of Rule of Law intervention—which even excludes "non-lawyerly aspects [of the state] such as public administration or non-state justice"[8]—has two consequences: on one hand, Rule of Law reformers try to develop the rule of law because the external ends it is thought to facilitate are valued; on the other hand, those ends are themselves outside the province of Rule of Law reformers. *We* do rule of law, that is, build the institutions that compose the formal justice sector; economists, sociologists, and politologists do the other stuff, dependent though that is thought to be on what we have done.

These three perspectives, and those many influenced by them and engaging with them, differ from one another substantially. However, they all have in common two core assumptions: (a) that the ingredients of the rule of law are legal institutions, rules, and official practices, and (b) that we are in a position to stipulate, in terms that apply generally, what aspects and elements of these institutions, rules, and practices add up to the rule of law. Many other accounts of the rule of law—among them "thick" versions that include substantive content of provisions, for example dealing with human rights, and more spare "thin" ones that focus on legal forms rather than substantive content—are even more specific than these. They mention particular configurations of institutions, presence or absence of bills of rights, and so on. Again, the focus is on features of the central legal order and what it proclaims.

I believe that there are problems with each of these approaches taken separately, but I also think, and have elsewhere argued, that what they share is as misleading as where they differ. They *start* with the wrong question, so their answers, however insightful, are often beside the point. The proper place to start, I believe, is with the question *why*, what might one want the rule of law *for?* not *what*, what is it made up of? And that matters, because no sensible answer to the second question can be given until one comes to a view on the first. And what counts as a sensible answer in one place might not be too sensible somewhere else. I have thought this for a long time and have argued it often.[9] The reasons have evolved, and I now have three of them, one conceptual, one empirical, and one practical.

The conceptual reason is this: the rule of law is not a natural object, like a pebble or a tree, which can be identified apart from questions of what we want of it. Nor is it even a human artifact you can point to, like the statement of a legal rule, though its realization or approximation might depend on such artifacts. The rule of law occurs insofar as a valued state of affairs exists, one to which we gesture by saying the law rules (not a simple notion and not one to be expounded simply by looking up two words in a dictionary, but let it lie for the moment). What we take to be its elements are supposed to add up to something, to be good for generating or securing that state of affairs. It is a *teleological* notion, in other words, to be understood in terms of its point, not an *anatomical* one, concerned with the morphology of particular legal structures and practices, whatever they turn out to do. For even if the structures are just as we want them, if the law doesn't rule, we don't have the rule of law. And, conversely, if the institutions are not those we expected but they do what we want from the rule of law, then arguably we do have it. We seek the rule of law for purposes, enjoy it for reasons. Unless we seek first to clarify those purposes and reasons and in their light explore what would be needed and assess what is offered to approach them, we are bound to be flying blind.

Should you have Fuller's octet, or Dicey's trio, or the World Bank's Rule of Law recipe book, but they happen to serve no salutary purposes in a particular society, or serve them ill, or do the opposite of what we believe the rule of law should do, or do nothing at all, or are overborne by hostile forces, it would be odd to say, with feeling: *that* society has the rule of law. It would be hard to find a nonacademic, at any rate, who would think to do so. The reason is simple and should be obvious: you might have law, but in such cases it doesn't rule.

It is in accord with the achievement that we postulate as the rule of law that we can sensibly say there is a lot of it about, say, in Scotland, less so in Russia; hard to find a living trace in, say, Belarus or Burma. And we can do so without too much knowledge of legal technicalities and intricacies. Knowing whether the rule of law is well realized in a society, then, is not in the first instance a question of the morphology of legal institutions, but rather a question of the existence, bare or flourishing, of the state of affairs in which the values of the rule of law are approached.

In another context, Gianfranco Poggi spoke of Durkheim's concept of society—what distinguishes it from a mere mass—as a contingent, "insofar as reality," "real *insofar as* certain things go on":[10] socially patterned behaviors, shared and internalized norms, and so on. I think of the rule of law that way. It is a relative and variable achievement, not all or nothing. But one can say it exists in good shape or repair insofar as a certain sort of valued state of affairs, to which law contributes in particular ways, exists. At this point I don't want to argue for a specific account of that state of affairs; I will just gesture in the direction. Putting it roughly for the moment, the rule of law is in relatively good order insofar as some possible behaviors, central among them the exercise of political, social, and economic power, are effectively constrained and channeled to a significant extent by and in accordance with law so that nonarbitrary exercises of such powers are relatively routine, while other sorts, such as lawless, capricious, willful exercises of power, routinely occur less often.

There is, of course, controversy about how that state of affairs should be characterized, how the law might contribute to it, and what it needs to be like to do that effectively. Such controversies are not unique to the rule of law, however. Recall democracy, justice, equality. Concepts that are contested, even "essentially contested,"[11] are not for that reason alone meaningless or useless. On the contrary, some of them are the most important we have.

My own specification cannot put an end to such controversy. Ends and means are both in play and disagreements are common in both domains. I want only to suggest that the rule of law needs first to be approached by asking after its *telos*. The purposes you postulate don't have to be moral purposes (though in my understanding of the rule of law they have moral value); it depends how you characterize them. But you can't usefully describe or explore the rule of law before clarifying what you think it's good for. Of course, those who make lists of the legal constituents of the rule of law think they add up to something, too. But they too easily assume an identity between the purposes and the institutional apparatus of the rule of law. They certainly have much more to say about the apparatus than the purposes.

This shades into my empirical point, directed both to analysts who seek to assess the extent of rule of law in different societies and to Rule of Law promoters, who seek to generate it. Social scientists who study the rule of law seek markers of it in various settings. This can be a sophisticated activity, full of indicators, data sets, and so on. But what do indicators indicate? Often, this is a seriously undertheorized question. Take one standard Rule of Law indicator, judicial independence. We know why people think it important that judges not be swayed by overweening overlords, outsiders, or off-siders. The judiciary is the institution where the legal buck stops, at least in principle, since judicial interpretations ultimately govern what the law is or becomes. And so it seems obvious that the more strongly the judiciary is shielded, institutionally, culturally, financially, from outside pressures, the better for the rule of law. As a result, judicial independence is a standard Rule of Law indicator. However, unless independence is assumed a priori to be good for the rule of law, the relationship between indicator and indicatee is altogether more problematic than it may seem at first blush.

Judicial independence is at best never more than part of what is required for judicial integrity and competence. More important, there are circumstances in which it works in precisely the opposite direction. It can be an effective shield for incompetence, political affiliations, and corruption, particularly in societies where these were rife before independence was institutionalized and where the notion that judges should be fundamentally creatures and speakers of the law had been the very last thing on anyone's mind. Thus, several postcommunist countries quickly institutionalized internal judicial self-government and independence from outside interference, as though their ideal of having a judiciary committed to the integrity and rule of law would best be reached by imagining it had already been attained. That made irremovable old, incompetent, corrupt, badly formed holdovers from earlier times. Indeed, in some legal orders "in transition," it seems that rendering judges irremovable was actually *intended*, by the first unrenovated ex-communist leaders, to have that result so that if they lost electorally, they would still have their people on the bench, independent of pressures from their opponents.[12]

Writing on some of the innocences of Technical Legal Assistance (TLA) programs, Stephen Holmes has pointed out that judicial independence is an ambivalent achievement. It is never all we want and in certain aspects not what we should want. Judges, he points out, are rightly dependent on the state to pay them; maintain court buildings, equipment, and so on; and faithfully and effectively enforce judicial decisions. None of these is a small undertaking, and we don't want judges to find ways to do them for themselves. Of course, we want the judges to make their decisions independently of all this routine dependency, and there are institutional ways to encourage this. However, unless it is accompanied by real deference to something outside their own interests—law, for example—independence can be a cure as bad as any disease. These are general truths, made all the more dramatic, as Holmes observes, in postauthoritarian regimes, where

> the judiciary is an "orphaned institution," suddenly freed from the tutelage of a now-defunct political authority, which it once approached on bent knees. Such surviving fragments of a dead authoritarian system are typically populated by sclerotic professionals wedded to old fashioned ways of doing business. The ideology of judicial independence, if accepted unthinkingly, can be used to obstruct or postpone their re-education.[13]

In such settings, Holmes goes on to note:

> [a] significant danger during transition, in fact, is *halfway reform.* Halfway reform occurs when the judiciary manages to free itself from authoritarianism without adapting to democracy. It can refuse orders from the executive branch without giving any particular deference to the interests of society expressed in the constitution or ordinary acts of the elected legislature. The post-authoritarian judiciary can instead work exclusively to perpetuate and augment its own corporate advantages. The private guild interests of judges can refuse all compromise with the common interest of society and, remarkably enough, can defend this recalcitrance with the language of liberalism. . . . To avoid such autistic corporatism, disguised as liberal orthodoxy and increasingly common in transitional regimes, should be, but is still not, one of the main objectives of TLA [Technical Legal Assistance].[14]

To the extent that these pathologies attend judicial independence, its existence can be an automatic "indicator" of the rule of law only if it is taken to be so as a matter of definition. The basis for selecting empirical indicators for the rule of law cannot itself be simply empirical. It must be theoretically guided, and central to the theorization must be some conception of the relationship between the indicator and what you are trying to indicate, or, in other words, whether it supports the rule of law or does not.

My third, practical, reason for suspicion of accounts of the rule of law that start with institutional means rather than valued ends follows from this tendency too readily to understand the rule of law in terms of institutional bits and pieces, often of distinguished but also often of distant and different provenance. The world of Rule of Law promotion is prone to a pathology well remarked by organization theorists, namely goal displacement. This occurs, simply put, when means are substituted for ends, often unconsciously, and people flap about with checklists (and checkbooks), recipes, "off-the-shelf blueprints,"[15] often modeled on alien and distant originals, with scant reflection on the purpose(s) of the rule of law or the proper purposes of their own enterprise. Are they to stock judicial libraries, increase the numbers of computers on judicial desks, teach judges some method or other of case management, all for their own sake, or are they supposed to promote the rule of law? Of course, we know what anyone would answer if asked. However, the link between what Rule of Law promoters promote and the rule of law is too often assumed rather than demonstrated or even questioned. Particular institutions and institutional forms are taken to contribute to the rule of law, and focus becomes fixed on those institutions rather than on the ends that, sometimes in a dimly remembered or clearly forgotten past, had inspired the development of those very institutions but which they may well not be serving in any way.

Where the rule of law is in good shape, and especially where it has been so for generations, we may not really understand why and still benefit from it. Philip Selznick cites Kenneth Winston's observation that, "we often don't know what it means to be committed to the value apart from the forms" to argue that "we often have more confidence in a particular form or practice, rooted in experience, than in an abstract statement of why the form exists or what values it upholds."[16] In such circumstances, there is a lot to be said for Michael Oakeshott's preference for the "pursuit of the intimations"[17] of traditions, over attempts to vindicate some rationalist plan. However, the project is different when people seek to institutionalize the rule of law where this has not happened before and where local traditions, though still of crucial importance because they are there and will need to be negotiated, are inhospitable to values one seeks to generate. Then pursuit of intimations is not enough. We need to think more deeply about first principles. In a context where the rule of law has been proposed for many societies where it was not strong or long embedded and where it often faces fierce competition from forces that have no concern with it and whose major interests allow no accommodation for it, my argument is that responses to such proposals that begin with what are taken to be the legal-institutional features of success stories are a bad way to start. We need to ask what values they do and should, particularly should, serve.

Of course, not everyone agrees on values, and the term "rule of law," we will see, is used by so many people to express so many different ambitions that it is important to get straight where they are coming from in this discussion. Given that the term is in common use, it is unhelpful to be too eccentric or solipsistic in one's use of it. However, given that it is in *such* common use, it is hard not to be stipulative to some degree. What follows are some of my noneccentric but particular stipulations.

Extrinsic and Immanent Ends

Now there is one constituency for the rule of law that might appear to have heeded my advice. That is the world of those many international agencies involved in Rule of Law promotion in "transitional," "postconflict," and "developing" countries. After all, the rule of law is today so popular among such agencies not for its own sake but because, as we have seen, it is thought to deliver other goods: economic development, human rights, democracy, and so on.

However, though I would be happy with any support, and while the popularity of the rule of law is welcome, I have something different in mind. As I mentioned a moment ago, the sorts of ends

just enumerated are *external* to the rule of law itself, benefits supposed to flow from it, what it is thought to do and facilitate, not
themselves part of what it means for it to exist. Moreover, those
ends don't affect promoters' understandings of what the rule of
law is or where it lies. The rule of law is treated as a kind of tech-
nology whose features can be specified independent of the ends
that are supposed to flow from them.[18]

Indeed, the literature discussing whether or not the rule of law
serves such ends typically jumps from an understanding of the rule
of law that identifies it with particular legal institutions to the external ends sought, ignoring that, in the gap in between, the question remains whether the rule of law's own proper purposes have
been achieved, even partially. This becomes particularly evident in
moments of disappointment, which in Rule of Law promotion are
very common. Promotional activity is undertaken, money is spent,
judges trained, and yet the economy does badly or a despot takes
over, or civil war breaks out again, and human rights are trampled.
"What did the rule of law do for *us?*" disgruntled reformers are
likely to complain. Thus, Frank Upham laments

> the likelihood that Western mischaracterization of the appropriate
> roles of law will be accepted by developing countries, thus leading
> to misallocation of domestic effort and attention, and perhaps most
> important, eventually to deep disillusionment with the potential of
> law. When the revision of the criminal code does not prevent war-
> lords from creating havoc in Afghanistan and the training of Chi-
> nese judges by American law professors does not prevent the deten-
> tion of political dissidents—or, perversely, enables judges to provide
> plausible legal reasons for their detention—political leaders on all
> sides may turn away from law completely and miss the modest role
> that law can play in political and economic development.[19]

Typically, Upham identifies the rule of law and exaggerated expectations of it, rather than an inadequate understanding of it, as
the source of his fears. However, what if the problem is less that
the rule of law was installed but failed to do much good than that
what was installed was not yet the rule of law but only bits of legal
apparatus not on their own up to the job? That is my view. When
legal institutional tinkering fails to prevent havoc, when people
who count bend or ignore the law, and those who don't count

have merely to suffer it or exercise of power without reference to it, the rule of law is in very poor shape if it exists at all, whatever the laws and institutional structures look like. For reasons to which we will come, that should not have been a surprise. On their own, the legal institutional features so often identified with the rule of law are not up to the task. On their own, they never are.

Surely one anticipates good consequences from the rule of law, if one does, because what it *does* has further benefits. It is because of something that the rule of law *offers* or *allows* that we anticipate salutary results for the economy, for democracy, for human rights, and so on. That might be a plausible hope or not. However, we will be able to tell only after we have the achievement, not merely some institutions hoped to produce it. Think of Max Weber on law and capitalism. He believed that formally rational law was more predictable than other sorts and that *from that predictability* flowed further benefits to modern capitalists. He might have been wrong about the connections, but that is the logic of the claim. We need to focus in the first instance on the *immanent* ends of the rule of law, its own *telos*, the point of the enterprise, goals internal to it. Further second-order effects on democracy, human rights, or the economy may or may not flow from the rule of law, and that would need investigation, but they are not intrinsic to it. Put in other words, economic development or even democracy is not in the first instance the goal of the rule of law. If either is favored by it, this is because immanent features of what it does, when it does what it should, favor it.

What ends are immanent in this sense? A first take on ends intrinsic to the rule of law, and one perhaps deepest in the Rule of Law tradition,[20] is that they involve legal reduction of the possibility of *arbitrary* exercise of power by those in a position to wield significant power. I have yet to provide or find a sufficiently complex and textured analysis of what arbitrariness includes (what degree of caprice? whim? unreasonableness? unreasonedness? discretion? If not all discretion, how much? And so on.) and excludes. At a general level, however, I am happy with Philip Pettit's definition:

> An act is perpetrated on an arbitrary basis, we can say, if it is subject just to the *arbitrium*, the decision or judgement, of the agent; the agent was in a position to choose it or not choose it, at their

pleasure. When we say that an act of interference is perpetrated on
an arbitrary basis . . . we imply that it is chosen or rejected without
reference to the interests, or the opinions, of those affected. The
choice is not forced to track what the interests of those others require according to their own judgements.[21]

Moreover, however difficult it may be to distinguish in detail, say,
between arbitrary and nonarbitrary choices, it is not hard to map
the territory roughly and to find examples, particularly of rank arbitrariness, if not of some perfect, imagined antipode of that. If
the edges are blurred, the importance of arbitrariness as an (and
perhaps *the*)[22] antivalue among those who have written about the
rule of law for centuries is not open to doubt.

Once I thought that reduction of the possibility of arbitrariness
was enough to locate the *telos* of the rule of law, and I still believe
that, but it needs to be spelled out a little more. For, taken too
simply, it might seem inconsistent with an element of legal orders
that goes deep, and for good reason. Neil MacCormick and Jeremy Waldron have reminded us that "law is an argumentative discipline,"[23] and that is not through accident or misadventure. People with legal interests at stake need to be able to speak for those
interests, whether they accuse or are accused. This requires a good
deal of provision from legal orders. Waldron stresses

> a deep and important sense associated foundationally with the idea
> of a legal system, that law is a mode of governing people that treats
> them with respect, as though they had a view or perspective of their
> own to present on the application of the norm to their conduct
> and situation. Applying a norm to a human individual is not like
> deciding what to do about a rabid animal or a dilapidated house.
> It involves paying attention to a point of view and respecting the
> personality and entity one is dealing with. As such it embodies a cru-
> cial dignitarian idea—respecting the dignity of those to whom the
> norms are applied as *beings capable of explaining themselves*.[24]

This is a moral value, but it is not simply a part of morality at
large. For it is not just randomly or fortuitously found in association with law. It is preeminently a *legal* value, fundamental to the
moral integrity of *legal* ordering, of what Fuller characterized as
"the enterprise of subjecting human conduct to the governance

of rules "[25] It is part, to use Fuller's words again, of the "internal morality" of law. To quote Waldron again:

> [A]rgumentation (about what this or that provision means, or about the effect of this array of precedents) is *business as usual* in law. We would be uneasy about counting a system that did not exhibit it and make routine provision for it as a legal system. . . . Courts, hearings and arguments—those aspects of law are not optional extras; they are integral parts of how law works, and they are indispensable to the package of law's respect for human agency. To say that we should value aspects of governance that promote the clarity and determinacy of rules for the sake of individual freedom but not the opportunities for argumentation that a free and self-possessed individual is likely to demand, is to slice in half, to truncate, what the Rule of Law rests upon: respect for the freedom and dignity of each person as an active intelligence.[26]

Is this, though, *another* legal value, in competition with reduction of arbitrariness, or is it rather an enrichment of our understanding of opposition to arbitrary power?

Often, opposition to legal arbitrariness is identified as pursuit of legal certainty. If we understand success in this quest as identical to increase of certainty, and if we thus think the more certainty the better, then the argumentative nature of law appears to be a major problem or, at least, a different, perhaps inconsistent value for law. For legal argument commonly upsets, indeed is often designed to upset, prevailing certainties. The more we can render contentious the possibilities offered by the law, it might seem, the less certain it becomes, and so the rule of law suffers.

However, the pursuit of maximum certainty is a vain and misleading one. First of all, law can never deliver it, both because the inherent uncertainties of legal interpretation make it impossible and because so many other sources of uncertainty in the world render it unavailable. For several reasons to which I will return, it is better to speak of reduction of uncertainties to a tolerable level rather than the attainment of ever-greater degrees of certainty. Neil MacCormick is wise here, as he so often was. Recalling his time as a Scottish deputy in the European Parliament, he writes:

> As a philosopher of law among the ranks of lawmakers, I always had a certain inclination to remind colleagues that certainty is

unattainable, and that the most one can do is aim to diminish uncertainty to an acceptable degree. What degree is acceptable depends on the fact that other values, including justice in the light of developing but currently unforeseen situations, is at stake.[27]

MacCormick's wisdom, like so many of his virtues, is not universally shared. Law can reduce many uncertainties that stem from arbitrary exercise of power and provide significant *thresholds* of security even in the absence of complete and unattainable certainty,[28] and that is all we should expect.

Moreover, *uncertainty* is only one index of arbitrariness in the exercise of power. Another, as is plain from Pettit's definition, is that those with power are free to ignore those affected, need give no thought to them as interested actors with their own "perspective on the world," in Simone Weil's phrase. That perspective is all the more crucial to take into account when its bearers are those likely to be affected by what the law does. The certainty that you and your views will be ignored, will count for nothing, in the exercise of power over you does not render that exercise nonarbitrary. Again, one can do no better than to allow MacCormick to make the point:

> If the Rule of Law is to be actually a protection against arbitrary intervention in people's lives, it seems clear that it is not in practice enough to demand that the operative facts did on some occasion actually happen or obtain. It is necessary that some specific and challengeable accusation or averment of relevant facts be made to the individual threatened with action. This in turn must be supported by evidence in an open proceeding in which the party charged may contest each item of evidence . . . and may offer relevant counterevidence as she/he chooses. Moreover, it must also be possible to challenge the relevancy of the legal accusation or claim.[29]

There is, then, a strong affinity between opposition to arbitrary exercise of power, which some have taken to suggest unchangeable, unchallengeable provisions and interpretations of law, and the argumentative character of law, which demands the opportunity for challenge, reinterpretation, and legally constrained and disciplined disputation by those affected by the exercise of power. At the point of contested application of laws to facts, which is *not* by the way where or how most law affects most life, provision needs to be made for the fact that power will be exercised arbitrarily unless those it affects are treated as *humans*, with legitimate differences over the meaning of the law, the existence and interpretation of the facts, and the application of that law to those facts. For that reason, for their reasons, I follow MacCormick and Waldron in taking openness to argumentation to complement and complete opposition to arbitrary exercise of power. Both the unpredictability or unreliability of the exercise of power and the inability to challenge it are obnoxious for several of the same reasons that having one's own perspective silenced or ignored is. Here are four.

One fundamental reason to wish for the possibility of arbitrary power to be strongly limited is that it imperils our liberty. It does so on most accounts of liberty, but perhaps most clearly in its republican conception, as *nondomination*. This conception is particularly law related, indeed law dependent. It has been emphasized by Philip Pettit[30] as the central republican contribution to political theory and by Gianluigi Palombella as the central achievement of the rule of law.[31] So understood, liberty is infringed not by every sort of interference but only by "arbitrary (reason-independent) interference,"[32] that is, precisely that sort contrary to the ideal of the rule of law. As Pettit puts it, "To enjoy non-domination is . . . to be possessed, not just of non-interference by arbitrary powers, but of a secure or resilient variety of such non-interference."[33] Such security and resilience are not likely to occur by accident but require institutional support. It is a task for the rule of law. Indeed, the link between law and liberty in this republican understanding depends on law denying the possibility of arbitrary exercise of power; "the right sort of law is seen as the source of liberty."[34] Only in circumstances where, and to the extent that, the "right sort of law" contributes to preventing arbitrary exercise of power is a republican citizen free, that is, not subject to the specific evil of domination.

Second, and perhaps the most basic and elemental consequence of arbitrary threats to one's liberty, is the simple *fearfulness* of life plagued by the potentially devastating impositions of power unrestrained by the need to give consideration to anything but the will and whim of the power-holder. Threats to liberty are obnoxious whether or not they cause fear, but if they do they are doubly so. Fear is the vice that Judith Shklar stresses most in her "liberalism of fear,"[35] and it is a great vice. Reduction of reasons for it is a great deliverance. And it is not enough, as the republican tradition has stressed, that as a simple matter of happy fact one is not actually subjected to acts of arbitrary power, though at any time one could be. On the contrary, as Joseph Priestley observed, "Having always some unknown evil to fear, though it should never come, he has no perfect enjoyment of it himself, or of any of the blessings of life."[36] To reduce the fear of it (as also its denial of liberty, dignity, and clarity), the limits on that power must be secure and so understood. A way of seeking to make it so is to institutionalize it.

A closely associated harm that flows from arbitrariness is the *indignity* of finding oneself the mere *object* of power, where one has to guess how one might be treated by those in power and/ or there is no way of asserting, defending, and claiming attention to one's own point of view in the face of its exercise[37]—all that flattery, bowing, and scraping, those forelocks to tug, caps to tip, favors to curry, to use (after Pettit) just some of the more evocative of the language's phrases for an undignified life. Law that avoids and curbs arbitrariness allows that citizens have their own points of view that must be attended to and treats them as active, self-directing *subjects*, not mere objects of sovereign will. By such laws, governments contribute to subjects' ability to further their own projects and to defend and pursue their self-chosen interests, without fear that at any time the rules might change without warning and without redress or might simply not matter.

A final and familiar reason for reducing possibilities of arbitrary power is that, faced with systematic arbitrariness, citizens lack reliable sources of *coordination* of expectations with others and between themselves and the state. It may only be in a disco that we do well when "the joint is rocking." Successful social coordination depends upon much besides a clear legal framework that cues in even those who might know nothing much else about others, but in large, complex and mobile societies, at any rate, it is hard to see it happening without such a frame. Among other things, the existence of Fullerian clear, prospective, etc., shared norms might (and is often assumed to) facilitate such coordination. This is a virtue that Friedrich von Hayek stresses, and, in large, modern, mobile, and complex societies, it falls to law to provide a great deal of it.

These four valuable outcomes—reduction of domination, of fear, of indignity, and of confusion—are not small reasons to value the rule of law. One might want more, and one might want other things. But, in the world we know, this is not a bad place to begin. One way of coming to recognize that is to think about life that doesn't benefit from the rule of law, because the law is irrelevant to the ways power is exercised or because it is of a sort that militates against the ends of the rule of law or because, as so often occurs, the rule of law is unevenly distributed within a society, rarely favoring those who might benefit from it most. Among examples where law doesn't rule are tyrannies, illiberal democracies, failed states, states strong enough to act arbitrarily but too weak to tame power, and societies with extralegal monsters beyond control by law. And, even where law is significant, where rule is, as the expression has it, more *by* law rather than *of* law, law is an instrument for the exercise of power but does not constrain it.[38] Again, we are talking about variations often of degree, but degrees count, and the variations in the role(s) law plays can be great. So, too, the pathologies associated with them. There are many reasons to want to avoid those pathologies. What might law contribute?

2. WHAT?

Accounts of the rule of law proliferate, and they differ greatly from one another. Some, we have seen, are institutionally "thin," others substantively "thick."[39] The first are often too spare to amount to much, the second too rich to allow one to sustain any useful distinction between the rule of law and whatever else you would like to find in a society.[40] A middle ground is available, however. It needs to have a special connection with *law*, lest the rule of law come to mean the rule of whatever is good, in which case we have no need for the concept;[41] we have already seen that there are values of this specifically law-related kind. And it has to address what might be needed for the law to *rule*, in ways that contribute to the particular *telos* one attributes to the rule of law.

The state of affairs that I have commended, where power can be effectively exercised but the possibility of its arbitrary exercise is securely limited, is unlikely to occur, particularly in large and complex societies, unless constraints on and channels for the exercise of power are institutionalized. Where such institutions are legal, the trick is to make law rule over those with significant degrees of power. That must include (though it should not be limited to) ruling over wielders of political power, even as laws are instruments of precisely that political power. And, if you think the bosses rule the law, the law must be able to rule them, too. The attempt to square these particular sorts of circles is the attempt to institutionalize the rule of law.

Lawyers and legal philosophers have suggested many ways in which law might be configured to aid in this attempt. I will mention three. One is by the law having particular formal characteristics. Another is by ensuring that it includes certain procedural guarantees. Legal philosophers have tended to emphasize the formal aspects, lawyers the procedural. Now that Jeremy Waldron has joined the lawyers, procedure is likely to get more philosophical attention. A third way, suggested by Gianluigi Palombella, is to institutionalize a specific "duality" within law, which balances law that is the instrument of government with a realm of law that it is not within even the ruler's power to alter, at least to alter routinely or easily or arbitrarily. I will sketch these in turn.

Law exerts its force in one or other or both of two directions. One is centrifugal. Law radiates signals of many kinds out to the wider society or segments of it, whether or not any contact develops between citizens and the world of officials at all. The other is centripetal, magnetic. It draws people into direct contact with agencies of the state, where in one way or another they are dealt with directly. There is, of course, significant overlap and interplay between these two functions. People's likelihood of direct engagement with officials and their understanding of what that might entail are affected by the signals sent out by legal institutions and how they are received and interpreted by citizens. Conversely, what happens in the legal institutions—in cases, trials, the behavior of police—obviously affects those who encounter them directly: litigants, petitioners, persons accused, defamed, assaulted, who come in voluntarily or are brought in by legal officials, among them police (who themselves are sent out into the community to extend the magnetic sweep of the law). However, it also sends signals to many more who never enter a court or even meet a policeman but nevertheless are affected by the law and their understanding of it.

One way of interpreting Lon Fuller's "internal morality of law" is to see it as primarily addressing the centrifugal functions of law. If messages are to be sent to indefinite numbers of persons assumed to wish and to be able to order their affairs within the frame and according to the injunctions of the law, they need to be able to know that law and confidently rely on it. Laws that conform to these eight conditions and are effective, it would seem, are knowable and can be more safely relied upon than laws or exercises of power that do not. Arbitrary effusions of a sovereign power or managerial direction that treats Fuller's features as contingent required only when useful to the wielders of power, fail these tests.

Recently, Jeremy Waldron has sought to supplement Fuller's list of formal characteristics with another group that he calls "procedural." His motivation is congenial to anyone who values the rule of law as more than an academic, or luxury, pastime. It has two aspects, both of which seem to me as important as they are often neglected by academics, even though I will later question whether Waldron's particular response satisfies them:

> Getting to the Rule of Law does not just mean paying lip service to the ideal in the ordinary security of a prosperous modern democracy it means extending the Rule of Law into societies that are not necessarily familiar with it; and in those societies that are familiar with it, it means extending the Rule of Law into these darker corners of governance, as well.
>
> When I pay attention to the calls that are made for the Rule of Law around the world, I am struck by the fact that the features that people call attention to are not necessarily the features that legal philosophers have emphasized in their academic conceptions.[42]

Waldron's list of procedural elements go to flesh out the normative ambition I referred to earlier, to ensure that, in their encounters with legal institutions, people are listened to, treated as human beings. They have, and we presume them to have, their own inner lives and particular "perspectives on the world"[43] that the law must accommodate. Such procedural values are many, but they include and revolve around the right to a fair trial by an impartial tribunal acting on the basis of evidence and argument, on one hand, and a host of rights to presence, voice, and representation during the trial, to examine witnesses, present evidence, hear reasons, and appeal, on the other.

A third way of trying to capture this complex ambition of constraining and channeling power, including lawful power, by law that is simultaneously an instrument of power is old in the English tradition of the rule of law and was imported with binding constitutions elsewhere more recently. Its rationale has recently been recovered and rearticulated by Gianluigi Palombella. According to this tradition, the point of the rule of law is "to prevent the law from turning itself into a sheer tool of domination, a manageable servant to political monopoly and instrumentalism."[44] It requires that, besides the laws that bend to the will of governments, " 'another' positive law should be available, which is located somehow outside the purview of the (legitimate) government, be it granted by the long standing tradition of the common law or by the creation of a 'constitutional' higher law protection, and so forth."[45] The common law as a higher law (though still law, not morality) that protects the right (*jurisdictio*) from being overwhelmed by rulers pursuing the ends of government (*gubernaculum*) is the most ancient institutionalization of this ideal. Written and binding constitutions are more recent examples. In all these, the ruler is constrained by something that is truly law but not his to rule, not able to be bent to his will. Such a conception, such a duality, Palombella stresses, was missing, until this century's spread of constitutions, from the European *Rechtsstaat*, which many, wrongly in his view, assimilate to the rule of law. Without this duality, a state may commit to Fuller's criteria of nonarbitrariness as its *form* of rule without any overarching constraint that renders anything beyond its power. Its ultimate goals might have nothing to do with reduction of domination, fear, indignity, or confusion. They might simply amount to tidy, reliable, and controllable ways for officials to extend state power and transact matters of state. This, to truncate grossly, is how Weber viewed the modern European state's interest in formal-rational law.

I choose these three accounts of what the rule of law is because each captures a significant way in which law might contribute to the rule of law and also represents a significant strand in distinguished traditions of thinking about the rule of law and how it is to be made good. Moreover, each ties the features chosen *in principle*, and not merely contingent *prediction*, to the values that the rule of law should serve. Indeed, each of these accounts eschews institutional particulars in favor of a teleological test that particular legal orders need to pass: you need to be able to know the law when you act; however in particular cases these goals are achieved, the law must treat you as a human with dignity and a perspective of your own; the law should institutionalize a balance between pursuing the good and securing the right through law. I envisage these three accounts as offering a cumulatively rich portrait of what is at stake in the rule of law and what are some of the generic features of law that might help us gain it. However, something fundamental about the rule of law still seems to me missing. Though I focus on these three as the most distinguished versions, most other accounts of the rule of law suffer from the same deficiencies.

3. WHERE?

I have recently noticed a tendency, or perhaps a recent tendency, for works on the rule of law to adopt geographical terminology. Palombella and Walker, for example, seek to "relocate" the rule of law.[46] The book in which this chapter appears hopes to be "getting to the rule of law." It is as though, after all this time, scholars have looked in all the usual places and not been able to find the rule of law in any of them. Perhaps they should look somewhere else.

That should not be surprising, for a great deal that matters most to whether law can rule is found outside legal institutions. It includes many of the *sources* of the rule of law, many *dangers* to the rule of law, and many of the *goods* the rule of law accomplishes. An account of the rule of law devoted only to features of legal institutions, rules and practices themselves, and one that sees it as an antidote to poisons that emanate only from those who wield the law is likely to miss a great deal of what makes it possible, what threatens it, and what makes it valuable.

This is a particular exemplification of a wise objection Lon Fuller made to the title of the "Law and Society Movement," and "law and society" study generally, on the grounds that it should speak not of "law and" but of "law in."[47] The point is not merely semantic.

Sources

A fundamental truth about the rule of law is that some of its deepest conditions and, even more, its most profound consequences are not found within legal institutions. I begin with conditions. The rule of law grows, needs nurturing, and has to be in sync with local ecologies. It can't just be screwed in, though it can be screwed up, and it depends as much on what's going on around it, on the particular things in that ecological niche, as on its own characteristics. This is a truth commonly ignored by those who fail to register the distinction nicely captured in the title of an essay by Robert Cooter, "The Rule of State Law versus the Rule of Law State."[48] It is the Rule of Law state that we want, the rule of state law and, at times, the nonrule of any law that we often get.

For the rule of law depends on a lot going right outside official practices and institutions, and a lot of what it depends upon is not what we conventionally take to be legal. As Amartya Sen has noted, in his influential speech to the World Bank:

> Even when we consider development in a particular sphere, such as economic development or legal development, the instruments that are needed to enhance development in that circumscribed sphere may not be confined only to institutions and policies in that sphere. . . . If this sounds a little complex, I must point out that the complication relates, ultimately, to the interdependences of the world in which we live. I did not create that world, and any blame for it has to be addressed elsewhere.[49]

This is not a truth restricted to countries struggling to see glimmers of the rule of law. It is universal, though not always registered by lawyers or legal philosophers. Thus, Waldron wants to keep faith with the way "the term is ordinarily used," and he says that law "comes to life in institutions," central among them judicial institutions.[50] And Tom Tyler's work suggests that the values Waldron stresses are those that people, at least when they go to court, value especially highly.[51] However, many ordinary people have little to do with such institutions and would ask for the law to have salutary effects in their everyday dealings both with one another and with officials. While the workings of the law clearly depend in many ways on its institutions, much of its life, even—perhaps especially

—in the well-appointed homes of its exporters, is lived outside official institutions as much as or more than within them.[52] When, that is, it has a life.

For many of the major effects of central legal institutions, where they *have* major effects (which is far from everywhere), occur outside those institutions. Those effects, in turn, are, to variable extents and in varying ways, dependent on the ways state laws interrelate with and are refracted, amplified, and nullified by existing nonstate structures, norms, networks, and attitudes. There is nowhere where everyone is straining to hear just what the legislature and the courts have to say on most actual or potential sources of conflict. Even if people saw a reason to pay special attention to these sources, there are many other generators of noise, some of it often louder and closer at hand than that generated by the law of the state. And states themselves make a lot of noise, much of it outside the law or contrary to the rule of law.

Whenever law stakes a claim to rule, then, there are many sources of potential normative, structural, cultural, and institutional collaboration and competition in every society, and they, and their interplay, differ markedly between (and often within) societies. How people will interpret the state's law and respond to it, how highly it will rate for them in comparison with other influences—these things depend only partly on what it says, how it says it, and what the law is intended by its makers to do. In complex and variable ways, people's responses to state law depend on how, in what form, and with what salience and force that law is able to penetrate all these intervening media, how attuned to it putative recipients are, and how dense, competitive, resistant, or hostile to its messages they might turn out to be.

This is not to say that state law is unimportant. It is often crucially important, but how important and, even if important, in what ways its effects work out in the world are heavily dependent on the complex social, economic, and political contexts into which it intervenes.

Dangers

Joseph Raz describes the rule of law as "essentially a negative value . . . merely designed to minimize the harms to freedom and dignity

which the law might cause in its pursuit of its goals however laud-
able these might be."[53] This seems to me doubly mistaken. The
harms for which the rule of law is a suggested antidote are abuses
of *power*, not merely of law. There are many ways in which power
can be exercised, used, and abused without the intervention of
law, even by the state, unless by definition everything the state does
is counted as done by law. The rule of law is intended to exclude
all those other ways from the start. More is necessary, but that exclusion is no small matter wherever arbitrary power is a concern.

   Moreover, there are many sources of abuse of power outside
the state and law altogether. Raz is clearly thinking only of state
power, and even those who might disagree with him over his negative characterization of the rule of law commonly view the primary
threat, to which the rule of law is a response, as coming from the
state. This is the common view, after all. But what about other
sources of power? Shouldn't the test be what they are likely to do,
not where they come from?

   As I have said, and as we often see, great threats and realizations
of unconstrained arbitrary exercise of power can have nothing to
do with the state. Indeed they require effective state interventions,
interventions to realize the rule "of law rather than men," where
these are possible and available, to tame. This is the gist of Robin
West's forceful response to Waldron:

> Law does a lot of things, but one of its core functions is to protect
> individuals against what would otherwise be undeterred privations
> against them—not by overreaching state officials but rather by un-
> deterred private individuals, corporations, or entities. Law does, as
> Waldron says, stigmatize, punish, impose liability, and so on. Law
> also, though, compensates individuals for private wrongs and pro-
> tects them at least much of the time against private violence. Some-
> times it does this well, and sometimes it does it only sporadically or
> not at all. In my view, a society that claims to regulate conduct under
> the ideal of the Rule of Law—as opposed to the rule of the stronger,
> or the rule of the more mendacious, or the rule of the more richly
> endowed, or the rule of the more vindictive, or the more manipu-
> lative, or the more fraudulent, or the more violent and so forth—
> should, seemingly, require that law do as much. Rule of Law scholar-
> ship, then, one would think, should reflect these ideals. . . .
>   . . . We want, from a liberal state that abides by the Rule of Law,
> not only a legal system that won't impose its will against us without

respecting our intelligence and seeking out our participation. We also want, from a liberal state that abides by the Rule of Law, some measure of safety in our homes and neighborhoods against private violence, some measure of fairness in our commercial dealings, and some measure of wellbeing in our private lives, free of the privations of more powerful private actors.[54]

West's point is true of every society, including my own (and yours), where the state is relatively effective and all the more so of many conflictual, postconflict, transitional, and failed states, where the miseries from which the rule of law would be a deliverance are closer to those imagined by Hobbes than to those understood by Locke.

Goods

The law never really rules unless it rules in the world around it. If that doesn't occur, no amount of internal elegance of design is worth a bean. Treating litigants well when you see them and have to judge them, is, of course, worth a whole string of beans, as Waldron rightly stresses. However, its social significance is dwarfed, certainly quantitively and arguably qualitatively, too, by what law does for or against people who never enter a lawyer's office, still less a court. Whether or not the rule of law has claim in a society is a matter found in the extent and quality of its reach and effects there: in interactions between citizens and the state, of course, but, of equal if not more importance, between citizens themselves.

This is well known to sociologists of law, sometimes too well known, since they can exaggerate the insignificance of states and their laws. Someone who didn't make this mistake but still understood the point was the historian E. P. Thompson. Thompson, as a man of the Left and a former Marxist, enraged erstwhile comrades with his encomium to the rule of law at the end of his, for this reason controversial, *Whigs and Hunters*.[55] I am all on his side on that issue, but I want to mention a less remarked aspect of his famous/notorious conclusion to *Whigs and Hunters*, in which he reflects on the

> difference between arbitrary power and the rule of law. We ought to expose the shams and inequities which may be concealed beneath

the law. But the rule of law itself, the imposing of effective inhibitions upon power and the defence of the citizen from power's all-
intrusive claims, seems to me to be an unqualified human good.[56]

Note where Thompson starts: with the *point* of the rule of law,
rather than its anatomy. Perhaps fortunately, Thompson was not
a lawyer, and, unlike most who write about the rule of law, he did
not seek to spell out just what legal elements allegedly produced
the salutary result he so praised. Rather, he insisted upon the "obvious point" that "there is a difference between arbitrary power
and the rule of law" and remarked that the latter was identified by
what it was claimed to achieve rather than by any recipe or précis
of ingredients. Thompson identified the rule of law by the good it
did—"the imposing of effective inhibitions upon power and the
defence of the citizen from power's all-intrusive claims." It was
only if and to the extent that law and the rule of law made that sort
of difference that it mattered.

And where did he look for evidence of that difference? Well,
not in particular legal forms and institutions, which he thought
were constantly being "created . . . and bent" by "a Whig oligarchy
. . . in order to legitimise its own property and status."[57] Still, that
oligarchy could not do as it wished; its hands were often tied by the
law it sought to exploit. How did Thompson show this? By describ-
ing the character of legal institutions and norms, or the experience of litigants, or internal legal balances? No. Rather, he called
in aid facts such as that

> [w]hat was often at issue was not property, supported by law, against
> no-property; it was alternative definitions of property-rights. . . .
> [L]aw was often a definition of actual agrarian *practice*, as it has been
> pursued "time out of mind." . . . "[L]aw" was deeply imbricated
> within the very basis of productive relations, which would have been
> inoperable without this law. And . . . this law, as definition or as rules
> (imperfectly enforceable through institutional forms) was endorsed
> by norms, tenaciously transmitted through the community.[58]

It is *social* facts like these that led Thompson to declare that "the
notion of the regulation and reconciliation of conflicts through
the rule of law—and the elaboration of rules and procedures
which, on occasion, made some approximate approach towards

the ideal—seems to me a cultural achievement of universal significance."⁵⁹ "Cultural achievement" is a well-chosen phrase, though much more than culture is involved.⁶⁰ And Thompson was right to seek his evidence where he did, rather than in descriptions of often contingent, historically specific, institutional particulars and still more to avoid taking these particulars to be the universal essence of the rule of law.

4. WHO CARES?

Up to now, I have contrasted my teleological-sociological approach to the rule of law with what I take to be the more common anatomical-institutional concerns that prevail in the literature. However, I have also emphasized that within that literature there are many competing views. Indeed, sitting in seminars and conferences about the rule of law over years, I have often recalled those clichéd scenes in Chicago gangster movies where cops bang on a door and demand, "Is a Mr. Capone in there?" to which a shouted reply rings out: "Who wants to know?" I can feel that way about discussions of the rule of law. A judge will point in one direction, a legislator in another, a tax lawyer in a third, a criminal defender in a fourth, a victim of Afghan warlords or Russian oligarchs somewhere else altogether, everyone all the while claiming to talk about the same thing. A lot of this can be explained by differences in local concerns and restricted views of a large reality, like the blind men and the elephant. And there are the conceptual contests we have already encountered.

However, I think that there is one systematic distinction between approaches to ideals such as the rule of law that matters across the board. It suggests different emphases and priorities, plays for different stakes, and requires and allows for different institutional strategies. The distinction I have in mind is between those whose first priority is to avoid as yet untamed evils and those who, fortunate to live where those evils have been largely stemmed or kept at bay, seek to secure and perhaps to refine and extend what goods they have. There are two points here. One is a general distinction between ways of approaching ideals; they might somewhat misleadingly be called "negative" and "positive" or "defensive" and "expansive" approaches. The second is between two different kinds of circumstance in which one thinks about, and might seek the ends of, the rule of law. One of these is where your need is to *establish* the rule of law to diminish the reign of arbitrary power, where that has not occurred or is not occurring. The other is where one seeks to improve or extend it, where legal constraints on arbitrariness are relatively well embedded.

Avoiding Evils, Pursuing Goods

One way to approach ideals is to attempt to capture what it is like for them to be properly and fully instantiated; John Rawls famously does that with justice, and he is not alone. Indeed, as Judith Shklar and Amartya Sen both observe, whereas philosophical writings on justice fill libraries, those on injustice might not fill a shelf. Thus, Shklar laments and notes of the countless works of philosophy and art devoted to portraits of justice:

> [W]here is injustice? To be sure, sermons, the drama, and fiction deal with little else, but art and philosophy seem to shun injustice. They take it for granted that injustice is simply the absence of justice, and that once we know what is just, we will know all we need to know. That belief may not, however, be true. One misses a great deal by looking only at justice. The sense of injustice, the difficulties of identifying the victims of injustice, and the many ways in which we all learn to live with each other's injustices tend to be ignored. . . . Why should we not think of those experiences that we call unjust directly, as independent phenomena in their own right? . . . Indeed, in all likelihood most of us have said, "this is unfair" or "this is unjust" more often than "this is just." Is there nothing much more to be said about the sense of injustice that we know so well when we feel it? Why then do most philosophers refuse to think about injustice as deeply or subtly as they do about justice? I do not know why a curious division of labour prevails, why philosophy ignores iniquity while history and fiction deal with little else, but it does leave a gap in our thinking.[61]

Another way to start, which Shklar favors, is to approach a value or ideal by exploring less where it might deliver us *to* when perfectly instantiated than what it might deliver us *from* and how that deliverance might be secured. Though he doesn't emphasize the point, Philip Pettit significantly casts the goal of republicanism as *non*-domination: "the condition of liberty is explicated as the status of someone who, unlike the slave, is not subject to the arbitrary power of another: that is, someone who is not dominated by anyone else."[62]

Amartya Sen approaches "the idea of justice" from similar beginnings. Most of us, he says, are moved not by "the realization that the world falls short of being completely just—which few of us expect—but that there are clearly remediable injustices around us which we want to eliminate."[63] Theory, he insists, should pay more attention to this disposition.

In a similar vein, Avishai Margalit explores the nature of a decent society. His account of decency is a deliberately *negative* one; a decent society is not characterized as one whose institutions treat members with respect; it is one whose institutions don't humiliate anyone dependent on them. Margalit deliberately and systematically avoids giving a positive version of these goals. His is an exercise in negative politics, approaching a value by seeking to avoid its negation. A decent society is one that is not indecent.

Margalit is quite explicit about this. He asks, "Why characterize the decent society negatively, as nonhumiliating, rather than positively, as one that, for example, respects its members?" He gives three reasons: one moral, one logical, and one cognitive. The first seems to me the most important and generalisable to other moral concepts. It is that "there is a weighty asymmetry between eradicating evil and promoting good. It is much more urgent to remove painful evils than to create enjoyable benefits."[64]

Apart from this asymmetry of urgency, I would add what might be called a kind of asymmetry of recognition. The importance of freedom from arbitrary intervention and oppression is often best understood in the light of experience or reflection on life without such freedom. Where fundamental evils have been tamed, it is hard to recall them. People living in civil and law-governed societies, not to mention just ones, might rightly have ambitions for more and better, but they frequently find it hard realistically to imagine less and worse. Yet, as Henry James, I think, has said, those without the "imagination of disaster" are doomed to be surprised by the world. Part of what is valuable in the rule of law consists in the possibility that it might mitigate some disasters. To lessen our surprise, and for a general understanding of the *value* of this value, we would do well to think about what might do that.

I think that's a good place to start—not to finish but to start. Hobbes started that way to understand the worth of a sovereign polity; he sought to imagine life without it. We might not agree with where he ended up, and Locke didn't, but, like Locke, we might learn from starting where Hobbes started. They were both threat experts, as was Shklar. It is an estimable skill, if not the only one you need.

One can learn a lot about the rule of law by experiencing or trying to imagine life without it. What does/would one miss? What might the rule of law contribute to improving matters? What would be needed for law to contribute what is needed from it? It is, after all, easy to miss what the rule of law does when it does it, easier to identify what it might be good for when one sees its lack. It is also easier to grasp its worth in its absence, even if just making up for that absence leaves us thirsting for more. If so, we should seek more. But we shouldn't settle for less.

It may turn out that, whether one starts positively or negatively, one will come to value what people who start elsewhere value. And it is a mistake to think that where one starts is where one should finish. A just society is one that avoids manifest injustice, but it is also one that does justice, and, since that is never a completed task, there is always more one might do.

Ultimately, my own conceptual bias is to follow Philip Selznick, who, though deeply concerned with identifying the conditions of social and institutional *flourishing*, starts, though he doesn't stop, at the same place as Shklar, Sen, and Margalit: we must understand and secure the conditions of survival or existence, baselines, he says, before we move on to flourishing. When such conditions are secure, we should aim higher, and we are also in a better position to do so. Risks are less risky. We should not, with melodramatic bad faith, settle for little because there could always be less if we are not seriously threatened with less. Ideally, the social-institutional complex in a society will not merely satisfy the minimum conditions for the rule of law plausibly to be said to exist but enable it to flourish as well. And, where such minimum conditions are satisfied, it is no answer to the goad that we can do better to be told that we can do worse. On the other hand, where those conditions are unsatisfied, avoiding worse is a major, immediate, and imperative goal; the rest might have to wait. First things first.[65]

Knowing Your Place

Now, whichever place one prefers to start as a conceptual matter, concerns with the rule of law are often very practical ones. And, at the level of practice, it is important to note the differences between the imperatives of seeking to establish, following Selznick's terminology, *baselines, conditions of existence, conditions of survival,* and those appropriate to *flourishing.* Aims are different, and differently exigent, threats to them similarly; what needs to be done to secure oneself against such threats will differ; the institutional means of deliverance from the worst evils might be quite different from those appropriate to enhance well-secured benefits. One's understanding of success will also vary. Minimal achievements don't sound like much when compared with maximal ones, but they may seem very precious when compared to no achievement at all, and they might be necessary for any further achievement. There are self-perpetuating spirals in institutional development: the further development and enhancement of the quality of the rule of law are much easier to attain if some of its elements already exist. Conversely, in their absence it can be difficult to develop, even at times to imagine, anything different. And, thus, successes of a "negative" kind can be of enormous moment for those concerned to establish baselines, while, once established, they can allow play for more positive ambitions.

Of course, we should where we can (without making matters worse), strive to do both—secure baselines and facilitate flourishing—and yet often people imagine that the same dangers are faced by both, the same goals are apt for both, and thus the same tools are needed by both. Why think that? What we might need to do to avoid the worst, or engage in "damage limitation," as Shklar implores, might be very different from what is needed to reach out to something better.

Legal orders differ greatly in the extent to which the values and practices of the rule of law are strongly embedded within them. Not every legal order is strongly embedded in institutions, professions, culture, and social structure, and so nor will the ways to make it so be everywhere of the same sort. That suggests two things. First, what Holmes has observed about Russia can be generalized to other societies that are poor in the rule of law:

> Lawyers are trained to solve routine problems within routine procedures. They are not trained to reflect creatively on the emergence and stabilization of the complex institutions that lawyering silently presupposes. Ordinary legal training, therefore, is not adequate to the extraordinary problems faced by the manager of a legal-development project in Russia. The problem is not Russian uniqueness and exceptionalism, but the opposite. In Russia, as everywhere else, legal reform cannot succeed without attention to social context, local infrastructure, professional skills, logistic capacities, and political support. . . . So legal knowledge alone is never enough.[66]

It may therefore be that the importance of attending to things other than law, when thinking about the rule of law, varies inversely with the latter's strength in a society.

However, and this is the second point, to the extent that lawyers' insights are relevant in "Rule of Law-poor" countries, they might favor emphasis precisely on those unnuanced conceptions of legality that conservatives make so much of, and progressives deride, in less threatened places and times. For, as Selznick has argued:

> Institutional autonomy, is, indeed, the chief bulwark of the rule of law. Judging, lawyering, fact-finding, rule-making: all require insulation from pressures that would corrupt them. The twentieth century has brought many reminders that legal autonomy of some sort is a necessary condition for justice. As the dictatorships of our time have shown, repressive law is hardly ancient history. In those regimes a primary victim has been the integrity of the legal process. High on the agenda in the struggle for freedom—in Eastern Europe, for example, or South Africa—is the building or rebuilding, of legal institutions capable of resisting political manipulation. For those who suffer oppression, criticism of the rule of law as "bourgeois justice" or "liberal legalism" can only be perceived as naïve or heartless, or both.[67]

On the other hand, in strong legal orders, such as those of the Western liberal democracies, for example, there are large cadres of people trained within strong legal traditions, disciplined by strong legal institutions, working in strong legal professions, socialized to strong legal values. Western legal orders are bearers of value, meaning, and tradition laid down and transmitted over centuries. Prominent among the values deeply entrenched in these legal orders are Rule of Law values, and these values have exhibited considerable resilience and capacity to resist attempts to erode them.

Members of a strong Rule of Law order may not need to have as great or immediate a concern with the extralegal foundations of what they have as those where legality is pervasively weak, simply because they have, as it were, been taken care of, if rarely by many in the generations that benefit from them. They may well, of course want to improve what they have, and, since the underlying conditions of legal effectiveness are to a considerable extent met, they are often right to concentrate on legal institutions. That is not because they live in a different world but because some universal problems have been dealt with in their part of the world and what the law is like counts here in ways it may not elsewhere. Other problems or opportunities have priority. It might be why so much talk of the rule of law, which emanates from such places, has so little to say about the extralegal conditions of legal effectiveness. It's not clear, however, how far their understandings will travel.

In these circumstances of relative luxury, moreover, the options open to partisans of the rule of law are also more open than is sometimes acknowledged. As Selznick again has argued:

> the very stability of the rule of law, where that has been achieved, makes possible a still broader vision and a higher aspiration. Without disparaging (to say nothing of trashing) our legal heritage, we may well ask whether it fully meets the community's needs. . . . So long as the system is basically secure, it is reasonable to accept some institutional risks in the interests of social justice.[68]

That suggests that not every potential source of threat will be equally salient in different legal orders: some will be much threatened, others less so. It also suggests that different threats might require different defenses. Not to mention that we might want to do more than ward off threats. Of course, the rule of law can be seriously threatened even where it appears to be in good shape. If we needed reminding, the war on terror reminds us of that, as it does of the dangers of complacency in such circumstances. Yet, there is still a lot to draw on, even there, which is unavailable in a tyranny, a failed state, an illiberal democracy, and so on.

Conservatives in Rule of Law-rich countries, suspicious of any falling off from some idealized version of it, often overreact to, say, injection of any substantive concerns into adjudication or discretionary authority in administration, indeed to any number of welfare state incursions on an idealized rule of Fuller-full-formal laws.[69] These are paraded as dangers to the existence of the rule of law as we know it, whereas they might be dangers only in circumstances where legality is already weak and has no other resources with which to defend itself. This shows little reflection on what the rule of law really depends upon, what it would be like to really threaten what they have of it, and what it would really mean to lack it. Radicals in the same societies, on the other hand, who treat some indeterminacy in appellate decision making as testimony to fraudulence of the Rule of Law ideal or at least to absence of the rule of law, exhibit a similar frivolousness about what it might really be to have to live without a good measure of it.[70] Perspective is all here.

Fuller spoke of the lawyer as a social architect. He appears to have had in mind both the lawyer's design of, say, contracts for clients and also the design of public legal institutions. In relation to the latter, at least, the term is sometimes an exaggeration, for there are at least two enterprises going on here. Rule of Law promoters in transitional and postconflict societies too often think about the rule of law as though establishing it where it has not existed or is being shot to pieces, at times quite literally, is in principle the same sort of job, if harder and more dangerous, as cultivating it where it has long grown and has deep roots and where its presence is an often unreflected-upon ingredient of everyday life. Yet, they are truly engaged in social architecture, often undertaken on hostile, unforgiving terrain.[71] Those fortunate to live where the rule of law is strong may have a lot to do to defend, secure, sustain, improve, and extend it, but those enterprises are, by comparison, more in the nature of running repairs. They may be major repairs, but there is something, often a great deal, of structure and helpful material there to work with and on. The ultimate goals of these activities and their common ambition—lessening the potential for arbitrary abuse of power—are not unrelated in these different circumstances, but the means appropriate to serve them can differ enormously.

And this points to one more difference between the two contexts I have sketched. In societies where the rule of law has long been secure, the fact that it is misconceived might not matter too much, since to a considerable extent it runs on its own steam. However, in conflictual, postconflict, and transitional societies, where efforts are made to generate, better to *catalyze* the rule of law, these problems can be catastrophic. For those most urgently seeking the rule of law are in the end concerned not with a package of legal techniques but with an *outcome*: that salutary state of affairs where law counts in a society as a reliable constraint on the possibility of arbitrary exercise of power.

More generally, and this is the conclusion of this article and not just this section, with regard to the rule of law it pays to be a contextual universalist: universalist about the value of it, deeply contextual about how to get there. What is precious about the rule of law, and a reason to start there, is not this or that bit of legal stuff but an outcome, a state of affairs, in which the law counts in certain ways. What conspires to generate such a state of affairs is complex and often mysterious and will vary from place to place and time to time. In particular, it will vary considerably between circumstances where the rule of law has yet to be *established* and those where the ambition is that it be improved. What doesn't vary is that it will depend on many things *outside* what we commonly regard as legal institutions.

NOTES

This chapter was delivered as the 2010 Annual Lecture of the Centre for Law and Society, University of Edinburgh. I am grateful to Neil Walker for inviting me to deliver the lecture and for extremely helpful comments on it. I also learned from participants in the discussion that followed the lecture. Drafts benefited much from several long and long-distance skypings with Gianluigi Palombella.

1. I am using shorthand here. The rule of law is not something you have or don't have. It comes in degrees, more or less, and not only on one scale. That is often important to recognize. When I use this shorthand, I

only mean that a society is comparatively well endowed with the rule of law. Other societies are less well endowed, some so poorly served that we say, also usually in shorthand, that they lack the rule of law.

2. See Lon L. Fuller, *The Morality of Law* (New Haven: Yale University Press, 1969).

3. See Judith Shklar, "Political Theory and the Rule of Law," in her *Political Thought and Political Thinkers*, ed. Stanley Hoffman (Chicago: University of Chicago Press, 1998), 26, on "Dicey's unfortunate outburst of Anglo-Saxon parochialism. . . . The Rule of Law was thus both trivialized as the peculiar patrimony of one and only one national order, and formalized, by the insistence that only one set of inherited procedures and court practices could sustain it."

4. *Introduction to the Study of the Law of the Constitution*, 10th ed. (first edition 1885) (London: Macmillan, 1959), 195–96.

5. See Randall Peerenboom, "Human Rights and Rule of Law: What's the Relationship?" *Georgetown Journal of International Law* 36 (2005): 809; *The New Law and Economic Development: A Critical Approach*, ed. David Trubek and Alvaro Santos (New York: Cambridge University Press, 2006); Stephen Golub, "A House without Foundations," in *Promoting the Rule of Law Abroad*, ed. Thomas Carothers (Washington, DC: Carnegie Endowment for International Peace, 2006), 105–36.

6. "Introduction" to *Constructing Justice and Security after War*, ed. Charles Call (Washington, DC: United States Institute of Peace Press, 2007), 4.

7. "In Defense of Imperialism? The Rule of Law and the State-Building Project," in this volume. See *Beyond Common Knowledge. Empirical Approaches to the Rule of Law*, ed. Erik Jensen and Thomas C. Heller (Stanford: Stanford Law and Politics, 2003), 1–2.

In legal circles in developing countries and in international development circles, *rule of law* has become almost synonymous with *legal and judicial reform*. Basic questions about what legal systems across diverse countries actually do, why they do it, and to what effect are either inadequately explored or totally ignored. In developed and developing countries, larger questions about the relationship of the rule of law to human rights, democracy, civil society, economic development, and governance often are reduced to arid doctrinalism in the legal fraternity. And, in the practice of the international donor community, the rule of law is reduced to sectors of support, the most prominent of which is the judicial sector.

During the past several years, we have witnessed an explosion of literature related to legal and judicial reform. Yet very little attention has been paid to the widening gap between theory and practice or to the disconnection between stated project goals and objectives and the actual activities supported.

8. Richard Sannerholm, "Rule of Law after War: Ideologies, Norms and Methods for Legal and Judicial Reform," *Örebro Studies in Law* 1 (2009), 131 and *passim*.

9. Most recently in "The Rule of Law: Teleology, Legality, Sociology," in *Relocating the Rule of Law*, ed. Gianluigi Palomella and Neil Walker (Oxford: Hart, 2009), 45–69.

10. Gianfranco Poggi coins the phrase to describe Durkheim's conception of society. See his *Durkheim* (Oxford: Oxford University Press, 2000), 35.

11. See Jeremy Waldron, "Is the Rule of Law an Essentially Contested Concept (in Florida?)," *Law and Philosophy* 21 (2002): 137.

12. See Pedro Magalhães, "The Politics of Judicial Reform in Eastern Europe," *Comparative Politics* 1 (October 1999): 32, 43, and my "The Rule of Law: An Abuser's Guide," in *The Dark Side of Fundamental Rights*, ed. András Sajó (Utrecht: Eleven International, 2006), 129.

13. "Judicial Independence as Ambiguous Reality and Insidious Illusion," in *From Liberal Values to Democratic Transition. Essays in Honor of János Kis*, ed. Ronald Dworkin (Budapest: CEU Press, 2004), 8.

14. Ibid., 9.

15. W. Jacoby, "Priest and Penitent: The European Union as a Force in the Domestic Politics of Eastern Europe," *East European Constitutional Review* 8 (1999): 62.

16. Philip Selznick, *The Moral Commonwealth* (Berkeley: University of California Press, 1992), 454.

17. "In politics, then, every enterprise is a consequential enterprise, the pursuit, not of a dream, or of a general principle, but of an intimation." Michael Oakeshott, "Political Education," in Oakeshott, *Rationalism in Politics and Other Essays* (Indianapolis: Liberty Press, 1991), 57. And see Oakeshott, "The Pursuit of Intimations," in ibid., 66–69.

18. See my "Approaching the Rule of Law," in *The Rule of Law in Afghanistan: Missing in Inaction*, ed. Whit Mason (Cambridge: Cambridge University Press, 2011).

19. "The Illusory Promise of the Rule of Law," in *Human Rights with Modesty: The Problem of Universalism*, ed. András Sajó (Leiden/Boston: Martinus Nijhoff, 2004), 281.

20. See John Philip Reid, *Rule of Law* (DeKalb: Northern Illinois University Press, 2004).

21 Philip Pettit, *Republicanism: A Theory of Freedom and Government* (Oxford: Oxford University Press, 1997), 55.

22 Goaded by Gianluigi Palombella, I am not sure that arbitrariness takes us far enough, but it's as far as I have so far worked out how to go, and I'm not sure we need to go any further.

23. *Rhetoric and the Rule of Law* (Oxford: Oxford University Press, 2005), 14.

24. "The Rule of Law and the Importance of Procedure," in this volume, 15–16 (emphasis in original).

25. *The Morality of Law*, 96.

26. Waldron, "The Rule of Law and the Importance of Procedure," 22–23 (emphasis in original).

27. *Rhetoric and the Rule of Law*, 11.

28. On the importance of securing thresholds as distinct from pursuit of formalistic certainty, see my "Ethical Postivism and the Liberalism of Fear," in *Judicial Powers, Democracy and Legal Positivism*, ed. Tom Campbell and Jeffrey Goldsworthy (Aldershot, UK: Ashgate, 2000), 59, esp. at 73ff.

29. *Rhetoric and the Rule of Law*, 25–26.

30. Pettit, *Republicanism*, 86.

31. "The Rule of Law as an Institutional Ideal," in *Rule of Law and Democracy: Internal and External Issues*, ed. G. Palombella and L. Morlino (Leiden: Brill, 2010), 3–37.

32. Ibid., 24.

33. Pettit, *Republicanism*, 69.

34. Ibid., 39.

35. In her *Political Thought and Political Thinkers*, 3–20.

36. *Political Writings*, ed. P. N. Miller (Cambridge: Cambridge University Press, 1993), 35 (quoted in Pettit, *Republicanism*, 86).

37. Cf. my "The Grammar of Colonial Legality: Subjects, Objects, and the Australian Rule of Law," in *Australia Reshaped: 200 Years of Institutional Transformation*, ed. Geoffrey Brennan and Francis G. Castles (Cambridge: Cambridge University Press, 2002), 220–60.

38. I discuss these in my "Approaching the Rule of Law."

39. See Randall Peerenboom, "Varieties of Rule of Law: An Introduction and Provisional Conclusion," in *Asian Discourses of Rule of Law*, ed. Peerenboom (London: Routledge Curzon, 2004), 1–10.

40. See Joseph Raz, "The Rule of Law and Its Virtue," in Raz, *The Authority of Law* (Oxford: Clarendon Press, 1979), 210.

41. Palombella is particularly good on the distinction between the rule of law as a legal, and not just a political or moral, ideal. See his "The Rule of Law as an Institutional Ideal."

42. "The Rule of Law and the Importance of Procedure," 3–4.

43. Raimond Gaita stresses the fact of our "inner lives" as a defining element of our common humanity. Simone Weil, an inspiration to Gaita, stresses a "perspective on the world." See Gaita, *Good and Evil: An Absolute Conception*, 2nd ed. (London: Routledge, 2004); Gaita, *A Common Humanity. Thinking About Love and Truth and Justice* (London: Routledge, 2000).

44. Palombella, "The Rule of Law as an Institutional Ideal," 4.

45. Ibid., 31.

46. See their edited book *Relocating the Rule of Law.*

47. Cf. Lon L. Fuller, "Some Unexplored Social Dimensions of the Law," in *Path of the Law from 1967*, ed. Arthur E. Sutherland (Cambridge, MA: Harvard University Press, 1968), 57: "The intensified interest in the sociology of law that has developed in recent years has come to assume the proportions of something like an intellectual movement. In the United States this movement has found a kind of sloganized expression in the title, *Law and Society.* . . . It would be captious indeed to pick any serious quarrel with this innocent renaming of the familiar. . . . At the same time there are, I believe, some dangers in this new title and in the allocation of intellectual energies it seems to imply. By speaking of law *and* society we may forget that law is itself a part of society, that its basic processes are *social* processes, that it contains within its own internal workings social dimensions worthy of the best attentions of the sociologist."

48. In *The Law and Economics of Development*, ed. E. Buscaglia, W. Ratliff, and R. Cooter (Greenwich, CT: JAI Press, 1997), 101–48.

49. "What Is the Role of Legal and Judicial Reform in the Development Process?" (Washington, DC: World Bank Legal Conference, 2000), 10. See, too, Brian Tamanaha, "The Primacy of Society and the Failures of Law and Development: Decades of Refusal to Learn," Keynote Address, Conference on the Rule of Law, Nagoya University, Japan, June 13, 2009, *Cornell Journal of International Law* (forthcoming).

50. Waldron, "The Rule of Law and the Importance of Procedure," 13, 14.

51. See Tom Tyler, *Why People Obey the Law* (Princeton: Princeton University Press, 2006).

52. See my "The Rule of Law and 'the Three Integrations,'" *Hague Journal on the Rule of Law* 1 (March 2009): 21–27. Here and elsewhere I have been much influenced by two classics of legal sociology where this point is splendidly made. See Sally Falk Moore, "Law and Social Change: The Semi-Autonomous Social Field As An Appropriate Subject of Study," in Moore, *Law as Process* (London: Routledge and Kegan Paul, 1978), 54–81; and Marc Galanter, "Justice in Many Rooms: Courts, Private Ordering, and Indigenous Law," *Journal of Legal Pluralism* 19 (1981): 1–47. As Galanter observes, "[t]he mainstream of legal scholarship has tended to look out from within the official legal order, abetting the pretensions of the official law to stand in a relationship of hierarchic control to other normative orderings in society. Social research on law has been characterized by a repeated rediscovery of the other hemisphere of the legal world. This has entailed recurrent rediscovery that law in modern society is plural rather

than monolithic, that it is private as well as public in character and that the national (public, official) legal system is often a secondary rather than a primary locus of regulation" (ibid., 20).

53. Raz, "The Rule of Law and Its Virtue," 228.

54. Robin West, "The Limits of Process," in this volume, 47–48.

55. *Whigs and Hunters. The Origin of the Black Act* (Harmondsworth, UK: Penguin, 1977).

56. Ibid., 266.

57. Ibid., 260–61.

58. Ibid., 261.

59. Ibid., 266.

60. See my "Approaches to the Rule of Law."

61. *Faces of Injustice* (New Haven: Yale University Press, 1990), 15–16.

62. *Republicanism*, 31.

63. *The Idea of Justice* (Cambridge, MA: Harvard University Press, 2009), vii.

64. *The Decent Society* (Cambridge, MA: Harvard University Press, 1996).

65. The distinction is pervasive in Selznick's writings. See *The Moral Commonwealth*.

66. "Can Foreign Aid Promote the Rule of Law?," *East European Constitutional Review* 8 (1999): 71.

67. *The Moral Commonwealth*, 464.

68. Ibid.

69. See, for example, Geoffrey de Q. Walker, *The Rule of Law, Foundation of Constitutional Democracy* (Melbourne: Melbourne University Press, 1988); F. A. Hayek, *Law, Legislation and Liberty*, vol.1 (Chicago: University of Chicago Press, 1973; vol. 2, 1974; vol. 3, 1979); E. Kamenka and A. E-S. Tay, "Beyond Bourgeois Individualism—The Contemporary Crisis in Law and Legal Ideology," in *Feudalism, Capitalism and Beyond*, ed. Eugene Kamenka and R. S. Neale (Canberra: Australian National University Press, 1975), 127–44. And, from a different political perspective, see Brian Tamanaha, *Law as a Means to an End: Threat to the Rule of Law* (New York: Cambridge University Press, 2006). A more complex appraisal of such developments is Philippe Nonet and Philip Selznick, *Law and Society in Transition: Towards Responsive Law* (Piscataway, New Jersey: Transaction, 2001).

70. I have particularly in mind Critical Legal Studies, a now dated movement but one that has occasional echoes. Cf. my "Critical Legal Studies and Social Theory—A Reply to Alan Hunt," *Oxford Journal of Legal Studies* 7 (1987): 26.

71. I discuss some of the difficulties of the task in "Hart, Fuller and Law in Transitional Societies," in *The Hart-Fuller Debate in the Twenty-First Century*, ed. Peter Cane (Oxford: Hart, 2010), 107.

PART II

MAINTAINING OR RESTORING THE RULE OF LAW AFTER SEPTEMBER 11, 2001

5

SEPARATION OF POWERS AND THE
NATIONAL SECURITY STATE

BENJAMIN A. KLEINERMAN

Although the constitutional struggles of the Bush administration now seem to be in our proverbial "rearview mirror," the constitutional questions that these struggles brought to the surface will surely remain. The essence of these struggles concerned the tenuous relationship between the rule of law and the preservation of national security. For the Bush administration, the preeminent importance of maintaining national security continually trumped concerns about the rule of law. And, if we are to be fair, this attitude made some sense for an administration that presided in its first year over an attack that killed so many citizens on domestic soil. Jack Goldsmith writes in his important and thoughtful book on the Bush administration: "It is hard to overstate the impact that the incessant waves of threat reports have on the judgment of people inside the executive branch who are responsible for protecting American lives."[1] Although Goldsmith's account, based in part on his own experience in the administration, ends up being critical, this criticism is mixed with a fair-minded awareness that the threat of another attack may have overwhelmed the administration's better judgment. He claims that the reactions of the administration were "natural responses by an executive branch entirely responsible for protecting the safety of Americans but largely in the dark about where or how the next terrorist attack will occur."[2]

In determining how we can restore the rule of law in the post-9/11 world, it is useful to start with this very natural reaction to these threats because they reveal the universality of the administration's response. In other words, contrary to what some might think, the restoration of the rule of law in the post-9/11 world requires more than Bush's departure. Goldsmith's argument actually reveals the extent to which any presidential administration, almost uniquely held responsible for preserving national security, will push the envelope in aiming to fulfill its responsibility. In a certain sense, then, one might say that the ultimate blame for the aggressiveness of the Bush administration in pushing beyond the Constitution actually lies in its constitutional duty itself.[3] Given that the Obama administration came into office under claims that it would be different from its predecessor, the number of questionable policies it has continued shows the extent to which the problem lies in the very nature of the office. Of course, Goldsmith also rightly notes that the aggressions of the Bush administration went further than those of other administrations, even those that were similarly singlemindedly concerned about security. Goldsmith claims that whereas other presidents—his preeminent example is FDR—concerned about national security remained sufficiently politically attuned that they were willing to work with the other branches, the Bush "administration's conception of presidential power had a kind of theological significance that often trumped political consequences."[4]

At the heart of this conception lay a far-reaching claim about the inherent constitutionality of all that the president thought necessary to conduct the "war on terror." While nearly every presidential administration has claimed independent and extensive executive power,[5] the Bush administration went further in its claim that it had a preclusive power that rendered unconstitutional any attempt by Congress to cabin executive discretion.[6] On the question concerning the relationship between the rule of law and national security, this meant that, for the Bush administration, the maintenance of national security was indistinguishable from the rule of law. Or, the rule of law, as conventionally understood, had to be reinterpreted in terms of the requirements of national security.

Insofar as this claim is the most far-reaching and dangerous but, at the same time, seemingly unique to the Bush administration, are we not back to the conclusion that all has been restored by his departure? I will suggest that we cannot rest satisfied with this conclusion for essentially two reasons, both of which derive from the twentieth-century turn toward the legalization of executive discretion and away from an understanding of this discretion as essentially extralegal—a decision that followed from and illustrated a new conception of governmental power as essentially unified, in which whatever any one branch decided must also be acceptable to the other two branches. First, the persistent need for "prerogative" means that the Bush administration's insistence on a preclusive power follows from this unified conception of governmental power. Legislation that aims to cabin presidential discretion would be unconstitutional insofar as there may indeed be situations when the necessities of national security require the executive to break certain laws. John Locke's insight remains true: there needs to be a power "to act according to discretion, for the public good, without the prescription of the Law, and sometimes even against it."[7] The unpredictability of political affairs requires a power capable of taking action that the laws either could not or should not have foreseen.[8] If the powers of government are unified, by which I mean if every action the government takes must be considered the action of the government as a whole, then the necessity of executive discretion would render unconstitutional any attempt Congress might make to establish permanent and unbreachable boundaries on executive discretionary action. If every action of the executive must also be approved by Congress and deemed constitutional by the Supreme Court in order to be considered legitimate, then the Bush administration was right to insist so strenuously on the preclusive nature of executive discretion. In typical circumstances, the restrictions placed by the other branches are completely acceptable. Executive discretion must, however, trump these restrictions in the extraordinary circumstance that requires the exercise of extraordinary power. If the ability to set aside the law must be contained within the law itself, then the Bush administration was right to insist on its legal ability to set aside the law. Conversely, even in those situations when presidents are not as inclined to insist so strenuously on the preclusive nature of executive discretion, a conception of unified governmental power will typically cause Congress and the Supreme Court, in its legislation and in its decisions, to give away too much power to the executive in order to give it sufficient leeway in its preservation of national security. Throughout much of the twentieth century, this has been the relationship between the branches on matters of national security. With all but a few exceptions, both Congress and the Supreme Court have acceded to the executive's demands. And, again, given the legitimate concerns about the powers needed to preserve national security, this accession is, for the most part, perfectly understandable. Given a notion of the unity of governmental power, the necessity of executive discretion acts like a runaway steam engine, destroying all of the fences we might attempt to create so as to hold it in check.

Because the demands of national security are not going to wane, especially given the continuing threat of terrorism, a restoration of the substantive rule of law requires that we somehow come to grips with these demands. I will suggest that the key to this restoration actually lies in rediscovering the nineteenth-century conception of the separation of powers and the "extralegal" notion of executive discretion that accompanied it. Within this conception, both Congress and the Supreme Court could be, paradoxically, more aggressive in restraining the executive precisely because their restraints were not understood as exhausting the executive's resource of potential power. Given the separation of powers, the executive retained an extralegal capacity to act in those exigencies that required action. Precisely, however, because it was extralegal, it did not need to be approved by the Supreme Court or authorized by Congress. And, at the same time, precisely because it was extralegal, the executive always risked himself in exercising it; that is, contrary to the Bush administration's claim to an inherent legal power to take whatever action it deemed necessary for the sake of national security, the executive's extralegal discretion is inherent only to the extent that it is inherently contestable.

In making this argument, I will concentrate specifically on the jurisprudence of the nineteenth century and contrast that jurisprudence with the different approach taken by the judiciary in the twentieth century. Because the judiciary typically decided cases in such a manner as to give legal effect in the decision itself to the laws that had been passed by Congress, the courts are the best place to start. Whereas one finds numerous cases in the early nineteenth century in which the Supreme Court was strikingly willing to rein in the actions of the executive branch, one now finds a Supreme Court whose acquiescence in both the actions and the claims of the executive is represented best, but not solely, by its decision in *Korematsu*.[9] As I will examine, the difference between the earlier and the later jurisprudence lies in the Court's conception of its power. The nineteenth-century Supreme Court did not understand itself as the final "decider" on the power that the government can exercise in the future. Instead, the Supreme Court decided only the question as to the adequacy of the government's actions in the past long after the action had taken place. The Court was not attempting to validate or "pre-approve" the government's action with a view to what might be necessary as a matter of national security: it was deciding only the right of the individual in the case before it as a matter of law. But, as Marshall makes clear in *Marbury v. Madison*,[10] his first articulation of judicial review, this is possible only in a system of separation of powers, in which both Congress and the president are free to act as they see fit, even as the judiciary is also free to act as it sees fit. In other words, paradoxically, the system of separation of powers allows the judiciary to assert itself much more than in a system in which it has the last word as to the power of the other branches.

1. Nineteenth-Century Separation-of-Powers Jurisprudence

In *Marbury*, Marshall articulates the doctrine of the separation of powers even as he also asserts the doctrine of judicial review. In the first place, it is worth noting, as others have noted prior to this, that Marshall's doctrine of judicial review is very different from the modern doctrine of judicial supremacy—notwithstanding *Cooper v. Aaron*'s contrary assertion.[11] But, beyond this, the case asserts the principle of judicial review only after a subtle and extended consideration of the political department's respective roles and powers; that is, the assertion of judicial review occurs only in the context of the separation of powers. Judicial review emerges only in the context of Marshall's discussion of the judiciary's function. One might say that judicial review is subordinate to the separation of powers, rather than, as so many scholars argue now, the principle that upholds the separation of powers.[12]

First, Marshall's decision in *Marbury* discusses the power of the president. Marshall writes: "By the constitution of the United States, the President is invested with certain important political power, in the exercise of which he is to use his own discretion, and is accountable only to his country in his political character, and to his own conscience." Marshall continues: "Whatever opinion may be entertained of the manner in which executive discretion may be used, still there exists, and can exist, no power to control that discretion. The subjects are political." So, in the first place, the executive's power is both discretionary and independent. And, in the exercise of his discretionary independence, the president is answerable only to the American people in his political capacity. As such, the acts of both the president and the president's officers "can never be examinable by the courts."[13]

That being said, however, Marshall is careful to limit its implications. So far from being a proponent of the far-reaching version of executive power proposed by the Bush administration, Marshall next suggests that the presidential administration's independence has certain limits, namely those imposed by the legislature. Marshall writes: "When the legislature proceeds to impose on that officer [appointed by the president] other duties; when he is directed peremptorily to perform certain acts; when the rights of individuals are dependent on the performance of those acts; he is so far the officer of the law; is amenable to the laws for his conduct." That is, the presidential administration's discretion is necessarily circumscribed by the laws of the legislature. So, even as Marshall asserts the independence of the executive, he also conditions that independence by noting the power of the legislature to impose legal duties on the executive branch.

These laws imposed by the legislature are especially pressing, Marshall implies here, "where a specific duty is assigned by law, and individual rights depend upon the performance of that duty." This concern for the connection between the laws imposed by the legislature on the executive and their effect on individual rights seems to arise from the specific and different function of the judiciary in these matters. Marshall writes: "The question whether a right has vested or not, is, in its nature, judicial, and must be tried by the judicial authority." It is clear "that the individual who considers himself injured, has a right to resort to the laws of his country for a remedy."[14] Where Congress can limit executive discretion directly by laws, the judiciary limits executive discretion only indirectly by deciding cases in which individuals who feel themselves injured have resorted to the laws of their country for a remedy. But, although Congress has a more direct way to limit the president, one might say that those limits will be effectual only in those cases in which individual rights have been injured. Congress's limitations will be effectuated by the judiciary.

But it is important to see that, contrary to the language of so many of the Supreme Court's separation-of-powers decisions in the twentieth-century, Marshall does not arrive at these limitations through some theory of the separation of powers that figures out the proper extent of the president's power. Instead, the only relevant question for him is whether an individual right has been injured and whether that individual has recourse to the laws of the country for reparation. Simply by exercising the judicial function, the judiciary ends up limiting the scope of presidential power. Paradoxically, although our modern jurisprudence is much more explicit in its aim to check and control presidential power, it ends up being much less effective insofar as it assumes unto itself the responsibility of determining the limits of that power. Marshall here is not determining the limits of presidential power. He claims explicitly that presidential power remains independent of his decisions. He claims the judiciary should decide only the concrete question about whether an individual has recourse to the laws for reparation to his rights. The limits on presidential power emerge, then, not in a doctrine of balance, as one finds for instance in the Court's decision in *Hamdi*,[15] but in the fact that an individual whose rights have been illegally harmed receives reparation. In other words, the limits on the president emerge not from the Court's theoretical pronouncements concerning the extent of the president's power—pronouncements that Marshall's decision in *Marbury* would seem to suggest the Court does not have the authority to make—but from the Court's fulfillment of its own function. The independence of the president's power remains untouched; the cases will decide only a narrower legal question: have individual rights been adversely affected in a manner that is incompatible with the existing law? The answer to this question does not affect the independence of the executive itself; it only repairs the effects of that independence.

Where the principle of separation of powers receives only what might be called theoretical consideration in *Marbury*—after all, the end result was that Marshall construed the judicial review of the Constitution to prevent the judicial reparation of rights—it comes into practice in Marshall's decision in *Little v. Barreme* (1804). In this decision, we see most clearly why the Bush administration's most far-reaching principle—the claim that the president's commander-in-chief power constitutionally preempts any attempt by Congress to create legal limits on the president's wartime power—must be incompatible with at least John Marshall's constitutional understanding. But, at the same time, we also see the combination of boldness and moderation that characterizes the jurisprudence of the nineteenth century.

The question before the court in *Little v. Barreme* was whether an officer could, under orders of the president, seize a vessel coming *from* a French port even though Congress had passed a law indicating only that vessels going *to* a French port could be seized. Importantly, Marshall notes: "that if only vessels sailing to a French port could be seized on the high seas, that the law would be very often evaded" and that, for this reason, the executive's construction was "much better calculated to give it effect." Marshall recognizes and explicitly notes that the executive's construction of the act, which extended the range of seizure, would be more successful in stopping French ships. But, nonetheless, Marshall concludes that "the instructions of the executive could not give a right" or "legalize an act which without those instructions would have been a plain trespass."[16] The executive's instructions, even though they were calculated only to give better effect to the law passed by the legislature, did not have any legal status and could not therefore protect the officer from being liable for damages.

Yet, even as the effect of this decision points to limits on presidential power, Marshall says absolutely nothing about those very limits, except in the passage previously quoted. He does not pontificate about the necessity of curtailing presidential power relative to the laws passed by the legislature. Nor does he speak about the needs of national security relative to those limits. Instead, he decides only on the question he first articulated in *Marbury*: were the rights of the individual affected by the exercise of discretion in a way that does not comport with the laws passed by Congress? Because they were, Marshall finds against the officer who carried out these orders. By deciding the case in this manner, Marshall fulfills the judicial function, protecting the rights of the individual while, for the most part, leaving alone the presidential function, protecting national security in these sorts of cases. Of course, he does not leave the presidential function entirely alone. By deciding against the officer in this case, he indicates that, whatever authority the president might have to issue orders to the subordinates within his administration, those orders do not have the force of law, especially if they are incompatible with the laws passed by Congress.[17] On the other hand, if the decision had gone the other way, then it would have had the effect of disabling the congressional function by allowing the executive to construe the laws passed by Congress in a manner beyond what Congress may have intended. By insisting on the inapplicability of the executive's construction of the law as independently relevant in determining the case, Marshall preserves one of the congressional functions, that is, passing laws that restrict what the executive can do in matters relating to national security.

There are two further reasons that Marshall can navigate the path that he does in *Little v. Barreme*. First, he decided this case long after the fact; thus, the decision in this case had no effect on the standing of the presidential orders he negated. Second, Marshall did not exclude the possibility of a congressional indemnity for the officer who owes reparations. Because the judicial branch is not the last word on these matters, the judiciary can simply resolve them as the law requires without worrying about the final justice of the matter. After all, as Marshall notes in the decision, one is tempted to think that the officer's seizure of the boat under orders from the president "might . . . excuse from damages."

The possibility of a further political remedy to a judicial decision becomes explicit in Taney's decision of *Mitchell v. Harmony* (1851). For the most part, Taney continues Marshall's separation-of-powers jurisprudence insofar as, like Marshall, he upholds the rights of the individual against illegal harms even as he also makes no claim about the independence of executive discretion. In this

decision, however, he goes somewhat further than Marshall ever
went insofar as he reflects on the conditions in which executive
discretion beyond the laws might be justified. The decision concerns the question whether a general was justified in seizing an
individual's property during the Mexican-American war. The Supreme Court determined that the fact of war does not justify the
seizure of property. This is similar to a decision Marshall also came
to in the war of 1812 case *Brown v. United States* (1814). Unlike
Marshall in *Brown*, however, Taney does reflect on the conditions
in which this seizure would be justified. He writes: "It is impossible
to define the particular circumstances of danger or necessity in
which this power may be lawfully exercised. Every case must depend on its own circumstances. It is the emergency that gives the
right, and the emergency must be shown to exist before the taking can be justified." But, unlike our contemporary jurisprudence,
Taney indicates that this question of necessity cannot ultimately
be determined by the Supreme Court. He writes: "This question
is not before us. It is a question of fact upon which the jury has
passed, and their verdict has decided that a danger or necessity,
such as the court described, did not exist when the property of the
plaintiff was taken by the defendant."[18] In other words, the question of necessity was determined by the jury deciding on the right
of the plaintiff in the initial case. It is a question determined by
judgment in the specific circumstances in which it is invoked. As
the initial argument itself implied, this judgment can be exercised
only through individual judgments by individual juries in individual cases. It is not a question that can be determined by abstract
legal principles announced by the Supreme Court. The argument
of necessity, Taney suggests, has a legal standing only in the context of the actual case when it is argued at trial. Only a jury can
determine that, although the general did take property, his taking
was justified by the necessities of the situation.

   That being said, Taney also indicates in this case that relief may
still exist even for the general who has been found to have unnec-
essarily and thus arbitrarily taken property during war. The key, for
Taney, is that such relief cannot and should not be found in the
courts. He writes: "It is not for the courts to say what protection
or indemnity is due from the public to an officer who, in his zeal
for the honor and interest of his country, and in the excitement

of military operations, has trespassed on private rights. That question belongs to the political departments of the government." The courts can determine, Taney continues, only what the law allows: "whether the law permits [property] to be taken to insure the success of any enterprise against a public enemy which the commanding officer may deem it advisable to undertake." In this case, "we think it very clear that the law does not permit it."[19] As in *Little v. Barreme* the controlling question is not what the situation might have required; there are any number of reasons why private rights might have been trespassed upon. These reasons are, however, beyond the cognizance of the courts. The courts, as legal bodies, can determine only what the law requires. They cannot remain legal bodies if they determine the ways in which the law must be bent to adjust to the requirements of national security. Although there is surely room for judicial discretion in the application of the law, the peculiarly political judgments involved in military matters are beyond the scope of this judicial discretion.

The jurisprudence of Taney and Marshall points to a somewhat different understanding of the "political question" doctrine than that which is often invoked by courts more recently. More recently, the "political question" doctrine has been invoked by courts as a way in which to avoid deciding any given case, claiming that resolution lies only with the political departments of government. I have suggested elsewhere that this approach to "political questions" is both natural and dangerous in the hands of a supremacist court. It is natural because it allows the court that claims final authority on any issue it decides to leave precisely the sorts of issues we encounter in *Mitchell* outside its jurisdiction. It is dangerous because its invocation by a court that determines the meaning of the Constitution suggests that there is no constitutional issue in these sorts of war powers questions.[20] But, in this nineteenth-century formulation, the "political question doctrine" does not preclude judgment by the courts. Unless, as Marshall writes in *Marbury*, the governmental action does not violate the law and affect the rights of the individual and is thus not a matter that relates to legal judgment, the courts have a role even in "political questions" like the seizure of property during war. But, instead of foreclosing judgment, the "political question" lies in the remedy that remains available to the political departments of government even after the courts have spoken. Because the courts are not the final source of authority, they can decide an issue without, at the same time, foreclosing the political departments from coming to a different decision. So, in this interesting example, Taney explicitly invites Congress to "say what protection or indemnity is due from the public to an officer who . . . has trespassed on private rights." By inviting the further judgment of the political departments, Taney can, at one and the same time, protect the sanctity of private rights and preserve the discretion of the political departments. He need not create a legal principle, fraught with so many difficulties, according to which private rights can be sacrificed in the proverbial interest of national security.

What I have called the nineteenth-century model of separation-of-powers jurisprudence continued to hold until the period of reconstruction after the Civil War, thus including the famous *Milligan* decision. Ian Zuckerman has recently suggested in a fascinating article that the essential juridical framework that led to *Korematsu* can be traced back to the "monist" conception of constitutionalism one finds in what would otherwise seem to be diametrically opposed to *Korematsu: Ex Parte Milligan*.[21] He writes: "In the framework established by *Milligan* the courts bear responsibility for regulating the use of emergency powers." But, "when reviewing the actual use of executive power in the midst of a crisis, courts are likely to come up against their ultimate lack of power to enforce rulings contrary to the government. Given this structure, courts are tempted to rule in favor of the government by interpreting the constitutional war powers expansively and flexibly, thereby 'normalizing' exceptional emergency powers." Thus, *Milligan*, even as it typically stands for a "rigid, rights-based doctrine," precisely by claiming that the Constitution and thus the courts regulate in war as much as in peace, actually creates the type of "expansive and flexible constitutional interpretation" we saw in *Korematsu*.[22]

Although there may be something to Zuckerman's argument insofar as *Milligan* has been appropriated by judicial absolutists who claim that it implies that the courts can regulate all power exercised by the government, it would be truer to the spirit of *Milligan* itself to understand it in light of the nineteenth-century model of separation-of-powers jurisprudence.[23] By this reading, the Court decided only on the legal issue of whether Milligan could be constitutionally tried by a military commission in this case in these circumstances. It did not decide on the bigger question as to whether the government could ever institute martial law. In fact, the decision says explicitly: "where war really prevails, there is a necessity to furnish a substitute for the civil authority, thus overthrown, to preserve the safety of the army and society; and as no power is left by the military, it is allowed to govern by martial rule until the laws can have their free course." Moreover, as with the rest of this jurisprudence, the Supreme Court decides on this legal question only after the conclusion of the Civil War, once security has been restored. Justice Davis writes:

> The temper of the times did not allow that calmness in deliberation and discussion so necessary to a correct conclusion of a purely judicial question. Then, considerations of safety were mingled with the exercise of power; and feelings and interests prevailed which are happily terminated. Now that the public safety is assured, this question, as well as all others, can be discussed and decided without passion or the admixture of any element not required to form a legal judgment.[24]

In other words, the choice to decide *Milligan* well after the war is over was not accidental. If the case had been decided during the war, it would have inevitably been affected by the circumstances of the war. The legal questions would have been obscured by political questions related to the immediate needs of security. By deciding the case after the conclusion of the war, the Supreme Court did two things at once: it protected the sanctity of the law and it allowed the government to proceed in the manner it saw fit during the war itself. By explicitly relating its decision to the circumstances that existed once peace had returned, *Milligan* differentiated itself from the twentieth-century jurisprudence we see, at its worst, in *Korematsu*: a decision during the war that the government explicitly sought so as to give its internment program legal sanction.

That Milligan should be understood in terms of the earlier model of jurisprudence is further confirmed by at least two decisions that come after it. In *Ex Parte McCardle* (1868), the Court determined that it could not decide an issue similar to the issue

decided in *Milligan* because Congress had stripped it of jurisdiction.[25] And, in *Mississippi v. Johnson* (1868), the Court laid out
the principle of separation of powers at the heart of nineteenth-
century jurisprudence with impressive clarity. The question in
that case was whether the Supreme Court could issue an injunction preventing the president from carrying into effect an act of
Congress alleged to be unconstitutional. In other words, could the
Supreme Court, if it agreed that the allegation was correct, act preemptively to prevent the president from undertaking the unconstitutional action? If Zuckerman's reading of *Milligan* were correct,
then there would seem to be no necessary reason why the deter-
miner of constitutional authority could not also prevent that action it believes has no such authority. But the Court did not come
to this conclusion in the case. Instead, following the model of
nineteenth-century jurisprudence, it explicitly denied its authority
preemptively to restrain the other branches of government. Justice Chase writes: "The Congress is the legislative department of
the government; the President is the executive department. Neither can be restrained in its action by the judicial department."
Paradoxically, however, but in keeping with this model of jurisprudence, the denial of preemptive restraint does not, at the same
time, deny ex post facto relief. Justice Chase continues: "The acts
of both, when performed, are, in proper cases, subject to its cognizance."[26] Even as there are general principles, the Court suggests,
"which forbid judicial interference with the exercise of Executive
discretion," those same principles do not forbid judicial relief if
executive discretion illegally runs afoul of individual rights. Again,
the separation-of-powers principle holds: the independence of
the executive branch guarantees that it can take whatever action
it deems appropriate without constraint from the other branches,
but this same independence does not protect it from accountability for that action by either Congress, if it runs afoul of its legislation, or the Supreme Court, if it takes illegal action that harms
individual rights. This arrangement allows the government to take
those actions it deems necessary for national security without sac-
rificing the rights of the individual to a legal principle that allows
these actions. Instead, it preserves executive discretion as an essentially extralegal power that, as such, can neither be enjoined nor
validated by the courts.

2. TWENTIETH-CENTURY SEPARATION-OF-POWERS JURISPRUDENCE

The new logic at the heart of what I am calling the court's twentieth-century separation-of-powers jurisprudence appeared first at the very end of the nineteenth. At the heart of the earlier jurisprudence is the understanding that the executive's action, whatever authority it might have, does not have any legal authority, unless the executive was acting according to an explicit law passed by Congress. Decided in 1890, *In re Neagle* departs from this model and gives to the actions of the executive branch a similar status to laws passed by Congress. The decision converts executive discretion from an extralegal capacity, over which the courts do not have control except to remedy the effects if the law is breached, into a legal capacity over which the courts do have control.

In re Neagle arose because Mr. Neagle, a deputy marshal from California, was asked by Attorney General William Miller to protect Judge Field from possible harm. The decision says: "Evidence [was] abundant that Terry and his wife [who feel they were wronged by Judge Field] contemplated some attack upon Judge Field during his official visit to California in the summer of 1889, which they intended should result in his death." While protecting Judge Field, Mr. Neagle killed Mr. Terry. Given the facts of the case, the Court decided that presidents have the power to protect judges of the courts of the United States, who, while in the discharge of the duties of their office, are threatened with personal violence or death. To ground this claim, the justices explicitly turn the take-care clause into a legal authority to take all those actions necessary for "the protection implied by the nature of the government under the Constitution." Justice Miller writes for the majority: "Any obligation fairly and properly inferrible from that instrument [the Constitution], or any duty of the marshal to be derived from the general scope of his duties under the laws of the United States, is 'a law' within the meaning of this phrase."[27] Justice Miller continues: "It would be a great reproach to the system of government of the United States, declared to be within its sphere sovereign and supreme, if there is to be found within the domain of its powers no means of protecting the judges, in the conscientious and faithful discharge of their duties, from the malice and hatred of those upon whom their judgments may operate unfavorably." Where nineteenth-century jurisprudence aimed only to discover the law and then to determine whether a governmental official's actions were in accord with this law, the Supreme Court now chose to determine what the law should be and to redeem the governmental officials' actions according to their reading of what power should exist. In the earlier jurisprudence, there was either an implicit or an explicit recognition that the Court's decision did not and could not exhaust the government's powers. The Court's decision could speak only to the question as to whether individual rights were injured and whether an executive official had explicit legal authority for his action—authority in the statutes passed by Congress. Here, the Court implicitly suggests that its decisions exhaust "the domain" of governmental power. If Mr. Neagle is not exonerated by the decision of this Court, then Mr. Neagle's "conscientious and faithful discharge" of his duties will be improperly punished.

The difference between the reasoning of the majority and that of the earlier jurisprudence can be seen by examining the dissenting opinion in the case. The dissent agrees with the majority insofar as "the personal protection of Mr. Justice Field, as a private citizen, even to the death of Terry, was not only the right, but was also the duty of Neagle and of any other bystander."[28] Instead, "our dissent is not based on any conviction as to the guilt or innocence of the appellee."[29] It was based only on the question as to whether there were congressional and, hence, legal, grounds for Mr. Neagle's actions; the dissent maintained that there were not. The dissent based itself on the older model of jurisprudence according to which the Court need ask only whether the action followed from an existing statute. By contrast, the majority invented a "statute" because it thought one should exist. Justice Miller writes, "We do not believe that the government of the United States is thus inefficient, or that its Constitution and laws have left the high officers of the government so defenseless and unprotected."[30] But the dissenters emphasize that they agree with this statement; their disagreement lay in the question as to how such power is exercised, not whether such power exists. Justice Lamar writes: "Powers must be exercised, not only by the organs, but also in conformity with the modes, prescribed by the Constitution itself." He continues:

"These great federal powers, whose existence in all their plenitude and energy is incontestable, are not autocratic and lawless."[31] Because of a conviction that each body of government must speak for the powers of the government as a whole, the majority subsumed the needs of the government into its decision. If government must exercise this power, then the Court must find it legal. But the dissent emphasizes that this jurisprudential procedure does damage to the "modes" by which the Constitution organizes power. In the old separation-of-powers model, the rights of the individual were "balanced" against the needs of the government, not through some judicial balancing act but through the competing modes of power. By sticking merely to what the law allows and what the law prevents, the old approach could better protect the rights of the individual. Moreover, it could do so without affecting the independence of the executive: after all, the flip side of this decision in *Neagle* is that, if the Supreme Court determines the legality of executive action, it can also determine its illegality. In other words, even as the executive administration gains the legal imprimatur of the judiciary, it also permits the judiciary to set the bounds upon it. The deeper problem, however, is not that, given its newly acquired power the judiciary will limit the executive power too much but instead the problem at which Zuckerman points: the judiciary, precisely because of its institutional situation, will tend to accede too much to the claimed needs of the executive.

In re Debs takes the logic of *Neagle* one step further. Whereas *Neagle* adduces the legal power of the executive from a hypothetical involving the "authority of the President or of one of the executive departments under him to make an order for the protection of the mail and of the persons and lives of its carriers" if the mail was "liable to be robbed and the mail carriers assaulted and murdered in any particular region of the country," *Debs* involves precisely this hypothetical. But, more than that, *Debs* also involves the question as to the legal status of, as Corwin writes, "an injunction from the United States circuit court forbidding the strike on account of its interference with the mails and with interstate commerce." Because of the gravity of the situation and the post-*Neagle* status of executive power, the Court found that the circuit court did have the power to issue this injunction. As Corwin notes, "The Court conceded, in effect, that there was no statutory basis for the injunction, but sustained it on the ground that the government was entitled thus to protect its property in the mails."[32]

The same jurisprudential logic that led the Court in *Neagle* to invent a statute where none existed led the Court to issue an injunction to support the needs of the executive. Justice Brewer writes for a now-unified Court: "The entire strength of the nation may be used to enforce in any part of the land the full and free exercise of all national powers and the security of all rights entrusted by the Constitution to its care." He continues: "If the emergency arises, the army of the Nation, and all its militia, are at the service of the Nation to compel obedience to its laws." Again, it is not that the earlier jurisprudence was unaware of the force of such arguments. But such arguments might have led the Court, as it did in *Mississippi v. Johnson*, to conclude only that it would not issue an injunction preventing executive action for the sake of national security. But, in the new jurisprudential mode, this same reasoning now led the Court to conclude that "every government, entrusted, by the very terms of its being, with powers and duties to be exercised and discharged for the general welfare, has a right to apply to its own courts for any proper assistance in the exercise of the one and the discharge of the other."[33] In the wake of *Neagle*, the Court thought itself responsible for articulating the powers that the government should have. Thus, it should not surprise us that the Court "assists" the executive in the exercise of the executive's duty by issuing injunctions for the sake of national security. The preservation of national security, understood in the earlier jurisprudence as the primary domain of the executive branch as regulated by Congress, had now become as much the domain of the judiciary as of the other two branches.

The legalization of executive discretion adopted by the Court in *Neagle* and *Debs* persists into the twentieth century and explains the Court's consistently deferential approach on war powers issues. Once the Court understands itself as having to decide whether to legalize that which the executive chooses to do as a matter of discretion in the realm of national security, it should not surprise us that the Court is rather forgiving of the exercise of executive power. Eric Posner and Adrian Vermeule justify this legacy of judicial (and congressional) deference to the executive on war powers issues because the institutional advantages of the executive branch, that is, secrecy, speed, and flexibility, allow it to manage best the necessities of wars and crises.[34] As they rightly argue: "In emergencies, then, judges are at sea. . . . The novelty of the threats and of the necessary responses make judicial routines and evolved legal rules seem inapposite, even obstructive."[35] There is no way for judges rightly to estimate the requirements of national security, and, as Posner and Vermeule also argue, there is no way for them rightly to find a balancing principle that will permit to the executive branch the right amount of power in the tradeoff between security and liberty. For this reason, they argue that judges should simply defer to the decisions of the executive branch. Given the twentieth-century model in which judges must decide whether any executive action is legal and thus acceptable, Posner and Vermeule may be correct. If judicial involvement would foreclose executive action in those situations where it is absolutely necessary for national security, the courts should defer to the executive branch. The difficulty with their argument lies in their failure to appreciate the older model of separation of powers, a failure they share with the newer model of jurisprudence.

Although *Korematsu* has not had the long-lasting and insidious effect on the law that Justice Jackson predicted in his dissent, it still stands, in a certain sense, as a model of the new jurisprudence insofar as the Court assumed that its decision would exhaust governmental power. Moreover, whereas, in the earlier jurisprudence, the Court often decided war powers cases well after the fact, in the World War II cases, the executive administration explicitly sought Supreme Court review during the internment itself. It wanted the constitutionality of the program to be settled and approved by the Supreme Court.[36] Finding the program constitutional, Justice Black writes in the majority opinion in *Korematsu*: "We are unable to conclude that it was beyond the war power of Congress and the Executive to exclude those of Japanese ancestry from the West Coast war area at the time they did."[37] That is, because the Court's decision could exhaust the war powers of Congress and the executive or because those powers did not exist independent of the Court's determination, the Court could not come to a decision other than this in this case. As Justice Black writes: "We cannot say that the war-making branches of the Government did not have ground for believing that in a critical hour such persons could not readily be isolated and separately dealt with, and constituted a menace to the national defense and safety."[38] These are questions that only the executive branch can determine; it is impossible for the judiciary to determine them adequately. Thus, if the judiciary's determination of these questions exhausts governmental power, then it is only natural that it will determine them constitutional. Because the courts see themselves as the final determinant of what can and cannot be done by the other branches, they have forced onto themselves the perspective of these branches, especially the executive branch's concern about national security. And, because the Supreme Court can speak to these issues only by articulating legal principles, this perspective almost inevitably forces it to permit whatever the political branches decide. So, whereas the uniquely limited perspective of the Supreme Court in the earlier period allowed it to determine only the legal and constitutional question before it, the broader perspective now adopted by the Court forces it into a situation where it must be more limited in its rulings. In the earlier jurisprudence, it need not determine the full scope of the government's war-making powers; it need only determine the constitutional scope of those powers from its important but limited perspective as the guardian of individual rights.

By creating legal principles that permit whatever the political branches decide, the modern Supreme Court has created principles that inevitably spread so that the government can shield more and more of its actions from accountability. In his book *In the Name of National Security*, Louis Fisher documents the articulation of such a principle and its subsequent spread in the case of the "state secret" doctrine in *United States v. Reynolds*. Once these legal principles are created by a Court that has adopted the executive perspective, they inevitably spread beyond the first case in which they were invoked. Fisher writes: "In *Reynolds*, the Supreme Court cautioned the government that the state secrets privilege 'is not to be lightly invoked.' That sense of self-restraint has long since disappeared. The federal government now invokes the privilege not merely for military and diplomatic secrets, or for national security in general, but for other categories that in the past would have been considered labored and far-fetched."[39]

Although *Korematsu* illustrates well the problem of courts thinking that they exhaust governmental power, it departs somewhat from the earlier model of jurisprudence insofar as the controlling question revolved around the constitutionality of both Congress and the executive's power. Where many of the earlier cases concerned situations where Congress had either prevented or failed to approve action that the executive had taken, this case concerned action that both Congress and the president had taken that the Constitution prevents.[40] For this reason, the more telling example of the new jurisprudence in relation to the old may come from a case such as *Dames and Moore v. Regan*. Claiming to base itself on the legal framework established in *Youngstown*—a case that comes closest to the older model of jurisprudence—the Supreme Court in *Dames and Moore* created a principle of statutory construction whereby powers not explicitly authorized can be construed from other explicit powers such that they enter into Jackson's first category in which "authority is at its maximum."[41] So, whereas Jackson had spoken of a "zone of twilight" in which presidents take action neither explicitly authorized by nor explicitly prevented by Congress, the Court here constructed a legal principle that effaces this category.[42] And, in doing so, the Court changed directions entirely from its earlier jurisprudence in which the Court had found that executive action that affects individual rights without statutory authorization was legally problematic. Where Marshall in *Little v. Barreme* explicitly avoided constructing a statute differently from the manner in which it was written, the Court in *Dames and Moore* chose to do the exact opposite.

Because the judiciary is understood as the last word on these subjects, one can understand the Court's approach in a case such as *Dames and Moore*. A decision such as *Little v. Barreme*, in which a general is held liable for following orders issued by the president —orders that the Court itself admitted were calculated better to give effect to congressional intent—would not sit well in an age when the Supreme Court, given its authority, is expected to issue decisions based not so much on what the law actually says as what the law should say, given what justice or necessity requires. The earlier Court knew that if justice required the general not to be held liable, then the model of divided power would allow Congress to act even after the Supreme Court acted. The fact that the Court was not the last word meant that it could simply contribute its own distinctive law-based view of the issue. Better that the Court adhere to what the law actually says than that it interject itself arbitrarily. The fact that the Court is now seen as the last word means that its decision must not be based so much on what the law says as on what the law should say.

At this point, defenders of the Bush administration would assert that they too deny the final authority of the Supreme Court as to all matters of governmental power. Instead, the crux of the robust theory of the "unitary executive" seems to rest on a notion of departmentalism, according to which the executive is fully sovereign in matters that fall within the executive sphere.[43] This notion of departmentalism is, however, ultimately still caught up in a conception of the unity of governmental power. As George Thomas has recently argued so persuasively, the founders were not "departmentalists" in this sense because they wanted the different branches to compete for power over some of the same issues. The Constitution intended to create, Thomas argues, "conflicting interpretations" between the branches over the scope and the limits of their respective powers.[44] For the founders' system of separation of powers, power is inherently divided and speaks in many different and conflicting voices. The fact that each branch has a different function, a different source of power, and different kinds of authority results in conflicting views about constitutional questions. The notion of departmentalist separation of powers that grounds the "unitary executive," on the other hand, still conceives of government as unified in its voice. Each branch simply speaks for a different part of that unified voice. The judiciary is supreme in matters of judicial power. The executive is supreme in matters of executive power. And the legislature is supreme in matters of legislative power.[45] But, again, the necessity of discretionary executive power reveals the most intractable difficulty in this departmentalist conception. Although the demands of national security are clearly executive in nature, the creation of limits on the exercise of the power that may be necessary for the preservation of national security must be both legislative and judicial concerns. In the face of these limits on executive concerns, these legal departmentalists are driven to the position that they must be unconstitutional.

It should be noted, however, that some theorists of the "unitary executive" have distanced themselves from any association with the claims made by proponents of the Bush administration. They claim that their understanding of the "unitary executive" does not necessitate the sorts of arguments put forth by John Yoo and others.[46] Without attempting to decide the issue here, the argument I have put forth does raise questions about the ultimate adequacy of the claim that there is no connection. After all, the proponents of the "unitary executive" are departmentalists who, at the same time, want to insist on an understanding of the separation of powers in which there are distinct and legally discernible spheres of power. So, the Bush administration claimed that there is a distinct sphere required to exercise the commander-in-chief power that makes unconstitutional any congressional inroads on that sphere. Is that not a natural consequence of their theory?

3. CONCLUSION

One might suggest that the restoration of the rule of law post-9/11 has already occurred. Rather than acceding to the claims made by the Bush administration, the Supreme Court issued a series of rulings that seemed to strike at the heart of both its claims and its actions. But, even as decisions such as *Hamdi, Hamdan,* and *Boumediene* seem to have attempted to limit executive power in the post-9/11 "war on terror," one has to wonder about the adequacy of these limits, both in the short term and in the long term. In the short term, it is not at all clear that, notwithstanding the overheated rhetoric, these decisions had quite the effect that is claimed for them.[47] At the heart of the "war on terror" are important legal questions concerning the rights of those the military holds given the threat they are said to pose to national security. Although the courts have intervened so as to establish that the executive did not have a free hand in determining the answer to these questions, the courts have not provided much of an answer themselves. In some ways, they are incapable of providing an answer. As Benjamin Wittes argues persuasively, the design of a legal architecture for the "war on terror" requires Congress's particular ability to fashion new law in a manner that the courts cannot. As we saw in the jurisprudence of the nineteenth century, the courts do well at upholding congressional law over and against extralegal executive discretion. They are simply ill equipped, however, to answer the tough political questions that must be answered in the "war on terror."

As Wittes writes, questions such as "whom can the military hold? For how long? With what kind of showing? Under what evidentiary rules?" have no obvious judicial answer insofar as they mostly apply to foreign nationals captured in foreign combat. Their answer requires a congressional framework that would then guide and delimit executive action. Within the system of separation of powers, the courts would then enforce that framework rather than creating it for themselves. To return to the cases, then, an even deeper problem with them is that, even as the courts have intervened in the "war on terror," their interventions have, at the same time, hindered Congress from attempting to answer these questions on their own insofar as the Court's interventions let members of Congress off the hook politically.[48]

This latter problem becomes even deeper when we consider the long-term implications of the Court's decisions in the "war on terror." As Wittes presciently predicted regarding the *Boumediene* decision, the essence of the decision would be that the Court would "merely have declared—yet again—that the Supreme Court has the final word." Although its interventions have neither created an adequate legal framework nor substantively restrained executive power all that much, they have consistently asserted, rather loudly, the Court's rightful role as the final word on these questions. In fact, one might conclude that the Court has abstained from going further in limiting executive power precisely because it understands itself as the final word and it wants to avoid the difficulties that would inhere in restraining the executive too much. As the final word, the Court has aimed to balance the requirements of national security against the concern for individual rights. The Court's limits on the presidency have emerged in the context of this balance. But, in the long term, it seems this balance would shift heavily toward national security in the wake of another attack. Thus, one wonders if the limits would remain.

All of this points us back to the past. Instead of expecting the Court to balance national security against individual rights by arriving at some perfect formula, the Constitution bequeathed us a system that allows that balance to emerge naturally from within the political contestation that exists between divided powers. In matters of national security, the need for this is most paramount. If the courts are understood as having the final word on the power of government, then the security-centered views of the executive branch will end up predominating. The combination of the preeminent importance of national security and the fact that the executive branch is uniquely suited to achieve it forces the other two branches to become deferential. The requirements of security and their relative incompetence to achieve them force both Congress and the Supreme Court to empower the executive. Once the Supreme Court legalized the previously extralegal discretion of the executive in *Neagle*, it pointed to both the judiciary's need to approve of executive discretion and Congress's need to legislate for it. In the old model of divided powers, the fact that each branch understood its power as independent of the rest and in contest with them allowed the executive to pursue national security even as Congress and the Supreme Court refused to defer to that pursuit. Precisely because they understood executive discretion as both independent and extralegal, the judiciary and Congress could actually afford to be less deferential to the executive. The other branches knew that if a situation arose that absolutely required the executive to act outside or even against the existing laws, the executive's extralegal independence would allow it to do so. Where the twentieth-century attempt to legalize executive discretion has forced the entire government to become complicit in the concern for national security, the nineteenth-century understanding of executive discretion as extralegal allowed the power to be exercised while simultaneously allowing the other branches to hold the executive accountable for the misuse of the power.

NOTES

1. Jack Goldsmith, *The Terror Presidency: Law and Judgment inside the Bush Administration* (New York: W. W. Norton, 2007), 72.

2. Ibid., 75.

3. Ryan J. Barilleaux, "Venture Constitutionalism and the Enlargement of the Presidency," in *Executing the Constitution: Putting the President Back into the Constitution*, ed. C. S. Kelley (Albany: State University of New York Press, 2006).

4. Goldsmith, *The Terror Presidency*, 212.

5. Steven G. Calabresi and Christopher S. Yoo, *The Unitary Executive:*

Presidential Power from Washington to Bush (New Haven, CT: Yale University Press, 2008).

6. David J. Barron and Martin S. Lederman, "Commander in Chief at the Lowest Ebb—Framing the Problem, Doctrine, and the Original Understanding," *Harvard Law Review* 121 (2008): 689; David J. Barron and Martin S. Lederman, "Commander in Chief at the Lowest Ebb—A Constitutional History," *Harvard Law Review* 121 (2008): 941; Benjamin A. Kleinerman, *The Discretionary President: The Promise and Peril of Executive Power* (Lawrence: University Press of Kansas, 2009).

7. John Locke, *Two Treatises of Government*, ed. P. Laslett (Cambridge: Cambridge University Press, 1988).

8. Kleinerman, *The Discretionary President*.

9. *Korematsu v. United States*, 323 U.S. 214 (1944); Louis Fisher, "Judicial Review of the War Power," *Presidential Studies Quarterly* 35 (2005): 466.

10. *Marbury v. Madison*, 5 U.S. 166 (1803).

11. *Cooper v. Aaron*, 358 U.S. 1 (1958); Michael W. McConnell, "Toward a More Balanced History of the Supreme Court," in *That Eminent Tribunal: Judicial Supremacy and the Constitution*, ed. C. Wolfe (Princeton: Princeton University Press, 2004); Robert Lowry Clinton, *Marbury v. Madison and Judicial Review* (Lawrence: University Press of Kansas, 1989).

12. David Gray Adler, "The Judiciary and Presidential Power in Foreign Affairs: A Critique," *Richmond Journal of Law and the Public Interest* 3 (1996): 1.

13. *Marbury*, 5 U.S. at 166.

14. Ibid.

15. *Hamdi v. Rumsfeld*, 542 U.S. 507 (2004).

16. *Little v. Barreme*, 6 U.S. 178 (1804).

17. A later decision, *Brown v. United States*, takes up the question as to whether the executive's actions, when taken without any authorizing congressional legislation, have the force of law. Interestingly, Marshall decided that they do not, while Story argued that they did. *Brown v. United States*, 12 U.S. 110 (1814).

18. *Mitchell v. Harmony*, 54 U.S. 115, 133–34 (1851).

19. Ibid., 135.

20. Benjamin A. Kleinerman, " 'The Court Will Clean It Up': Executive Power, Constitutional Contestation, and War Powers," in *The Supreme Court and the Idea of Constitutionalism*, ed. S. Kautz, A. Melzer, and J. Weinberger (Philadelphia: University of Pennsylvania Press, 2009).

21. Ian Zuckerman, "One Law for War and Peace? Judicial Review and Emergency Powers between the Norm and the Exception," *Constellations* 13 (2006): 522.

22. Ibid., 526.

23. Jeffrey Tulis, "Deliberation between Institutions," in *Debating Delib-*

erative Democracy, ed. J. S. Fishkin and P. Laslett (Malden, MA: Blackwell, 2003). Although they do not speak of the decision in the framework I have adopted in this paper, Bessette and Tulis make a somewhat similar suggestion regarding the underappreciated constitutional flexibility that also exists in the *Milligan* decision. Joseph M. Bessette and Jeffrey Tulis, "The Constitution, Politics, and the Presidency," in *The Presidency in the Constitutional Order*, ed. J. M. Bessette and J. Tulis (Baton Rouge: Louisiana State University Press, 1981). See also Herbert J. Storing, *Toward a More Perfect Union: Writings of Herbert J. Storing*, ed. J. M. Bessette (Washington, DC: AEI Press, 1995), 381–83.

24. *Ex Parte Milligan*, 79 U.S. 109 (1866).

25. Samuel Isaacharoff and Richard H. Pildes, "Between Civil Libertarianism and Executive Unilateralism: An Institutional Process Approach to Rights during Wartime," in *The Constitution in Wartime: Beyond Alarmism and Complacency*, ed. M. Tushnet (Durham, NC: Duke University Press, 2005).

26. *Mississippi v. Johnson*, 71 U.S. 500 (1866).

27. *In re Neagle*, 135 U.S. 59 (1890).

28. Ibid., 80.

29. Ibid., 76.

30. Ibid., 70.

31. Ibid., 82.

32. Edward Corwin, *The President: Office and Powers, 1787–1984*, 5th ed., ed. R. W. Bland, T. T. Hindson, and J. W. Peltason (New York: New York University Press, 1984).

33. *In re Debs*, 158 U.S. 582 (1895).

34. Eric A. Posner and Adrian Vermeule, *Terror in the Balance: Security, Liberty, and the Courts* (New York: Oxford University Press, 2007).

35. Ibid., 18.

36. Dennis Hutchinson, " 'The Achilles Heel' of the Constitution: Justice Jackson and the Japanese Exclusion Cases," *Supreme Court Review* (2002): 455.

37. *Korematsu v. United States*, 323 U.S. 214, 217–18 (1944).

38. Ibid., 218.

39. Louis Fisher, *In the Name of National Security: Unchecked Presidential Power and the Reynolds Case* (Lawrence: University Press of Kansas, 2006), 245.

40. Isaacharoff and Pildes, "Between Civil Libertarianism and Executive Unilateralism."

41. Rebecca A. D'Arcy, "The Legacy of *Dames and Moore v. Regan*: Twilight Zone of Concurrent Authority between the Executive and Congress and a Proposal for a Judicially Manageable Nondelegation Doctrine," *Notre Dame Law Review* 79 (2003): 291.

42. Thomas A. O'Donnell, "Comment: Illumination or Elimination of the 'Zone of Twilight'? Congressional Acquiescence and Presidential Authority in Foreign Affairs," *University of Cincinnati Law Review* 51 (1982): 95.

43. Gary Lawson and Christopher D. Moore, "The Executive Power of Constitutional Interpretation," *Iowa Law Review* 81 (1996): 1267.

44. George Thomas, *The Madisonian Constitution* (Baltimore: Johns Hopkins University Press, 2008).

45. Steven G. Calabresi and Kevin Rhodes, "The Structural Constitution: Unitary Executive, Plural Judiciary," *Harvard Law Review* 105 (1992): 1153.

46. Calabresi and Yoo, *The Unitary Executive*, 405–15.

47. Benjamin Wittes, *Law and the Long War: The Future of Justice in the Age of Terror* (New York: Penguin Books, 2008).

48. Kleinerman, " 'The Court Will Clean It Up.' "

6

JUDICIAL OVERSIGHT, JUSTICE, AND EXECUTIVE DISCRETION BOUNDED BY LAW

CURTIS A. BRADLEY

In his interesting and provocative essay, "Separation of Powers and the National Security State," Benjamin Kleinerman contrasts a purported nineteenth-century approach to separation of powers with a purported modern approach, and he suggests that it would be desirable to return to the earlier approach. He contends that under the nineteenth-century approach, the courts would not claim to have the final say about the national security powers of the national government and would instead simply decide individual rights questions, and, when they found a violation of rights, they would still leave to Congress the ability to reach its own conclusions about justice through the means of indemnification of the defendant government officials.[1]

Under the modern approach, by contrast, Kleinerman contends that courts have moved to a "conception of unified governmental power," whereby one branch of the federal government must be the ultimate decider on issues of national security.[2] This approach has at least two undesirable consequences, he contends. First, when the unified conception is applied by the executive branch, it leads to the claim that Congress is barred from regulating the executive, a claim made on a number of instances by the Bush administration.[3] Second, when courts claim to have the

135

ultimate decision-making authority, they end up being unduly deferential to government claims of authority, and here Kleinerman gives in particular the example of the infamous *Korematsu* decision involving the Japanese internment during World War II.[4]

To the extent that Kleinerman is suggesting that the courts should avoid unnecessary rulings about the ultimate constitutional authority of the government in national security matters, I agree. For example, it seems to me that the Court in the famous Civil War-era decision *Ex Parte Milligan* should have rested its decision simply on the proposition that President Lincoln's use of a military trial in that case was contrary to the 1863 Habeas Act, as Justice Chase argued in his four-Justice concurrence.[5] By going further and opining that the military trials would have been unlawful even if approved by Congress, the Court set itself up for having its decision disregarded—first by the Reconstruction Congress, and later by the Supreme Court itself in the *Ex Parte Quirin* case involving the Nazi saboteurs.[6] Among other things, subsequent national security decisions, whether by courts or by political actors, are likely to be affected by the perceived necessities of the time,[7] making it unwise for the Supreme Court to issue general proclamations out of the context of a particular situation.

Despite this point of agreement, in general I found Kleinerman's description of the purported contrast between nineteenth-century and modern approaches to separation of powers to be problematic, both in its characterization of the Supreme Court and in its characterization of the executive branch.

First, consider the Supreme Court. There is little evidence showing that the modern Supreme Court adheres to a unified conception of governmental power in national security cases, as Kleinerman contends. Rather, its approach is generally the one advocated by Justice Jackson in his concurrence in the *Youngstown* steel seizure case, whereby governmental power is dependent on how the two political branches have interacted.[8] This is the approach expressly cited by the Court, for example, in the *Dames and Moore* hostage-crisis case in the early 1980s[9] and in the *Hamdan* military-commissions case in 2006.[10]

By relying too much on a data point of one—namely *Korematsu* —Kleinerman may also be overstating the extent to which the modern Supreme Court has been deferential to governmental claims of national security authority. There is certainly some deference, although usually that simply means that courts leave it to Congress to override the executive if it so chooses. But not all decisions are like *Korematsu*. Indeed, the same day that it issued the *Korematsu* decision, the Court issued its decision in *Endo*, in which it concluded that there was no legal authority to continue the internment of concededly loyal Japanese Americans.[11] Moreover, during the Korean War, the Court decided *Youngstown*, holding that President Truman had exceeded his authority in seizing the steel mills. Furthermore, the Court repeatedly rejected the Bush administration's claims in the war on terror, especially in the *Hamdan* decision concerning military commissions and the *Boumediene* decision concerning habeas rights at Guantanamo.[12]

Kleinerman's contrast between the individual-rights focus of the nineteenth-century approach and the broader, forward-looking focus of the modern approach also appears to be overdrawn, for two reasons. First, Kleinerman seems to assume that a resolution of an individual-rights claim does not represent a judicial decision about the scope of executive authority, but this assumption is questionable. The nineteenth-century damages decisions had prospective importance in at least two respects: they made clear that Congress could regulate the executive's actions, which is itself a constitutional issue, and they also affected the future incentives of government officials. It is true that broad-based injunctive relief would create greater potential conflict between the judiciary and the executive than decisions awarding only retrospective relief, but courts even in the modern era do not readily enjoin national security programs. Moreover, in the rare instance in which the courts have done this, such as in the *Youngstown* steel seizure case, the verdict of history seems to be that it was warranted, and Kleinerman himself appears to approve of the decision.[13]

Second, the modern national security cases, like the nineteenth-century cases, typically also involve individual-rights claims. Many of them, including all of the major cases involving the war on terror, involve claims for habeas corpus relief, a type of relief that has potentially been available against the federal government since the beginning of the nation and of course was utilized extensively during the Civil War. Other cases, such as *Youngstown* and *Dames and Moore*, involve claims of private property and contract rights.

Moreover, the Court has not been issuing abstract advisory opinions in these cases, and, in fact, most of its decisions have been narrowly framed. For example, the Court made clear that the settlement of claims authority in *Dames and Moore* was specific to the facts of that case,[14] and the plurality in the 2004 *Hamdi* decision made clear that it was deciding only the government's authority to detain someone picked up in the fighting in Afghanistan.[15]

Kleinerman's broader idea that the modern courts no longer leave the ultimate evaluation of *justice* to the political branches also does not seem quite right. Even when courts do say that the national government as a whole has the constitutional authority to act, as in *Korematsu*, they are not saying that the actions are just or wise, and they still leave to the government the final authority on that question. Indeed, subsequent congresses came to conclude that the Japanese internment was wrong, and they were able to make that final decision, not the courts. I think Kleinerman also errs in suggesting that the flip side of this is true—that is, that, under the modern approach, governmental actions are considered legitimate only if blessed by the courts. Kleinerman criticizes in his essay the idea that "every action of the executive must also be approved by Congress and deemed constitutional by the Supreme Court to be considered legitimate"[16]—but that is a red herring, since no one has ever suggested that. To take just one example, President Obama did not need to have a judicial blessing of his troop surge in Afghanistan to have it considered legitimate.

Now, consider the executive branch. Kleinerman contends that, under the nineteenth-century approach, executive actions would have no legal authority unless done pursuant to an explicit act of Congress.[17] This is an overgeneralization. First, the executive's commander in chief power and recognition powers allowed the president to do some things unilaterally that would have had legal effect, particularly effects under international law. To take just one example, President Madison made a binding agreement with Great Britain concerning the exchange of prisoners during the War of 1812.[18] So, at most, Kleinerman's claim applies only to situations involving an invasion of common law rights. Second, by the time of the Civil War, courts had begun to construe the president's authority even in this regard more broadly. A good example is a decision called *The Prize Cases*, in which the Court upheld Lincoln's authority, as Commander in Chief, to seize merchant vessels that violated his blockade order at the outset of the Civil War. The Court noted that if congressional action was needed, Congress's after-the-fact approval of Lincoln's blockade was sufficient, but the Court also said that it did not think Lincoln needed that congressional approval.[19]

Kleinerman equates support in the executive branch for a "unitary executive" with support for a unified conception of governmental power,[20] but those are actually distinct concepts. Kleinerman seems to envision that "unitary executive" means an executive that cannot be limited by Congress. The standard usage of the term "unitary executive," however is somewhat different: it is that, when the executive is acting *within the limits of the law*, Congress cannot regulate the chain of command and reporting in the executive branch.[21] That is why a paradigm concern of unitary executive proponents is an interference with the president's power over appointments and removal of officers.[22] Of course, the Bush administration did sometimes claim that Congress was limited in its ability to regulate executive action, just as the Clinton administration sometimes made that claim and now the Obama administration has made that claim,[23] but this is *not* a claim about a unitary executive. Rather, it is a claim about the Constitution's particular assignments of authority.

Finally, and perhaps most fundamental, Kleinerman does not persuasively establish a general need of the executive branch to break the laws, something that is an undercurrent of his essay and a key theme of his book. Congress understands the desirability of presidential discretion in foreign affairs and thus often delegates broad discretion to the president—for example, in the International Emergency Economic Powers Act, which is one of the statutes at issue in the *Dames and Moore* hostages case. It also quite readily grants the executive broad discretion when crises emerge —for example, its broad grant of military authority after the September 11 attacks. In addition, the Constitution can reasonably be construed as vesting discretion over certain matters with the executive—for example, in regulating the conduct of a war pursuant to the commander in chief power.

To be sure, there is an important question lurking here, which is whether it is better to say that some necessary actions are legal or to say that some illegal actions are necessary. As an initial matter, it is not clear to me how often this issue really comes up. I suppose the most obvious contemporary issue would be waterboarding of terrorist suspects, where one could ask whether it is better to distort the meaning of the word "torture" to make this legal or to treat it as illegal subject to some sort of post-hoc immunity. But it may be a false choice, given that many people do not believe that waterboarding was in fact necessary. Moreover, if we think it *was* necessary, it is not self-evident that we should nevertheless prohibit it in all circumstances with the hope that brave CIA officials will flout the law. In fact, as those who have worked in the government have observed, such officials are likely to avoid taking aggressive action if they perceive the possibility of criminal prosecution, especially since they correctly understand that the political climate could easily change and undermine whatever hope for post-hoc immunity they might otherwise have.[24]

Perhaps the most famous historical example that raises the issue of whether the executive branch needs to operate outside the law is President Lincoln's suspension of the writ of habeas corpus at the outset of the Civil War. He famously justified this action in his "all the laws but one" speech to Congress—that is, he asked whether he should have allowed the country to collapse just to respect the one law about congressional power to suspend the writ. But people tend to forget that this was his fall-back argument; his main argument was that, when the United States is being invaded and Congress is out of session, the president has some constitutional authority to suspend the writ until Congress acts.[25] This constitutional claim is hardly frivolous, and an important postscript to that event was that Congress did eventually regulate the suspension of habeas corpus, and the Lincoln administration accepted Congress's ability to do so. In any event, I think we should hesitate before developing a general theory of constitutional law based on an event as unique as the Civil War, just as I think we should hesitate before developing a general theory based on the ticking-time-bomb scenario.

So, at least on the basis of these examples, I am not convinced that we need to accept a regime that understands the executive branch as having the discretion to violate the law.[26] Kleinerman favors having the president justify to the nation the reasons for his national security actions,[27] but that can and will be the case even within the ambit of law. Many historical examples show that getting congressional authorization or judicial approval does not protect the president from public scrutiny of his actions; to take just one example, President Bush had congressional authorization for the war in Iraq, and yet that did not insulate him from the need to persuade the nation of the legitimacy of the war.

NOTES

1. Benjamin Kleinerman, "Separation of Powers and the National Security State," this volume, 110–20.

2. Ibid., 109–11.

3. Ibid., 108–11.

4. Ibid., 125–26.

5. See *Ex Parte Milligan*, 71 U.S. 2, 136–37 (1866) (Chase, J., concurring).

6. See Curtis A. Bradley, "The Story of *Ex Parte Milligan*: Military Trials, Enemy Combatants, and Congressional Authorization," in *Presidential Power Stories*, ed. Christopher H. Schroeder and Curtis A. Bradley (New York: Foundation Press, 2009).

7. See, e.g., Robert J. Pushaw Jr., "The 'Enemy Combatant' Cases in Historical Context: The Inevitability of Pragmatic Judicial Review," *Notre Dame L. Rev.* 82 (2007): 1005.

8. See *Youngstown Sheet & Tube Co. v. Sawyer*, 343 U.S. 579, 635–38 (1952) (Jackson, J., concurring). See also Curtis A. Bradley, "Clear Statement Rules and Executive War Powers," *Harvard Journal of Law and Public Policy* 33 (2010): 139–40; Samuel Issacharoff and Richard H. Pildes, "Between Civil Libertarianism and Executive Unilateralism: An Institutional Process Approach to Rights during Wartime," *Theoretical Inquiries in Law* 5 (2004): 1.

9. See *Dames and Moore v. Regan*, 453 U.S. 654, 669, 674 (1981).

10. See *Hamdan v. Rumsfeld*, 548 U.S. 557, 593 n.23 (2006); see also ibid. at 638 (Kennedy, J., concurring).

11. See *Ex Parte Endo*, 323 U.S. 283 (1944); see also Patrick O. Gudridge, "Remember *Endo*?," *Harv. L. Rev.* 116 (2003): 1933.

12. It is difficult to know from his essay what Kleinerman thinks of decisions like *Boumediene*. He criticizes the Supreme Court for insisting on having the last word in national security matters and cites *Boumediene* as an illustration of this phenomenon, but he does not suggest that the Court should have immunized the Guantanamo detention facility from judicial

review, as the executive had sought. See Kleinerman, "Separation of Powers," 129–31. Indeed, it is unclear how the judiciary could fulfill what Kleinerman describes as its nineteenth-century function of vindicating individual rights if the Court had come out the other way in *Boumediene.*

13. Inexplicably, Kleinerman describes *Youngstown*, a broad constitutional ruling in which the Supreme Court upheld an injunction against a governmental measure that the president claimed was necessary for national security during an ongoing war, as "com[ing] closest to the older model of jurisprudence." Ibid., 127.

14. See *Dames and Moore*, 453 U.S. at 688.

15. See *Hamdi v. Rumsfeld*, 542 U.S. 507, 516 (2004) (plurality). Kleinerman seems critical of the plurality's balancing approach in *Hamdi*, but he does not suggest how the Court should have determined the scope of the due process rights in question if not through a balancing of considerations. See Kleinerman, "Separation of Powers," 113, 129–30.

16. Ibid., 109.

17. Ibid., 121.

18. See Cartel for the Exchange of Prisoners of War, U.S.-Gr. Brit., May 12, 1813, reprinted in 2 *Treaties and Other International Acts of the United States of America, 1776–1818*, ed. Hunter Miller (Washington, DC: U.S. Government Printing Office, 1931).

19. 67 U.S. (2 Black) 635, 670–71 (1863).

20. See Kleinerman, "Separation of Powers," 128–29.

21. See, for example, Cass R. Sunstein, "What the Unitary Executive Debate Is and Is Not About" (Aug. 6, 2007), at http://uchicagolaw.typepad .com/faculty/2007/08/what-the-unitar.html. See also Steven G. Calabresi and Christopher S. Yoo, *The Unitary Executive: Presidential Power from Washington to Bush* (2008), 4 (showing "that all of our nation's presidents have believed in the theory of the unitary executive").

22. See Calabresi and Yoo, *Unitary Executive*, 3, 6.

23. For an Obama administration claim to this effect, see David J. Barron, Acting Assistant Attorney General, Office of Legal Counsel, "Constitutionality of Section 7054 of the Fiscal Year 2009 Foreign Appropriations Act" (June 1, 2009), at www.justice.gov/olc/2009/section7054.pdf. For a Clinton administration claim to this effect, see Walter Dellinger, Assistant Attorney General, Office of Legal Counsel, "Placing of United States Troops under United Nations Operational or Tactical Control" (May 8, 1996), at www.usdoj.gov/olc/hr3308.htm.

24. See, e.g., Jack Goldsmith, *The Terror Presidency: Law and Judgment Inside the Bush Administration* (New York: Norton, 2007), 94.

25. See Message to Congress in Special Session of July 4, 1861, in 4 *The*

Collected Works of Abraham Lincoln, ed. Roy P. Basler (New Brunswick, NJ: Rutgers University Press, 1953), 421, 429–30.

26. Contrary to what Kleinerman suggests, Chief Justice Marshall's recognition in *Marbury v. Madison* that the Constitution vests the president with some discretionary political authority does not mean that *Marbury* supports a presidential authority to violate the law. See Kleinerman, "Separation of Powers," 112–13. As Marshall made clear, the U.S. Constitution "establish[es] certain limits not to be transcended by [the three governmental] departments." *Marbury v. Madison*, 5 U.S. (1 Cranch) 137, 176 (1803). If the president is acting pursuant to discretion vested in him by the Constitution, he is not transcending those limits.

27. See Benjamin Kleinerman, *The Discretionary President: The Promise and Peril of Executive Power* (Lawrence: University Press of Kansas, 2009), 10.

7

THE INSTABILITY OF
"EXECUTIVE DISCRETION"

LIONEL K. McPHERSON

In the United States, terrorism—particularly terrorism that originates in the Muslim world—is widely believed to constitute an unprecedented menace. Post-9/11 doctrine holds that the country can no longer afford to rule out national security measures that many citizens in the past would have dismissed as disreputable. Such measures, we are told, might be necessary to preserve "our way of life" in "the age of terrorism," even when they are at odds with basic tenets of domestic or international law. If this necessity is seen as a perverse irony, the perversity is widely taken to reflect the fanatical evil of the country's terrorist foes, not the corruption of the ideal of American values. Efforts to defeat aggressive opposition to U.S. foreign engagement have eroded the civic notion that respecting the rights of individuals, even when doing so might not be legally expedient or ensure public safety, is a fundamental moral and political commitment. Thus, ideas and practices such as "harsh interrogation" or torture, "indefinite detention" without or despite trial, and "retroactive immunity" from criminal liability have become normalized as fit for serious public debate and acknowledged government policy.

　　Linked to such practices had been an explicit attempt by the Bush-Cheney regime to constitutionalize a very strong version of the "unitary executive theory" of presidential power. This version, which maintains that courts and Congress cannot impose real limits on the president's exercise of executive power, is now especially unfashionable. Yet Benjamin Kleinerman's focus on executive power through the lens of evolving separation-of-powers jurisprudence is hardly less timely. In the realm of national security, the spirit of a strong version of the unitary executive theory lives on through Barack Obama. For example, the Obama administration has asserted a "state secrets privilege" that would deny alleged torture victims a court hearing "any time a complaint contains allegations, the truth or falsity of which has been classified as secret by a government official."[1] The executive branch continues to insist, shifting to a purportedly pragmatic rationale, that government actions can lie outside judicial review.

Kleinerman is sympathetic to wide latitude for executive power on matters of national security—which is to say, he broadly accepts post-9/11 doctrine. At the same time, he envisions executive power being kept in check by cultivating in citizens a proper veneration of the Constitution. He favors a separation-of-powers model in which each branch of government conceives of its power as independent from and in contest with the powers of the others. This model, he claims, is most in line with a traditional understanding of the Constitution and best balances national security and protection of individual rights and liberties.[2] Setting aside the matter of American constitutional interpretation, an obvious question is how this balancing is supposed to work.

According to Kleinerman, the people's "love of the limiting aims of the Constitution" would politically embolden Congress "to cite the Constitution as it calls on the president to justify extralegal or illegal activities."[3] Why he believes this is not clear. Congress is unlikely to become unusually responsive to ordinary citizens on such amorphous grounds. Presidents are already in the habit of citing the Constitution, under some interpretation or other, to justify activities that might appear to be illegal. Moreover, Congress seems to view its role less as an independent branch of government than as an institution divided along party lines, with Democrats and Republicans overwhelmingly dedicated to advancing their own political interests first and their party's interests second. A deeply divided citizenry seems largely to share the priority of aligning with one's party politics and aims over consistent, conscientious application of the Constitution (see, e.g., *Bush v. Gore*). In short, the notion that popular love of the Constitution will support a separation-of-powers check on executive power is wildly optimistic.

But Kleinerman has pressing reason for concern about unchecked executive power. He seems to grant that the president can have the authority to engage in illegal activities—by virtue of the singular, distinctive authority of the president. While post-9/11 national security doctrine urgently appeals to "the unknowable threats of a dangerous world,"[4] the argument sounds more rhetorical than substantive. The world has always been a dangerous place, and the knowableness of threats is mostly beside the point. If the president is to have the authority to engage in illegal activities, this surely must be due to the existence of exceptionally high stakes.

The question, then, is how high the stakes must be. Sotirios A. Barber and James E. Fleming argue that "the executive power is constitutionally obligated to restore or maintain the conditions for constitutional democracy and the rule of law"; they find, for instance, that Lincoln "acted without constitutional authorization to save the Union and the Constitution."[5] On their view, "There is no paradox, because fidelity to the Constitution always presupposes material conditions that the Constitution cannot guarantee."[6] Such a view of executive power exceedingly rarely leads in the direction of post-9/11 doctrine. Every threat to national security is not plausibly a threat to the material conditions for a constitutional democracy. Nor does every national security threat represent an affront to the executive's power and responsibility to protect the country.

I am skeptical that the president has distinctive authority to engage in illegal activities, even when the stakes are highest. This skepticism seems to me compatible with the Barber-Fleming nonparadox of executive power, whereby the president has a positive duty to protect the Constitution.[7] Positive duties are not necessarily accompanied by special authority to violate the law in order to satisfy them. I will not argue for the primacy of domestic or international law; nor will I argue that granting the president authority to violate the law diminishes individual rights and liberties. Rather, I will argue that the very notion of "executive discretion"—namely as a function of distinctive authority to justify illegal activities on grounds of national security—is conceptually unstable.[8] If and when there is a morally extraordinary rationale for violating the law, no special authority to violate that law would appear to be required.

Either post-9/11 doctrine does not require only the highest stakes to trigger executive recourse to illegal activities or the doctrine embraces an expansive understanding of the highest stakes. The source of distinctive authority for executive discretion is practical in nature, Kleinerman suggests. He looks to Eric Posner and Adrian Vermeule, who "justify [the] legacy of judicial (and congressional) deference to the executive on war powers issues because the institutional advantages of the executive branch, i.e. secrecy, speed, and flexibility, allow it to manage best the necessities of wars and crises."[9] Kleinerman endorses the corresponding argument that "[t]here is no way for judges rightly to estimate the requirements of national security."[10] But appeals to national security necessity usually underdescribe fundamental questions about the concrete stakes and the extent of acceptable measures. For example, Kleinerman makes the case as follows: "Was it truly necessary to undertake an illegal action like torture so as to preserve the nation's security? [O]ne must show more than that crucial information was gathered by harsh interrogation methods. One must also show . . . that these methods were the only feasible manner in which to gather this information; that is, other legal methods failed."[11]

In contrast to Posner and Vermeule, Kleinerman rejects a very strong unitary executive model of unified sovereignty whereby each branch of government ostensibly is supreme in its own domain. Proponents of this model use the word "deference" as a euphemism for what actually is submission. While Kleinerman worries that judicial and congressional submission to the executive would create a "national security state," he does not question "the necessity of discretionary executive power."[12] The debate, as he frames it, presupposes license to protect national security through means that admit of no prior specification. We are to believe that "'[t]he novelty of the threats and of the necessary responses'" defies constructive judicial imagination. This might be true in the absence of an account of national security necessity.[13] There is a range of possibilities about what could be thought to activate the

license—from immediately securing the nation as a viable, autonomous political entity to preventing any politically motivated, violent attack on the homeland or on state officials or property any-
where in the world.[14] The latter seems the prevalent understanding in the United States.

Nonetheless, societal fear of a "new ordinary, where vast and
unthinkable destruction remains a constant possibility," implies
neither a cogent conception of national security necessity nor a
justification for executive discretion.[15] A particular society's phe-
nomenological experiences of political violence are subjective.
Objectively, the destruction done through terrorism in fact has
been exponentially less than that done through conventional warfare. Given "the brute reality of war for noncombatants," as I have
described it elsewhere, noncombatants generally have more to
fear from conventional warfare than from terrorism.[16] Not unrea-
sonably, they might morally reject the sharp distinction that traditional just-war theory draws between intentionally harming noncombatants, which never is permitted, and foreseeably and avoid-
ably but unintentionally and "collaterally" harming them, which
typically is permitted.[17] That there has been a dramatic change in
worldly circumstances for societies backed by military power—and
whose civilians had been unaccustomed to reckoning directly with
political violence of any kind—does not indicate that the moral
universe has changed.

A blunt "law of necessity" argument for overriding domestic
or international law does not take seriously the laws of war, let
alone the idea of just-war theory.[18] Claiming necessity, any nation
that exhausted legal methods could invoke a prerogative to torture, for example, in confronting some national security threat,
nonconventional or conventional. Post-9/11 doctrine appears to
base claims of necessity not only on the sheer scale of harm that
might be done by an attack but also, and independently, on the
difficulty of detecting and deterring certain types of threat. This
difficulty does not constitute a new and unanticipated phenomenon, though some manifestations of the difficulty—such as international terrorist networks, operating out of rogue, dysfunctional,
or failed states insufficiently responsive to standard methods of political and military suasion—might be new. Law proper already reflects judgments about limits to expediency in a dangerous world.

If a law of necessity were always implicitly in effect, we would have trouble explaining how a settled legal prohibition of torture could ever have developed so as to require distinctive license to torture.

Let's back up, though, and consider another difficulty: call it the "double-dipping" problem. The ultimate institutional advantage of the executive branch is its systematic capacity to employ political violence and massive human and technological resources. This systematic capacity is the practical essence of executive power. Barber and Fleming suggest a similar point in distinguishing between "the delegated powers of the presidency and the resulting powers . . . from the president's strategic position in the constitutional scheme."[19] Lincoln had the power, de facto, by virtue of his normal authority as president, to violate the Constitution in respects that he deemed necessary to win the Civil War. Our crucial judgments here are moral: they depend on our assessment of the moral urgency of the president's ends and the apparent necessity, under the circumstances, of illegally using certain means.

In other words, the political legitimacy to employ vital mechanisms of the state is constitutive of the executive's distinctive authority. This same capacity cannot plausibly ground justification for executive discretion to break (or rewrite) the law: the judicial and legislative branches have already "deferred" by accepting the executive's initiative in exercising the capacity on matters of national security. Their deference enables the executive to act first and answer questions later, confidentially and under the presumption that its actions are legally justifiable. The domestic legal barriers can be set low or with creative ambiguity—which would help to explain why the legal fiction of "harsh interrogation" took as long as it did to give way to the indisputable reality of torture. On what distinctive basis could the president insist on the further power of executive discretion to violate the law?

Compare civilian police, who are vested with authority to enforce the law and to maintain public order. Toward these ends, they have powers to investigate, command, arrest, interrogate, and use lethal force. Yet, such powers are supposed to be exercised within the limits of the law; and the law, which in the United States is increasingly permissive about "exigent circumstances," already gives police wide latitude to perform their duties. The legal constraint holds despite the institutional advantages of the police

—namely their law enforcement powers, which generally put the police in the best position to manage ordinary crime and public order. We would be disinclined to accept the argument that, given their law enforcement powers and the inability of judges and legislators always to anticipate the field requirements of law enforcement, the police justifiably can undertake illegal actions if they can show, after the fact, that illegal methods were the only feasible manner of trying to accomplish highly important law enforcement goals.[20]

A likely objection is that national security is different, rendering inapt the analogy between the executive branch and civilian police. But how national security is relevantly different is not obvious, especially in the absence of an account of national security necessity. Terrorism, for instance, does not pose more of a danger than ordinary violent crime. Between 16,000 and 17,000 reported murders were committed in the United States each year between 2004 and 2008, for a total of roughly 83,000 murders over those five years.[21] The totality of terrorism directed against the United States has not caused anything close to this extent of bodily harm, and no such realistic threat currently exists.

If the expressly political nature of political violence, as opposed to ordinary violent crime, is supposed to make the difference, this needs to be elaborated—largely against a background where terrorists lack the capacity directly and profoundly to destabilize the United States as a political entity. Shifting the discussion away from terrorism will not be easy, since the types of threats posed by state violence are longstanding, and the public has been led to believe that severe departures from the law would extend only to confirmed or suspected "unlawful combatants," "insurgents," or "radical" noncombatants. If fixation on nonstate political violence is motivated primarily by the difficulty of detecting and deterring nonstate actors, this seems uncomfortably analogous to the expediency rationale nonstate actors have for resorting to terrorism —which is the near-futility of militarily weak groups or peoples using conventional means to fight militarily powerful states. I am not trying to minimize the threat or consequences of terrorism. I am arguing that simply appealing to national security necessity does not go far in justifying discretionary executive power to violate domestic or international law.

A state, of course, has a responsibility to protect persons and things within its purview from unlawful violence. Kleinerman suggests, as do Posner and Vermeule, that new types of threats posed by terrorism strengthen the case for executive discretion. This implies that older types of threats posed by states are not compelling enough. I have suggested that emphasis on terrorism actually weakens the case for executive discretion. Supporters of executive discretion who emphasize terrorism risk exaggerating its significance. Insofar as an argument from national security necessity is solid in its own right, rhetorical maneuvers that fuel fear and anxiety about terrorism are gratuitous.

To be clear, Kleinerman shares with proponents of a strong version of the unitary executive theory the view that executive discretion can be justified with respect to national security. Terrorism does not play a theoretically essential role on this view. Kleinerman's disagreement with strong unitary executive theorists turns mainly on how to interpret the Constitution or, more broadly, how to understand the rule of law under pressure of crisis. He defends a model of separation of powers on which the potential for abuse of executive discretion is held in check through active contestation by the judicial and legislative branches. But this debate deflects attention from a basic, more limited question: what kinds of violations of the law would executive discretion be justifying?

My argument is that the case for executive discretion—as reflective of the president's distinctive authority—becomes less plausible as the illegal actions to be justified become morally more problematic and not because morally problematic actions should never be undertaken. The reason might seem counterintuitive: if the national security stakes truly are high enough to open the door to actions that otherwise would be not only legally but also morally objectionable, then it is hard to see why any distinctive authority would be needed to undertake such actions. A credible "law of necessity" would recognize no constitutional or authority limits.

The debate that Kleinerman joins conflates two questions of executive discretion: I describe these as the procedural question and the substantive question. Roughly, the distinction marks procedures themselves rather than the nature of certain actions in themselves. The procedural question of executive discretion is whether and why the executive justifiably may act outside the procedural boundaries of the law. *Miranda* warnings are a straight-forward example of the procedural dimension of the law. A more controversial example is warrantless domestic wiretapping—construed as a violation of the Fourth Amendment to the Constitution (which addresses unreasonable searches and seizures) and, more specifically, a criminal violation of the Foreign Intelligence Surveillance Act (FISA). The substantive question of executive discretion is whether and why the executive justifiably may violate the law by engaging in actions that by their nature are morally objectionable, if not absolutely morally prohibited. Torture is an example of an action covered by the substantive dimension of the law.

Discussions of executive discretion confuse and mislead by failing to distinguish the procedural question and the substantive question. Kleinerman's discussion has this flaw. An adequate account of executive discretion cannot be given, nor even can an adequate discussion proceed, unless the domain is specified. The idea that the executive can have distinctive authority to violate the law with respect to procedure does not seem deeply startling: this would be a matter of weighing the national security stakes against the short- and long-term stakes of violating legal procedures. On any particular occasion, procedural violations of the law do not directly and greatly threaten anyone's life or liberty. But these are not the violations that generate the most controversy, and they are not the violations that Kleinerman seems mostly to have in mind.

I am not at all suggesting that procedural violations of the law are technicalities. Nor am I insisting that there is always sharp distinction between procedural violations and substantive violations. For instance, willingness to allow in criminal prosecutions putative evidence that "might not meet every jot and tittle of American criminal law," as Jack Goldsmith and Neal Katyal put it,[22] might well go from a procedural to a substantive issue when that putative evidence was gained through torture. The judicial and legislative branches have an important role to play in guarding against executive abuse of power on the purportedly procedural front. They maintain the integrity of the law by compelling the executive to demonstrate the national security necessity that would justify exercising executive discretion. Whether this is done prior to or after the fact of a procedural violation of the law seems a secondary consideration when the executive has a legitimate case. When the executive does not have a legitimate case, the after-the-fact discovery of a procedural violation would not be of immediate consequence in terms of life or liberty. Further, the judicial and legislative branches could then respond by being less deferential going forward to the particular executive regime. None of this seems at odds with Kleinerman's view of executive power.

By contrast, the idea that the executive can have distinctive authority to violate the law with respect to actions that by their nature are morally objectionable is a very different story. Torture is not merely, and indeed is not fundamentally, a legal or constitutional matter; and no universal, objective conception of morality must be posited in order to make the point. This is because, in general, moral permissibility does not depend on legal proceduralism or constitutional theorizing, not because the law as such or the Constitution lacks gravitas.

The ultimate question regarding the substantive question of executive discretion is whether an action that is by its nature morally objectionable can be morally justified on some occasion, whether on grounds of national security stakes or other, utilitarian grounds. But if the human stakes truly are so high, this seems to destabilize the very idea of executive discretion as a function of the distinctive authority of the president or of any other specific office or officeholder. The exceptionally high human stakes and not any distinctive authority would be doing the decisive work of moral justification under conditions of crisis. Any person or entity that happens to have the practical capacity to undertake actions for the sake of a greater good, actions that typically are morally objectionable, should be—at least by a "law of necessity" type of argument —deputized to do so. True necessity, on whatever construal, cannot afford to care who gets the job done and how. Of course, this is also a reason to be extremely wary about politically launched necessity claims in the morally substantive domain.

In sum, if moral limits can be cast aside when the human stakes are high enough, it is implausible to hold that the lines of authority culminating in the executive branch cannot be cast aside, as well. This supports the conclusion that the notion of executive discretion as a function of distinctive executive authority is stable only regarding actions immediately confined to the procedural domain. In the morally substantive domain, the notion of executive discretion is both destabilized by and superseded by necessity claims that are supposed to justify violating the law.

NOTES

1. The Ninth Circuit Court of Appeals rejected "the Government's theory [that] the Judiciary should effectively cordon off all secret government actions from judicial scrutiny, immunizing the CIA and its partners from the demands and limits of law." See *Mohamed v. Jeppesen Dataplan, Inc.*, 579 F.3d 943, 955 (9th Cir. 2009).

2. Benjamin Kleinerman, "Separation of Powers and the National Security State," this volume, 110–11, 130–31.

3. Benjamin Kleinerman, *The Discretionary President: The Promise and Peril of Executive Power* (Lawrence: University Press of Kansas, 2009), 17.

4. John Yoo, *The Powers of War and Peace: The Constitution and Foreign Affairs after 9/11* (Chicago: University of Chicago Press, 2005), 21 (cited in Sotirios A. Barber and James E. Fleming, "Constitutional Theory, the Unitary Executive, and the Rule of Law," this volume, 157.

5. Barber and Fleming, "Constitutional Theory," 157.

6. Ibid., 158.

7. Ibid., 157–58.

8. I am distinguishing between "extralegal" and "illegal": my argument here concerns the illegal, that is, that which exceeds the limits of the law as compared to that which lies in a legal grey zone.

9. Kleinerman, "Separation of Powers and the National Security State," 124–25.

10. Ibid., 125.

11. Kleinerman, *The Discretionary President*, 9.

12. Kleinerman, "Separation of Powers and the National Security State," 128.

13. Eric A. Posner and Adrian Vermeule, *Terror in the Balance: Security, Liberty, and the Courts* (New York: Oxford University Press, 2007), 18 (cited in Kleinerman, "Separation of Powers and the National Security State," 125).

14. Cf. Michael Walzer's "supreme emergency" exception to the rules of war, *Just and Unjust Wars*, 3rd ed. (New York: Basic Books, 1997), 259–60.

15. Kleinerman, *The Discretionary President*, 12.

16. Lionel K. McPherson, "Is Terrorism Distinctively Wrong?" *Ethics* 117 (2007): 524, 529.

17. Ibid., 537.

18. See, e.g., Richard A Posner, *Not a Suicide Pact: The Constitution in a Time of National Emergency* (Oxford: Oxford University Press, 2006), 158 (cited in Kleinerman, *The Discretionary President*, 9).

19. Barber and Fleming, "Constitutional Theory," 159.

20. The comparison is not undermined by the U.S. Supreme Court's unanimous decision in *Virginia v. Moore* (2008), which held that police may use evidence obtained through illegal searches during traffic stops. This case does not authorize illegal searches but, rather, concerns the admissibility of evidence.

21. U.S. Department of Justice, Federal Bureau of Investigation, "Crime in the United States, 2008," http://www.fbi.gov/ucr/cius2008/data/table_07.htm.

22. Jack L. Goldsmith and Neal Katyal, "The Terrorists' Court," *New York Times*, July 11, 2007.

8

CONSTITUTIONAL THEORY, THE UNITARY EXECUTIVE, AND THE RULE OF LAW

SOTIRIOS A. BARBER AND JAMES E. FLEMING

This essay, part of a larger project, considers theories of the unitary executive and what the best of these theories imports for the rule of law and the future of constitutional theory as a whole. As we see it, at least in a sense that predates Bush administration apologist John Yoo,[1] the unitary executive is here to stay. Precisely because the American constitutional executive is a unitary power, President Obama can close Guantánamo unilaterally, without Congress's leave. President Obama, on his own, can also revoke Bush's executive orders regarding secrecy. He can renounce Bush administration memoranda attempting to justify torture, and he can prohibit further acts of torture during his tenure in office. Obama cannot, however, coherently renounce the unitary executive at the same time that he acts unilaterally to undo excesses of the last unitary executive. In any case, to recall Justice Robert Jackson's formulation from *Youngstown Sheet and Tube Co. v. Sawyer*, the "imperatives of events and contemporary imponderables" are going to require strong executive power.[2] The same basic thought appeared some five generations before Justice Jackson's time when Alexander Hamilton, an early proponent of a unitary executive, said in *The Federalist* that because "[t]he circumstances that endanger the safety of nations are infinite . . . no constitutional shackles can wisely be imposed on the power to which the care of it is committed."[3]

John Yoo claims to derive his theory of the unitary executive from *The Federalist*.[4] We share his assumption that *The Federalist* is a good place to start. Unlike *The Federalist*, however, Yoo fails to embed the unitary executive in proper context: a broad theory of coordinated institutions. When Yoo says that "Federalists defended the centralization of the executive power in the president precisely in order to enable the federal government to respond to the unknowable threats of a dangerous world,"[5] he relies on Hamilton's argument in *The Federalist* No. 70 that good government is impossible without "energy in the executive," that unity in the executive is essential to energy in government, and that unity in the executive is conducive to "[d]ecision, activity, secrecy, and dispatch."[6]

But Yoo does not think like Hamilton. Yoo is an advocate for policies of a particular administration or party during a particular historical period. Because Hamilton thinks holistically, as a Framer, he situates his unitary executive in a broad theory of coordinated institutions in which different sets of power shape and limit one another. Yoo fails to embed his unitary executive in a general theory of coordinated constitutional functions like that articulated in *The Federalist*.

This broader context of executive power has three parts. One is an institutional context that includes the Congress, the courts, and institutional norms like democracy and the rule of law. Another is a substantive context, oriented to constitutional goods or ends to which constitutional institutions are committed. A third is a philosophical context: the view of the human good and the human condition that is believed to justify the constitutional ensemble of substantive goods and institutional means. Insensitive to this broader context, Yoo's partial and distorted understanding of executive power has a striking payoff: the actions of a giant like Lincoln become precedents for the acts of an incompetent like Bush. In this essay we explain why academic constitutional commentary should be prepared to make judgments of this kind.

We begin with the *philosophical* context. Elsewhere, we invoke Lincoln and argue that the executive power is constitutionally obligated to restore or maintain the conditions for constitutional democracy and the rule of law.[7] Our claim is that Lincoln acted without constitutional authorization to save the Union and the Constitution. Acted extraconstitutionally in order to save the Constitution? There is no paradox, because fidelity to the Constitution always presupposes material conditions that the Constitution cannot guarantee. Lincoln felt that the Civil War might be lost unless he displaced Congress's powers to initiate the raising of armies and navies, to authorize spending, and to suspend the writ of habeas corpus. The conditions of the Civil War brought various constitutional provisions into irresolvable conflict.[8] Abiding by the letter of some provisions meant disobeying others; namely the clause requiring the president to "take Care that the Laws be faithfully executed"[9] and the president's oath to preserve and defend the Constitution.[10] The Constitution is silent as to how to resolve these conflicts—under some conditions, therefore, fully constitutional conduct is impossible. For some situations, all one can hope for are pro-constitutional actions or, as we refer to them, *constitutionalist* actions—actions that restore the conditions for honoring the Constitution—actions that are *constitutionalist* though not *constitutional.* This kind of argument is easier to accept in war than in peace because war exposes the essentially *positive* nature of the Constitution—its overriding commitment to substantive ends like security and the general welfare—and the corresponding *positive duties* of those who take the oath to preserve and defend it.

Bush did not disagree. He acted as a positive constitutionalist when he compromised constitutional restraints to secure the nation against terrorism. But conservative constitutional theorists have yet, officially, to face that fact. Positive constitutionalism has an openly favorable view of government as the agent of collective aspirations. Conservative constitutionalism purports to view government as a necessary evil, with exceptions in the areas of foreign and military affairs, criminal justice, and, for many conservatives, sexual morality. The exceptions are big enough to expose the libertarianism of conservatism as a pretext. Conservatives are as pro-government as anyone else when it comes to ends they seek to promote, like national security, law and order (for individuals if not for corporations), and selective forms of sexual restraint. Yet, among conservatives, the antigovernment mask is effective. Conservatives see themselves as moderate libertarians, not as positive constitutionalists committed to a view of society different from that of their openly pro-government counterparts on the left. As a consequence, they do not fully explicate and defend the society to which their constitutional doctrines point. They have a positive constitutionalism of their own, but they downplay that fact, and they fail to expose their positive agenda for all to see.

Chief Justice William Rehnquist, the author of the Supreme Court's opinion in *DeShaney v. Winnebago County Department of Social Services*,[11] was the most visible proponent of negative constitutionalism. Yet, in his book, *All the Laws but One: Civil Liberties in Wartime*, Rehnquist practically embraced the idea *inter arma silent leges*—that, during war, constitutional restraints are silent.[12] For Rehnquist, when constitutional forms, rights, and limits are suspended indeed the laws are silent, and everything is permitted to the executive.[13] Rehnquist thus subscribed to part of Lincoln's view but not all of it. He failed to see, as Lincoln saw, that when the Constitution is suspended, the executive has restorative obligations—affirmative obligations to work actively toward restoring conditions in which the Constitution can function as law once again. These affirmative obligations include the pursuit of domestic conditions (in Lincoln's case, the end of the secessionist threat) that would permit government by constitutional forms, rights, and limits. In sum, unlike Lincoln, Rehnquist failed to see that executive power must be committed to restoring or maintaining the conditions for constitutional democracy and the rule of law.

President Bush may or may not have realized this, but conservative constitutional theory denies affirmative constitutional obligations. In *DeShaney*, Chief Justice Rehnquist denied even a minimal duty of the night-watchman state: the protection of a four-year-old child from the perfectly predictable (because it was repeated and well-reported) violence of a deranged father.[14] And Bush's conception of the war on terror as permanent brought into question the possibility of restoring the conditions for the rule of law.

Next, we will sketch the *institutional* context of the unitary executive. The Constitution does put the president in a strategic setting for exercising the kind of power that Yoo contemplates. We can distinguish between the delegated powers of the presidency and the resulting powers that Yoo contemplates—those powers resulting from the president's strategic position in the constitutional scheme. But a president's exercise of strategic power can be constitutional only if it can eventually take a form that comports with constitutional criteria. It has to express itself in a way that can be expressed in generally applicable statutory laws that meet constitutional tests and can be applied by courts. Eventually, strategic power must be reconciled to delegated power and the rule of law.

More generally, we need a theory of the unitary executive that situates the executive in the context of an institutional theory of the conflictual Constitution.[15] Bush, together with the theory upon which he acted, was contemptuous of Congress and the courts and would brook no disagreement from, conflict with, or limitation by those institutions. Indeed, the Republican-controlled Congress capitulated to that view. Republican Speaker of the House Dennis Hastert, rather than conceiving of Congress as an institution with responsibilities to check executive power, publicly proclaimed that his job was to enact the president's agenda.[16] Hastert spoke and acted as if the nation had a parliamentary system, rather than a presidential system with institutional checks and balances.[17]

Within institutional theories of the conflictual Constitution of the sort elaborated by Mariah Zeisberg and Jeffrey Tulis, Congress has responsibilities not simply to defer to or serve as an agent of executive power but also to contest exercises of executive power.[18] President Bush, Vice President Cheney, and Karl Rove all made a serious effort to establish a de facto parliamentary system in place of a presidential system of institutional checks and balances. They aspired to install a permanent Republican majority led by a unitary and unilateral executive and supported by a permanently pliant Congress and judiciary—contrary to the separation of powers and the deliberative politics reflected in the American constitutional regime. They sought to govern through secrecy and by leveraging fear—exploiting a permanent war on terrorism, keeping the public in the dark about the formation of major policies, and maintaining a permanently fearful citizenry.[19] To achieve their ends, they promoted the political power of those religious evangelicals who treat disagreement with their beliefs as either sinful or unpatriotic. There were no clearer signs of their hostility to constitutional institutions than their secrecy and their treatment of critics as traitors and heretics. They could not conceive of a loyal opposition; opposition to them meant disloyalty to the country.

These ambitions reflected Bush's sense that his instincts were in tune with God's will and the market's hidden hand, an attitude at odds with the scientifically informed political planning exemplified by the American Founding.[20] Indeed, Bush created a modern analogue to the divine right of kings: certain and infallible executives with direct communications from God do not need deliberative processes for governance; they need only executive processes for carrying out their infallible convictions.

In light of the results of the Bush years at home and abroad, constitutional commentary should be open to an alternative model of presidential power. One such alternative is the Hamiltonian model sketched earlier—the strong but institutionally situated executive. This model includes legislators with a sense of institutional identity and loyalty, along with courts that are committed to contesting and checking executive power. We have no objection to a Hamiltonian presidency—one that remains situated within an institutional scheme and responsible to its norms. Within such a scheme, checks on presidential power are best seen in a positive light, as means for preventing mistakes. This view might have spared the nation the consequences of the Bush era.

To recapitulate: the executive exists in an institutional context that includes Congress and the courts. The president does not float on a detached pedestal. Even when emergencies force the president to act extraconstitutionally, he or she must return to Congress and the courts for post-hoc approval, as Lincoln did. This means that the president's actions must meet the formal and substantive moral standards requisite for constitutional laws. Secrecy might be essential in times of war, but secret institutions (like Bush's foreign prisons) defeat the visibility that is essential to democratic responsibility and the rule of law. By assuming that the "war on terror" would be more or less permanent, Yoo depreciated the institutions and principles of public responsibility represented by Congress and the courts. This transformed Hamilton's unitary-but-attached-and-checked executive into Bush's unitary-but-detached-and-elevated executive.

Finally, we turn to the *substantive* context of the unitary executive, the context of constitutional goods or ends. This context has three aspects: a hierarchy of *goods*—the goods of the large commercial republic;[21] a set of appropriate *attitudes* held by the citizens or at least the leadership community of the large commercial republic; and certain *virtues* that these goods and attitudes presuppose.

The Federalist situates executive power in an overarching picture of the good life, the social ends to which the Constitution is an instrument. Constitutional goods or ends presuppose certain attitudes, virtues, and character. Most liberals who criticize Yoo's theory (and Bush's execution of it) criticize it in the wrong way.[22] This is because these liberals, like conservatives, have lost touch with the broader concept of constitutional ends and the personal character traits that accompany appreciation of these ends. Thus, current constitutional commentary—both conservative and liberal—largely ignores substantive constitutional ends and personal character.[23]

Yoo invokes not only *The Federalist* but also Lincoln as authorizing Bush's theory and practice of executive power.[24] The big difference between Abraham Lincoln and George Bush lies in Bush's failure to appreciate the broader constitutional context of executive power and to display the attitudes associated with the pursuit of real goods by actors who are aware of their fallibility and their responsibilities to others. Had Yoo appreciated all aspects of this context, he would have been able to articulate in theoretical terms what, we venture, everyone knows: George W. Bush was no Abraham Lincoln! Put another way, the problem with Bush and Cheney, in addition to their view of executive power, is that they lack appreciation of constitutional ends and the attitudes and character presupposed by those ends and requisite for their competent pursuit.

Post-Bush, theorists of executive power will have to rethink the connection between power, the ends of power, and the character of those who wield power. That connection can be established only by reconnecting constitutional institutions to constitutional ends. Constitutional power must be dedicated to public purposes, like those listed in the Preamble. And, because the content of these ends is controversial, constitutional power must be dedicated to a healthy politics—a politics through which the system elaborates the best conceptions of constitutional ends in changing circumstances. After the Bush administration, we must reconnect our understanding of executive power to an understanding of the constitutional ends that such power is to pursue and the intellectual and moral virtues requisite to that pursuit.

The obstacles to any such project are intellectual and cultural. The intellectual obstacles include relativism, moral skepticism, preference utilitarianism, and dogmatic religiosity. Why? Because each of these forces in its own way obscures the deliberative and self-critical manner in which rational actors should pursue real goods—goods about whose content they can err and about whose means they can err. Academic moral relativism and skepticism in academic law and the social sciences have largely ignored developments in modern philosophy (moral constructivism and moral realism) that justify the assumption of ordinary political life, including the assumption of the American constitutional Framers, that the ends of political life are real goods, not apparent goods or goods determined by subjective preferences.

The cultural obstacles have been fostered by the market economy, which underwrites or reinforces relativism, moral skepticism, and preference utilitarianism. The economic crisis wrought by deregulatory policies that began in the Carter years, together with the larger tragedy to the country wrought by the Bush presidency, should motivate the intellectual community to rethink philosophically dated orthodoxies that divert intellectual energy from questions of value and character, in the abstract and regarding particular historical figures, movements, and developments. Put differently, academics must rethink orthodoxies that rule out propositions like "Bush was no Lincoln," for such orthodoxies blind observers to what we have strong arguments to regard as dimensions of reality. Rethinking academic orthodoxies could be a step toward overcoming the cultural obstacles we've mentioned.

In the wake of the Bush presidency, the time for "normal science" has passed, and constitutional theorists should be prepared to think in unconventional terms. In doing so, constitutional theorists need to develop a deeper understanding of the broader context of constitutional commitments, institutional checks, and constitutional goods, attitudes, and virtues. Theorizing about the unitary executive and maintaining or restoring the rule of law must reckon with that broader context.

NOTES

In this essay, we have drawn extensively from an essay we published in the Randolph W. Thrower Symposium "Executive Power: New Directions for the New Presidency?" held at Emory University School of Law. See Sotirios A. Barber and James E. Fleming, "Constitutional Theory and the Future of the Unitary Executive," *Emory Law Journal* 59 (2009): 459. We gratefully acknowledge Eric Lee and Jameson Rice of Boston University for research assistance.

1. See generally John Yoo, *The Powers of War and Peace: The Constitution and Foreign Affairs after 9/11* (Chicago: University of Chicago Press, 2005). Other prominent recent works defending Bush's vision of the unitary executive include Steven G. Calabresi and Christopher S. Yoo, *The Unitary Executive: Presidential Power from Washington to Bush* (New Haven: Yale University Press, 2008).

2. 343 U.S. 579, 637 (1952) (Jackson, J., concurring).

3. *The Federalist* No. 23, at 147 (Alexander Hamilton), ed. Jacob E. Cooke (Middletown, CT: Wesleyan University Press, 1961).

4. Yoo, *War and Peace*, 21.

5. Ibid. (further citing twice in the same paragraph Hamilton's *The Federalist* No. 70). Yoo also stated in an essay published by the Heritage Foundation:

> But the text and structure of the Constitution, as well as its application over the last two centuries, confirm that the President can begin military hostilities without the approval of Congress. The Constitution does not establish a strict war-making process because the Framers understood that war would require the speed, decisiveness, and secrecy that only the presidency could bring. "Energy in the Executive," Alexander Hamilton argued in the *Federalist Papers*, "is a leading character in the definition of good government. It is essential to the protection of the community against foreign attacks." And, he continued, "the direction of war most peculiarly demands those qualities which distinguish the exercise of power by a single hand."

John Yoo, *Energy in the Executive: Re-examining Presidential Power in the Midst of the War on Terrorism*, First Principles Series No. 4 (Heritage Foundation, Washington, DC), April 24, 2006, at 2 (footnote omitted) (quoting *The Federalist* No. 70, at 423 (Alexander Hamilton)), *available at* http://www .heritage.org/Research/PublicDiplomacy/fp4.cfm.

6. *The Federalist* No. 70, at 472 (Alexander Hamilton).

7. Sotirios A. Barber and James E. Fleming, "War, Crisis, and the Con-

stitution," in *The Constitution in Wartime: Beyond Alarmism and Complacency,* ed. Mark Tushnet (Durham, NC: Duke University Press, 2005), 232, 236–37, 242–43.

8. Ibid.

9. U.S. Const. art. II, § 3, cl. 4.

10. U.S. Const. art. II, § 1, cl. 8.

11. 489 U.S. 189 (1989).

12. William H. Rehnquist, *All the Laws but One: Civil Liberties in Wartime* (New York: Knopf, 1998).

13. Ibid.

14. *DeShaney,* 489 U.S. at 189–90.

15. This sort of theory has been proposed by political scientists Mariah Zeisberg and Jeffrey Tulis. See, e.g., Mariah Zeisberg, "Constitutional War Authority: A Relational Conception" (2009) (unpublished manuscript, on file with Professor Zeisberg, University of Michigan, Dept. of Political Science) Mariah Zeisberg, "The Relational Conception of War Powers," in *The Limits of Constitutional Democracy,* ed. Jeffrey K. Tulis and Stephen Macedo (Princeton: Princeton University Press, 2010), 168; Jeffrey K. Tulis, *Democratic Decay and the Politics of Deference* (Princeton: Princeton University Press, forthcoming); Jeffrey K. Tulis, "On Congress and Constitutional Responsibility," *B.U. L. Rev.* 89 (2009): 515. We interpret Benjamin Kleinerman's view, both in his recent book and in his essay for this volume, similarly as reflecting an institutional theory of the conflictual constitution. See Benjamin A. Kleinerman, *The Discretionary President: The Promise and Peril of Executive Power* (Lawrence: University Press of Kansas, 2009); Benjamin A. Kleinerman, "Separation of Powers and the National Security State," this volume.

16. As Thomas Mann and Norman Ornstein put it: "Speaker Hastert . . . proclaimed that his primary responsibility was not to lead and defend the first branch of government but to pass the president's legislative program." Thomas E. Mann and Norman J. Ornstein, *The Broken Branch: How Congress Is Failing America and How to Get It Back on Track* (New York: Oxford University Press, 2006), 139.

17. Ibid., 7 ("In its highly centralized leadership and fealty to the presidential agenda, the post-2000 House of Representatives looks more like a House of Commons in a parliamentary system than a House of Representatives in a presidential system."); Alan Wolfe, *Does American Democracy Still Work?* (New Haven: Yale University Press, 2006), 60.

18. See sources cited in note 15.

19. See, e.g., Andrew Bacevich, *The New American Militarism: How Americans Are Seduced by War* (New York: Oxford University Press, 2005); Benjamin R. Barber, *Fear's Empire: War, Terrorism and Democracy* (New York:

Norton, 2003); Jack Goldsmith, *The Terror Presidency: Law and Judgment inside the Bush Administration* (New York: Norton, 2007); Stephen Holmes, *The Matador's Cape: America's Reckless Response to Terror* (New York: Cambridge University Press, 2007); Robert M. Pallitto and William G. Weaver, *Presidential Secrecy and the Law* (Baltimore: Johns Hopkins University Press, 2007); Jane Mayer, *The Dark Side: The Inside Story of How the War on Terror Turned into a War on American Ideals* (New York: Doubleday, 2008).

20. Sotirios A. Barber and James E. Fleming, *Constitutional Interpretation: The Basic Questions* (New York: Oxford University Press, 2007), 36.

21. Elsewhere we have elaborated these goods. See ibid., 35–55.

22. See, for example, the otherwise excellent book by Peter M. Shane, *Madison's Nightmare: How Executive Power Threatens American Democracy* (Chicago: University of Chicago Press, 2009).

23. For an important exception, see Clement Fatovic, *Outside the Law: Emergency and Executive Power* (Baltimore: Johns Hopkins University Press, 2009). Fatovic's study of *The Federalist* and its philosophic precursors from Machiavelli to Locke discloses a clear expectation that power in the executive would be accompanied by character traits that would serve as a substitute for the rule of law in emergencies whose challenges exceeded the capacity of established constitutional norms.

24. See John Yoo, *War by Other Means: An Insider's Account of the War on Terror* (New York: Atlantic Monthly Press, 2006), 97, 113–14, 121, 122, 148, 238. Jack Goldsmith, a leading conservative lawyer and academic who served in the Department of Justice during the Bush administration, has contrasted Bush with Lincoln. Goldsmith, *Terror Presidency*, 210–15.

PART III

BUILDING THE RULE OF LAW AFTER MILITARY INTERVENTIONS

9

JUSTICE ON THE GROUND?
INTERNATIONAL CRIMINAL COURTS
AND DOMESTIC RULE OF LAW BUILDING
IN CONFLICT-AFFECTED SOCIETIES

JANE E. STROMSETH

1. INTRODUCTION

Building the rule of law after military interventions is a central pre-occupation in many parts of the world today. From Afghanistan to Iraq, from Sierra Leone to East Timor to the Balkans, and else-where, national leaders and international actors are struggling to strengthen fragile governance structures, establish genuine secu-rity, improve justice systems, and build public confidence and faith in these institutions in the midst or the aftermath of violent con-flict. As difficult as it is to build institutions crucial to the rule of law, including courts capable of functioning in ways that are pro-cedurally fair and consistent with basic human rights, convincing skeptical publics that new and reformed institutions are worthy of their trust can be even harder.

The challenge is made even greater when conflict-affected so-cieties have endured horrific atrocities that have left families and communities reeling in their wake. Mass atrocities inflict unspeak-able pain upon individuals and families and often leave a legacy of deep distrust of neighbors, state authority, and justice institu-tions. Reassuring citizens that, henceforth, such abuses will not be permitted to recur and that people will be protected from predatory state and nonstate actors alike is crucial to building any degree of public confidence in the rule of law.

The challenge, of course, is how to do this. As fragile societies struggle to consolidate peace and move forward, the issue of accountability and redress for past abuses can be divisive and difficult. Different groups and individuals may disagree quite strongly over how hard to press for justice, particularly in the face of limited resources, weak domestic justice systems, and fragile peace settlements. Some victims may demand trial and punishment of perpetrators, while others may place greater emphasis on public acknowledgment of their suffering and on reparations or some tangible form of assistance. Furthermore, in societies where impunity has reigned, where the rule of the gun has been predominant, where legal institutions have been used by particular factions to control and subordinate others and are deeply discredited and distrusted or are otherwise dysfunctional, domestic legal institutions may simply be unable to provide a credible bulwark against impunity or to deliver fair justice for atrocities. In such situations, international criminal courts increasingly have stepped in to fill the vacuum.

Over the past two decades, international criminal courts—and "hybrid" or mixed courts that combine national and international judges and lawyers—have become part of postconflict transitions in a number of countries, particularly after conflicts involving large-scale violence against civilians. The United Nations Security Council created the International Criminal Tribunal for the Former Yugoslavia (ICTY) in 1993 and the International Criminal Tribunal for Rwanda (ICTR) one year later. These courts were followed by innovative hybrid criminal courts located not in some far-off place but directly in societies recovering from conflict—in East Timor, Sierra Leone, Bosnia-Herzegovina, and Cambodia. Establishment of the International Criminal Court (ICC), whose jurisdiction took effect in 2002, added a permanent international tribunal with the potential to have an even greater long-term impact in a wider set of circumstances. These tribunals focus on investigating individuals suspected of committing international crimes—genocide, crimes against humanity, and war crimes—and on delivering justice in fair and impartial trials that accord with international standards of due process.

The international and mixed criminal courts created over the past two decades have produced significant developments internationally. These tribunals have indicted, tried, and convicted a number of high-level political and military figures—including former heads of state—for egregious international crimes, eroding the prospect of impunity for such offenses. These courts have played an indispensable fact-finding role—establishing an official record of the horrendous crimes committed, the criminal responsibilities of those involved, and the suffering of victims—a record that cannot simply be denied or overlooked in the future. These trials also have set some groundbreaking legal precedents and have played an educational role in focusing world attention on fundamental rules of international law prohibiting genocide, crimes against humanity, and war crimes. Despite these courts' limitations and challenges, their work is changing the landscape of international justice.

Far less clear, however, is the impact of these courts *on the ground* in the societies that endured the atrocities. Are the criminal trials before these tribunals influencing public understanding of and confidence in fair justice in the affected societies? Are international criminal courts—and the hybrid tribunals that combine national and international judges and lawyers—contributing in any enduring way to building domestic capacity for justice and the rule of law? These are hugely important questions because, ultimately, the key to preventing future atrocities is building domestic capacity for justice and the rule of law. Yet, despite the considerable resources and expertise devoted to these courts over the years, we still know surprisingly little about their tangible domestic effects. Thus, a crucial challenge in the years ahead will be to better understand and to strengthen the contribution of international and hybrid criminal tribunals to justice on the ground in the countries most directly affected.

But how should we even think about "justice on the ground" —what might it entail, and how can we evaluate whether progress to advance it is being made? And how concretely can tribunals do better, in very practical ways, to try to realize it? These are

the questions I will address in this essay. I take as a starting point
the agreed international law prohibiting genocide, crimes against
humanity, and war crimes and the international standards of due
process and focus on the far less examined question of the contribution of international and mixed tribunals to "justice on the
ground" and domestic Rule of Law building. In so doing, I will
draw upon and build upon my coauthored book (written with
law professors David Wippman and Rosa Brooks) titled *Can Might
Make Rights? Building the Rule of Law after Military Interventions.*[1] Our
book seeks to understand the enormous challenges that external
interveners and local reformers face in struggling to strengthen
the rule of law in conflict-ridden societies and to offer modest suggestions for what might be done better. In conceptualizing the
rule of law, our book offers a deliberately practical definition that
not only includes basic physical security and functioning legal institutions that operate in ways that are procedurally fair and consistent with fundamental human rights but also emphasizes that
building the rule of law is also a matter of cultural commitments to
and public confidence in the very idea of the rule of law.[2] This is a
theme I will also stress in this essay.

2. FROM INTERNATIONAL CRIMINAL COURTS TO JUSTICE ON THE GROUND

When international or hybrid criminal tribunals prosecute atrocity
crimes, they must, of course, focus on their core purpose of bringing individual perpetrators to justice in fair and impartial proceedings that accord with international standards of due process.
These complex and important trials inevitably require substantial
time, financial support, dedication, and expertise. Yet, seemingly
modest efforts to enhance their *domestic* Rule of Law impact potentially can make a real difference in building public understanding
and confidence that the law can be fair. After all, the people on
the ground endured the atrocities, and providing meaningful justice to them should surely be an important factor in how we evaluate the contribution of international criminal justice. Otherwise,
international and hybrid criminal trials run the risk of simply being a "spaceship" phenomenon: they arrive, do their business, and
take off, leaving a befuddled domestic population scratching their

heads and wondering what, if anything, their "visitors" had to do with the dire realities on the ground—realities that all too often include desperately underresourced national judiciaries; limited public awareness or dissemination of laws; a dearth of well-trained judges, police, prosecutors, and defense attorneys; abysmal prisons; inadequate governmental accountability or transparency; and limited public access to justice in rural areas, just to name a few recurring problems.[3] Indeed, the ultimate impact of international and hybrid courts will be uncertain if their work is completely disconnected from the challenges of strengthening the rule of law domestically in conflict-affected societies. Furthermore, if these tribunals fail to address public concerns about their work and simply ignore local perceptions about justice, they may undermine public confidence in fair justice, reinforcing cynicism and despair rather than helping to build public trust in justice and the rule of law.

The importance and urgency of these questions hit me directly when I visited Sierra Leone in the summer of 2004, just as the Special Court for Sierra Leone—the hybrid criminal court made up of both international and national judges, lawyers, and administrators—was beginning its first trial.

The Special Court's stunning new courthouse—a building whose gently curved shape echoes the graceful hills of Sierra Leone's capital city, Freetown—had just opened. Former interior minister Sam Hinga Norman and two others were in the dock. Sitting in the gallery with a full-house of Sierra Leoneans and a smattering of ex-pats, I leaned forward to hear the first anxious witness testify about the cruel atrocities he had seen and endured. But, as the day's proceedings began, several spectators in the gallery boisterously cheered support for defendant Norman, whom many viewed as a defender of the nation against rebels from the brutal Revolutionary United Front (RUF). And, during a break in the proceedings and in later conversations, many Sierra Leoneans expressed to me their frustration that others were not also on trial: what about the person who actually cut off my hand and is living right down the street?, implored one amputee. So the complicated messages about justice that people were taking away from the new court's proceedings were evident from the very start.

And what about the domestic justice system? The Special Court's sparkling new courthouse, air-conditioned buildings, and ample computer terminals stood in marked contrast to the swelteringly hot, dilapidated old Victorian structure that houses Sierra Leone's struggling national courts. The domestic Supreme Court justices with whom I met could barely contain their frustration over their lack of resources and administrative support when they compared them to those allocated to the Special Court. Lawyers and citizens alike talked to me about the lack of public confidence in the domestic justice system and the endemic problems of delay, political influence, and limited capacity. So, hard questions about how the new hybrid court might contribute to strengthening domestic legal capacity—rather than competing with it—were immediately on my mind.

In short, having arrived in Sierra Leone full of hope for the project of international criminal justice—and for the prospects, in particular, of a mixed tribunal located in the affected country—I immediately came face to face with the complicated realities on the ground. And, in reflecting on my experiences in Sierra Leone and elsewhere, I've been struck over and over again by the enormous gap between the resources and attention lavished upon the international and hybrid criminal courts themselves and the far more limited attention given to how those courts might concretely have an impact on the ongoing struggles within the affected societies to build justice systems, to strengthen the rule of law, and to deepen public confidence in the possibility of fair justice.

With this as background, I will do four things in this essay:

(1) I will explore the question of "justice on the ground"— how can we best think about this, and how might we realistically expect international and hybrid courts to make a contribution?

(2) I will look at recent experience, particularly in Sierra Leone, East Timor, and Cambodia, to better understand some of the difficult challenges in actually advancing "justice on the ground."

(3) I will examine how the arrival of the International Criminal Court is starting to have an impact on "justice on the ground," with particular reference to the ongoing situation in Uganda.

(4) I will conclude with some concrete suggestions for action and for further research, with the aim of identifying practical ways that those involved in—and interested in —international and hybrid courts can better contribute to advancing "justice on the ground."

Before launching into these questions, let me start with a note of humility about the prospects for international criminal justice. In the years since the ICTY was created, in 1993, we've learned important lessons about the complexity of international criminal justice. The first is that we need to be far more humble and realistic about the goals that international trials can be expected to accomplish. Such trials can focus on only a limited number of potential defendants, the jurisdiction of the tribunals is restricted (often for political reasons) to limited time frames that may be only a snapshot of a larger conflict, and international rhetorical support often is not matched by an equal willingness to provide resources, political support, or tangible assistance in arresting indictees. As a result, these tribunals inevitably achieve only limited and imperfect justice, and the resulting trials often leave a "justice gap" that undermines their credibility among local audiences and that may not resonate with preferred local approaches to accountability. In short, we can't simply assume that the proceedings before these courts necessarily will convey positive messages about fair justice to diverse and skeptical domestic audiences; more systematic efforts to understand and address their criticisms and to convey the value and purpose of the proceedings will be needed.

A second lesson that has become clear since 1993, moreover, is that criminal trials are only part of the picture. They often need to be supplemented by other mechanisms of postconflict accountability and justice. Truth and reconciliation commissions, for example, can provide a fuller account of a conflict and its causes and consequences, offer a greater opportunity for direct participation by victims, recommend far-reaching reforms, and may also —as in East Timor—seek to promote reconciliation and reintegration of lesser perpetrators into the community through reconciliation agreements and rituals.[4] Particularly where large numbers of perpetrators will never realistically be brought to trial and where victims struggle with poverty and urgent need on a daily basis, other mechanisms will be needed to address local concerns about justice and fairness.

A third lesson international actors have begun to learn (belatedly, I'm afraid) is to pay more attention to the goals and priorities of the domestic populations that endured atrocities and must now chart a new future. The question of how best to face the past—and what forms of accountability to pursue—is a difficult one, and different societies ultimately may have quite different goals and priorities. Within those societies, moreover, various actors and groups may disagree quite strongly over priorities. In East Timor, for example, Prime Minister and former president Xanana Gusmao has long stressed the importance of reconciliation and forward-looking social justice, whereas others (including the Commission for Reception, Truth, and Reconciliation, in its report)[5] continue to emphasize the importance of criminal prosecution of major offenders. And, of course, each country's unique circumstances and capacities will profoundly shape the possibilities and mechanisms for postconflict justice. Furthermore, although international funds and attention often flow more generously to international and hybrid accountability proceedings than to the desperate needs of national justice systems, these needs must be addressed if a stable rule of law is to take root.

If these and other lessons underscore the need for multifaceted accountability procedures, they also signal a growing concern on the part of both international and domestic actors to leave behind a continuing legacy—skills and capacities, new habits of thought and practice—when accountability proceedings conclude. But, the impact of different accountability initiatives on strengthening the domestic rule of law in war-torn societies is not straightforward. Much will depend on how accountability processes are conducted, the extent to which local perceptions of justice are altered by the proceedings, and whether those proceedings contribute in any enduring way to domestic capacity for justice.

3. JUSTICE ON THE GROUND

So let's turn now to the difficult question of "justice on the ground." How can accountability proceedings contribute to strengthening the rule of law in postconflict societies? What concrete messages about justice and what tangible impacts on struggling domestic justice systems can international and hybrid trials realistically hope to imprint? In exploring these challenging questions, I will focus on two possible contributions of these trials: first, what I call their *demonstration effects,* and, second, what I call their domestic *capacity-building effects.* Advancing justice on the ground in these ways ought to be at least part of what we look at in assessing the contribution of international criminal justice to domestic Rule of Law building. Let me elaborate each in turn.

Demonstration Effects

Criminal atrocity trials inevitably convey messages about justice to the multiple audiences who are aware of the proceedings—messages that can either build or undermine public confidence in the rule of law. Substantively, it seems to me, international and hybrid criminal trials ideally should convey three key messages:

First, *trials should convey the message that certain conduct is out of bounds and is subject to criminal law and individual accountability.* Specifically, no matter what your cause or grievance, genocide, war crimes, and crimes against humanity are unacceptable and universally condemned.

Second, *trials should make it clear that impunity for those who commit such crimes is being punctured.* Given all the constraints, impunity is far from over, but justice and accountability is possible, and those who commit these crimes—whether high or low on the totem pole —cannot presume on impunity. The possibility of trial and accountability, if not now, then in the future, exists.

Third, *trials for atrocity crimes should aim to demonstrate and to reassure people that justice can be fair.* Fair justice, of course, must include impartial procedures and due process. If trials are shams, if procedures are deeply flawed, then the proceedings will undercut the message of fair justice for universally condemned atrocities. But fair justice is not only about fair procedures. It is also about *substance:* are comparable offenses being prosecuted evenhandedly regardless of who or which groups committed them? Are high-level perpetrators as well as those who directly committed the atrocities facing justice? In short, accountability proceedings aim to demonstrate through fair trials of individual defendants that atrocities are unacceptable, condemned, and not to be repeated. They aim to substantiate concretely and to demonstrate a norm of accountability.[6]

Why are such demonstration effects important to "justice on the ground"? For very tangible reasons. For victims of atrocities and for the larger population of a society recovering from conflict, demonstrating through fair trials that impunity is being punctured for egregious crimes—even if only partially—provides a concrete example of justice that may begin to build greater public confidence in the rule of law. Most tangibly and directly, by removing individual perpetrators of atrocities from positions in which they can control and abuse others, criminal trials (and processes such as rigorous vetting) can begin to reassure the population that old patterns of almost total impunity and exploitation are no longer tolerable. This can help to break patterns of rule by fear and begin to build public confidence that justice can be fair.[7] Furthermore, procedurally fair trials underscore the importance of respect for *all* persons, including defendants accused of severe atrocities, and provide an example of fair justice to domestic populations that understandably often are skeptical of judicial processes based on bitter past experience.

Such demonstration effects are important not only to victims and perpetrators but also to the public more generally, including those who were bystanders to atrocities. By concretely showing that certain conduct is condemned and that individual accountability is possible, trials can reinforce the illegality and "*moral unacceptability*" of atrocities and help counter potential indoctrination of ordinary citizens into supporting or tolerating acts of mass violence, as Mark Drumbl argues.[8] Likewise, as the ICTY explained in the Blaskic case, among the purposes of punishment is "individual and general affirmative prevention aimed at influencing the legal awareness of the accused, the victims, their relatives, the witnesses, and the general public in order to reassure them that the legal system is being implemented and enforced."[9] Particularly in societies that have been wracked by persistent impunity and in which little confidence exists in justice or the rule of law, demonstrating through fair trials that even those with political and economic power can face accountability for egregious crimes may give citizens reason to expect (and to demand) accountability and fairer justice processes in the future.

Whether such positive demonstration effects are possible in specific postconflict societies will depend significantly, however, on whether the affected population is aware of the trials and comes to understand them as fair and legitimate, even if incomplete and imperfect, responses to the atrocities endured. The substantive issues of fairness may be especially important to local audiences: if "big fish" go free while much lesser offenders are held accountable—or, alternatively, if direct perpetrators face no justice or accountability of any kind—the proceedings may have negative, counterproductive demonstration effects. They may send a message that justice is not fair, that previous patterns of impunity are continuing, and that deep-seated grievances will not be addressed. The complete failure to pursue accountability at all can send a similar message, contributing to a continuing distrust of justice institutions and pessimism about the rule of law. In Afghanistan, for example, impunity is a persistent problem in those parts of the country where regional commanders and warlords function as a law unto themselves. Accountability for current abuses is probably of greater immediate concern for many Afghans than accountability for the past, but the two are clearly related when, in many instances, warlords who grew accustomed to operating with impunity in the past brazenly continue to do so in the present.[10]

This raises the question of deterring misconduct, which is another hoped-for benefit—or demonstration effect—of prosecuting those who commit atrocities.[11] Ideally, with respect to actual perpetrators and also others who might become involved in (or tolerate) such behavior in the future, a credible demonstration that certain conduct is unacceptable—and that impunity is no longer ensured—can begin to alter calculations of the consequences of behavior over time. When a powerful man like former president Charles Taylor of Liberia is on trial for egregious crimes, he is disempowered and sidelined—and his ability to wreak havoc in West Africa is constrained. Beyond this, other higher-ups cannot completely discount that they too might meet the same fate. Those lower on the chain might also think twice about committing atrocities.

But we need to be realistic here. Although trials can deny and prevent specific individuals from again committing atrocities, broader evidence about deterrence and dissuasion remains elusive and uncertain.[12] And, even in most cases of serious atrocities, the prospect of punishment is still minimal, and prosecution remains selective, at best. Furthermore, in truly desperate circumstances, such as in Uganda's long conflict in which rebels in the Lord's Resistance Army (LRA) forcibly recruit child soldiers and force them, by pain of death, to kill other people, it is obvious that much, much more than a few criminal trials far from the conflict zone is needed to halt impunity.

Prevention requires more than just taking steps to dissuade individuals from committing crimes by prosecuting offenders. Effective prevention over time is broader and generally requires more far-reaching initiatives. These include, among others, stopping the hemorrhaging violence, overcoming a legacy of impunity by building the rule of law—including the institutions and cultural attitudes that help reinforce new norms of behavior and new patterns of accountability—and addressing grievances and inequalities that may underlie long-standing conflicts. (I will turn to domestic capacity building in a moment). Individual accountability for atrocities, while very important, clearly is only one piece of such larger efforts at prevention.

In short, we need to acknowledge the enormous challenges of overcoming impunity and demonstrating fair justice to domestic populations in conflict-affected societies. We cannot simply presume that reassurance about fair justice inevitably will flow from holding international or hybrid trials. On the contrary, particularly given the imperfect and limited nature of international justice and the enormous challenges in achieving meaningful accountability for devastating atrocities, the tribunals must work harder to engage local populations, which are often deeply pessimistic about justice institutions as a result of prior domestic experience. Furthermore, even international trials that international leaders regard as procedurally completely fair may be viewed with skepticism by domestic audiences within the affected societies: for example, explaining why a lengthy international trial culminating in incarceration in a Swedish prison is fair justice may require considerable effort. And, while domestic disillusionment over international and hybrid trials can feed cynicism about the possibility of fair justice—there is plenty of anecdotal evidence of this—we need much better research to begin to fully understand how credible accountability proceedings might actually contribute to building public confidence and trust in justice institutions. More systematic efforts to understand the criticisms and concerns of skeptical domestic audiences—and meaningful outreach that engages honestly and fully with these concerns—are essential if tribunals hope to build rather than undermine public confidence in fair justice.

Capacity-Building Effects

Pursuing justice on the ground is not only a matter of demonstrating through fair trials that impunity is being punctured for egregious crimes. A second way that international and hybrid tribunals can influence development of the rule of law domestically is through concrete *capacity building.* Accountability proceedings should not simply be an "aside"—standing totally apart from ordinary and ongoing processes of reform. Instead, over time, accountability norms—the condemnation of brutal atrocities, the importance of fair proceedings for determining responsibility, and the need for effective and impartial procedures for resolving future disputes more generally—must become *embedded in domestic practices.* Such capacity building is vital because preventing future atrocities and building public confidence in nonviolent conflict resolution and in the rule of law will depend on the real capacity to deliver at least a semblance of fair justice in domestic justice systems.

Yet, all too often, well-resourced international tribunals and struggling domestic justice systems are two completely separate and unrelated worlds. As noted earlier, the comfortable, well-stocked, air-conditioned offices, the computers, the ample administrative staff, and the other resources available to the international and hybrid tribunals stand in stark contrast to the dilapidated, sweltering courtrooms, limited legal resources, poorly paid judges, and minimal administrative support or supplies in many domestic systems. Furthermore, expensive international and hybrid trials can compete for international funding and attention with struggling domestic justice systems, creating tensions and resentments when domestic needs are shortchanged. In Rwanda, for instance, the government and ordinary citizens alike resent the millions of dollars spent on the international tribunal in Arusha, Tanzania, while Rwanda's own domestic legal system languishes desperately in need of aid. But, these challenges argue all the more for thinking systematically and creatively from the start about how international tribunals can advance their fundamental goal of justice through fair trials while *also* contributing, concretely and more substantially, to justice on the ground.

If international and hybrid courts aim to have any lasting impact in advancing justice on the ground, they should give greater attention to how they can assist domestic capacity building in two crucial ways. First, these courts can make tangible, even if modest, contributions to the domestic justice systems in the societies affected by the atrocities being prosecuted. This can be called the *supply side* of justice on the ground. International and hybrid criminal courts typically enjoy a degree of international support that domestic, postconflict justice systems can only dream of. These international resources understandably are focused on the fundamental task of prosecuting defendants in fair trials that meet international standards of justice. But there are opportunities for *synergies*—that is, for international and hybrid tribunals to contribute concretely to domestic legal capacity while doing their own important work to advance justice.

The possibilities for such synergies will vary, of course, depending on the type of tribunal and the circumstances in the affected country. Hybrid courts located in the country that survived the atrocities may be most able to directly build domestic capacity by increasing the skills and experience of local legal professionals involved in the court's work—such as judges, prosecutors, defense counsel, administrators, and investigators—at least if the national participants ultimately remain in the country to contribute to the domestic system. Hybrids can have additional impacts on the domestic justice system, as well—for instance, by offering educational workshops for national judges and lawyers, training investigators in witness protection, and so forth. But, realizing these benefits does not happen automatically; it requires astute planning, resources, and sensitivity to the many practical and political challenges that can arise when a tribunal locates directly in the country most affected by the atrocities.[13] Even when trials are held before the ICC in The Hague, valuable opportunities to contribute to domestic capacity building still exist, for example through workshops, discussions, and outreach (including via radio) aimed at domestic jurists, lawyers, civil society leaders, and the general population. Whatever particular form this assistance takes, those involved should look for synergies that will help strengthen domestic capacity for justice on the ground in enduring ways.

A second kind of domestic capacity building is also crucially important, and that is educating and empowering civil society—individuals and groups—to expect justice and accountability from legal and political institutions. We can call this the *demand side* of justice on the ground. Building the rule of law is as much about strengthening public demand for and confidence in justice as it is about building better legal institutions. If the people have little awareness of their rights or confidence or belief in a developing justice system, they are unlikely to turn to the system to resolve disputes or to give any degree of loyalty to the ongoing project of building the rule of law.[14]

By putting legal accountability for international crimes on the national agenda, criminal trials (as well as other accountability mechanisms) can be an important focal point for public engagement on vital questions of justice. Thoughtful public outreach by tribunal staff can increase public understanding of the proceedings and issues before the court; local and international nongovernmental organizations (NGOs) can magnify these effects by working to inform and empower ordinary citizens about the importance of accountability and fair justice and by keeping pressure on postconflict governments to abide by fundamental norms of international law prohibiting war crimes, genocide, and crimes against humanity. By engaging with local NGOs that work on issues of justice and accountability, by encouraging discussions at schools and via radio, and by reaching out to populations that might otherwise have limited access to justice and political power, tribunals can have *empowering ripple effects* by strengthening public demand for justice in ways that may continue long after a tribunal's work is over.

The political scientist Beth Simmons, in her important new book, *Mobilizing for Human Rights: International Law in Domestic Politics*,[15] shows how ratifying human rights treaties can change the dynamics of domestic politics by placing compliance with international norms on the domestic agenda of political leaders and by providing a basis for mobilizing civil society in support of compliance. Citizens are most likely to become engaged when they have reason to believe that mobilizing around rights may concretely improve their situation. Similar dynamics may be possible when war-ravaged countries commit themselves, even if imperfectly, to fair trials for international atrocity crimes.

Yet, trials held far from the people most affected by atrocities inevitably will have a difficult time advancing justice on the ground in the ways I've described, at least in the absence of systematic domestic outreach or direct capacity-building efforts. Even if they prosecute and thereby remove major perpetrators from domestic power structures, these trials must also be seen domestically to be doing justice if they are to have positive demonstration effects on the ground. (The growing impact of the ICC—and its ability to prod and catalyze domestic trials—is discussed later, in part 6 of this chapter). Hybrid tribunals located in the affected country —with strong domestic participation and outreach—have some built-in advantages in leaving a tangible legacy on the ground.[16] Yet, they too have faced obstacles in demonstrating that impunity for international crimes is being punctured and that justice can be fair, or in strengthening domestic capacity for justice. Examining the experiences in several different postconflict societies can help to illuminate some of the many practical difficulties in actually advancing justice on the ground.

4. THE RECORD ON THE GROUND: DEMONSTRATING FAIR JUSTICE?

Even hybrid tribunals established in countries that have lived through atrocities have confronted many challenges in building public confidence in fair justice or in contributing to domestic capacity. Looking at the diverse experiences in Sierra Leone, East Timor, and Cambodia shows some of the hardest challenges, as well as some promising practices.[17]

a. Sierra Leone's Special Court

Sierra Leone endured a violent, decade-long civil war, in which civilians suffered enormously: the war claimed the lives of an estimated 75,000 people and displaced a third of the country's population and was marked by brutal crimes against humanity and war crimes, including forced recruitment of child soldiers, amputations, summary executions, rapes, abduction of women into "forced marriages," terrorizing the civilian population, and other offenses.

In 2002, once peace was restored after a British-led military intervention, the government of Sierra Leone and the United Nations agreed to create the Special Court for Sierra Leone. The court was given jurisdiction to try those who bear "the greatest responsibility for violations of international humanitarian law" committed in Sierra Leone since November 30, 1996.

Sierra Leone's Special Court was a deliberate effort to design a tribunal that could overcome some of the limitations of purely international or purely domestic accountability trials. The court is a "hybrid" tribunal whose four components—judicial chambers, office of the prosecutor, defense office, and registry—include an interesting blend of both international and Sierra Leonean staff.

Located in Sierra Leone's capital, Freetown, the Special Court is less distant, physically and psychologically, from the people of the country than an international tribunal located far away would be. The participation of local judges, lawyers, and other Sierra Leonean nationals (such as the dynamic group of outreach officers, who are all Sierra Leonean) has helped to give the tribunal greater local legitimacy, giving citizens of Sierra Leone a greater stake and sense of ownership. As a result, the court has the potential to demonstrate accountability in a way that resonates effectively with local populations.

Second, locating the court in Sierra Leone—and including national participation in its work at all levels—provides a better opportunity for building capacity and leaving behind a tangible contribution to the national justice system, including resources, facilities, and training. It also facilitates extensive outreach efforts designed to deepen public understanding of the tribunal's work, producing a more direct impact on the local population.

International involvement in the court has important benefits, as well. Supported by the UN and contributions from many states, the Special Court has substantially greater resources and credibility than the country's struggling domestic justice system, which suffers from problems such as low public confidence, and corruption. International participation and resources help ensure that the Special Court's proceedings are fair and satisfy international standards of due process.

Demonstration Effects: Puncturing Impunity

By indicting those who bear the greatest responsibility for orchestrating the brutal conflict in Sierra Leone, the tribunal has helped to disempower and prevent them from again committing such atrocities. Sierra Leoneans agree to a remarkable extent on who these people are. They put former Liberian president Charles Taylor at the top of the list, followed by two others: RUF commander Foday Sankoh and General Sam Bockarie. All were indicted, but only Taylor is still alive to stand trial. (Sankoh died of natural causes in custody; Bockarie was murdered in Liberia along with his family, allegedly on Taylor's orders.)[18]

The trial of Charles Taylor before a panel of the Special Court (sitting in The Hague) is a very big deal in demonstrating that even leaders at the highest level are not above the law. Taylor is being tried on eleven counts of crimes against humanity, war crimes, and other serious violations of international humanitarian law, including terrorizing the civilian population, murder, rape, sexual slavery, and use of child soldiers. Throughout Sierra Leone, people overwhelmingly support prosecuting him before the Special Court. His trial is a dramatic demonstration of the puncturing of impunity—that even "big men" are not above facing justice.

Indeed, hundreds of Sierra Leonean citizens gathered in the hills of Freetown near the Special Court to witness the dramatic moment in March 2006 when Charles Taylor was finally taken into custody and flown into Freetown. Security concerns about trying Taylor in the region led the Special Court and the government of Sierra Leone ultimately to request that his trial be held at The Hague, and Taylor was transferred there in June 2006, where he is currently on trial. Certainly, many Sierra Leoneans are disappointed that he is not being tried in the country, making the proceedings less accessible to the local population.[19] And the physical distance has put some limitations on possibilities for direct outreach to the local population. But the Special Court's public affairs and outreach offices have taken measures to relay the proceedings and summaries of the proceedings to the people in various ways.

Demonstration Effects: Reassurance about Fair Justice?

Without question, the Special Court has faced some distinct challenges. To demonstrate meaningful accountability and fair justice for atrocities to the people of Sierra Leone, the court's proceedings must be widely viewed as legitimate—both in terms of their substance (who is being prosecuted for what offenses) and in terms of process. In this respect, the fact that the prosecution indicted and the court has tried and convicted leaders from all the major groups in Sierra Leone's conflict—the Revolutionary United Front (RUF), the Armed Forces Revolutionary Council (AFRC), and the Civilian Defense Forces (CDF)—has been important in demonstrating that no one is above the law and in avoiding the perception of "victor's justice." Even so, there are several difficult issues that have complicated the perceived legitimacy of the trials among the Sierra Leonean population.

First, many Sierra Leoneans express frustration that specific individuals who did the actual chopping, raping, and killing remain free. As one amputee put it during a town hall meeting I attended in Sierra Leone: "the person who chopped off my hand lives down the street; if there is no justice, my children may seek vengeance." There are an estimated 35,000 or so such perpetrators who are very unlikely ever to face justice in the domestic justice system. When pressed—as they often are—by victims who ask why the person who chopped off their hand is not being prosecuted, the Special Court's outreach staff discusses the principle of command responsibility to explain that somebody is answering for the crime. And, while Sierra Leoneans understand that the court's mandate is to try those "most responsible," there remains frustration that lower-level offenders are not facing any accountability, as well.

Second, the trial of CDF leader and former interior minister Sam Hinga Norman generated controversy, at least initially: many regarded him as a hero who acted to defend Sierra Leone from the RUF, and the court's outreach staff had to work hard to explain that he was being tried for serious crimes in violation of international law—that, regardless of one's cause, there are clear limits on how one can fight. Outreach staff also stressed that prosecution of Norman and two other CDF defendants showed that the Special Court was not a court controlled by the government. Norman ultimately died of natural causes before his trial concluded, and the Special Court's original chief prosecutor, David Crane, believes that the strong evidence against Norman ultimately showed Sierra Leoneans that Norman was an "offender" against the nation, rather than its defender.[20]

But the sentencing proceedings of Norman's two codefendants in October 2007 highlighted the sensitivity that still surrounds the CDF trial. The Sierra Leonean judge on the CDF trial panel, Judge Thompson, in a troubling opinion, ruled that the "necessity defense" completely absolved the CDF defendants of the many atrocities of which they were accused because they were acting to defend the nation. The trial panel majority, in contrast, convicted the defendants of multiple counts of war crimes, which included "killings and other atrocities against unarmed civilians . . . including children fleeing for their lives and for safety from the bloody exchanges of enemy fire, and further, that these civilian captives or fugitives, were unarmed and were not in the least, participating in hostilities."[21] Yet, the trial panel sentenced the defendants to only six and eight years, respectively, concluding that punishment should be mitigated by the fact that the defendants' forces "defeated and prevailed over the rebellion of the AFRC that ousted the legitimate Government [and] contributed immensely to re-establishing the rule of law in this Country where criminality, anarchy and lawlessness . . . had become the order of the day."[22] The prosecution appealed this sentencing ruling, and the appeals chamber increased the sentences of the two CDF defendants to fifteen and twenty years, respectively. The three AFRC defendants, in contrast, were sentenced to forty-five to fifty years. The three RUF defendants were sentenced to twenty-five, forty, and fifty-two years, respectively.

Outreach: Demonstrating Accountability and Fair Justice

In confronting the many challenging issues that have arisen, one of the most impressive features of the Special Court's work has been its innovative and dynamic outreach program to the citizens of Sierra Leone. A talented staff of Sierra Leonean outreach officers travels regularly throughout the country to discuss the work of the court, with the explicit goal of "promot[ing] understanding of the Special Court and respect for human rights and the rule of law in Sierra Leone."[23] With ten district offices, this substantial outreach program has been vital in engaging the Sierra Leonean people in the work of the court and stands in contrast to the lack of systematic outreach in other postconflict contexts.

In community town hall meetings and focused workshops around the country, outreach officers aim to demonstrate and illustrate, using the actual proceedings before the court, that "law can and should be fair, that no one is above the law, and ultimately that the rule of law is more powerful than the rule of the gun."[24] The court's outreach officers work hard, for example, to explain what "fair justice" looks like. A prosecution and defense before an impartial tribunal is an important concept to convey to a population deeply skeptical of the fairness of justice systems and inclined, from bitter experience, to believe that people are simply "on the take." The outreach staff also uses the concrete cases before the Special Court to illustrate key principles of law and justice. These lively, wide-ranging discussions—led by dynamic Sierra Leonean outreach officers—often are not easy, but they do wrestle forthrightly with difficult challenges and public questions concerning fair justice and accountability.

There is no doubt that the Special Court's ambitious outreach efforts have had an impact in building public awareness of the court's work. In a society where travel to rural areas is difficult and access to media is limited, the outreach staff has engaged the population, creatively and thoughtfully, on critically important issues of justice and accountability. An early opinion poll indicated that significant majorities were aware of the court and viewed its work positively.[25] As the three combined trials of RUF, CDF, and AFRC leaders took place and as the important trial of Charles Taylor continues, the Special Court's public affairs office has produced weekly audio summaries highlighting critical developments in the proceedings, which are widely broadcast over the radio throughout Sierra Leone.

The outreach and public affairs efforts have not been immune

from criticism, however. Some members of the defense staff at
the Special Court have expressed frustration that they have not
had more opportunity to engage in outreach, particularly after
the early efforts by the prosecution.[26] (Recently, however, defense
counsel for Charles Taylor held an outreach session in Sierra Leone.) The weekly radio broadcasts of trial proceedings have not
been as frequent as some observers would like. And the ability of
most Sierra Leoneans to actually attend Special Court proceedings in the capital was limited, despite court-sponsored programs
to bring groups of citizens to Freetown to attend the trials.[27] Furthermore, a number of studies offer a more mixed and critical
account of the outreach program.[28] As outreach efforts continue,
additional survey research hopefully will enable further analysis of public perceptions of the court and its work, and more research is needed to assess the longer-term impact of the outreach
program.[29]

b. Mixed Demonstration Effects in East Timor

Meanwhile, in East Timor (now Timor-Leste), the hybrid Special
Panels for Serious Crimes had a much harder time demonstrating
fair accountability, in large part because neither political support
nor resources (international or domestic) for East Timor's hybrid
tribunal were as forthcoming as many originally hoped.

An independent country since May 2002, East Timor had chafed
under Indonesian occupation since the mid-1970s. In the period
surrounding East Timor's historic referendum for independence,
in 1999, militias operating with the aid and support of the Indonesian army committed severe atrocities against Timorese independence supporters: murders, rapes, looting, burning. The UN, with
Indonesia's reluctant consent, authorized an international military force, led by Australia, which helped restore stability to East
Timor, and this was followed by a UN Transitional Administration
that helped East Timor prepare for and ultimately make the transition to independent statehood.

Key states and UN leaders—involved in delicate negotiations
with Indonesia to secure its consent to the military intervention
—opted not to establish an international tribunal but instead
pressed Indonesia to bring those responsible to justice domesti-

cally. Within East Timor itself, the UN established the Special Panels for Serious Crimes—special hybrid judicial panels within the Dili District Court consisting of two international judges and one Timorese judge—to try cases of crimes against humanity, war crimes, and other atrocities. The UN also established the Serious Crimes Unit, a UN-funded prosecutorial and investigative office for serious crimes.

The international support for the hybrid panels was always lukewarm. As a result, the Special Panels faced chronic shortages of administrative, legal, and linguistic support from the beginning, and support for the defense counsel was especially limited. Some improvements occurred over time, but a shortage of resources, support personnel, and translators continued to hamper the tribunal which concluded its last trials in 2005, with appeals continuing through 2006. Also, the UN Security Council decided to shut down the panels when the UN mission in East Timor ended, even though many suspects had never been investigated or tried. In the end, the UN-funded Serious Crimes Unit was able to investigate fewer "than half of the estimated 1,450 murders committed in 1999."[30]

Substantively, the hybrid tribunal's impact in terms of demonstrating the puncturing of impunity and fair justice has been ambiguous, at best. The tribunal did try a significant number of individuals for crimes against humanity and other offenses in proceedings that an international commission of experts concluded generally accorded with international standards.[31] The Serious Crimes Unit also issued many indictments, including against high-level Indonesian military officials.[32] However, the vast majority of the more than three hundred accused reside in Indonesia, and they are unlikely ever to be extradited to East Timor for trial or credibly tried in Indonesia, absent substantial international pressure, which has not been forthcoming, particularly since 9/11 and international interest in counterterrorism cooperation with Indonesia.

The net result is that East Timor's tribunal tried only mid- and lower-level indictees, mostly Timorese ex-militia members involved in the violence surrounding the referendum, but did not reach the higher-level suspects in Indonesia. This sent a very mixed message about accountability to Timorese citizens when those at the top never face justice.

Furthermore, within Indonesia, there has been no meaningful accountability for the atrocities committed in East Timor. On the contrary, in August 2004, an Indonesian court overturned the convictions of four Indonesian security officials previously found guilty of crimes against humanity in the violence in East Timor.[33] These acquittals mean that no Indonesian security officials are serving time for the horrific violence perpetrated against the East Timorese in the period surrounding its referendum.[34] The only individual convicted and serving time in Indonesia for these offenses, Eurico Guterres, a former Timorese pro-Indonesian militia leader, served less than two years of his ten-year sentence before he was pardoned in Indonesia and released.

The mixed results of East Timor's Special Panels for Serious Crimes reflect the broader ambivalence of UN officials, major governments, and Timorese leaders themselves about pressing Indonesia too hard. Other goals—consolidating independence, forging political and economic ties, resolving outstanding border issues, counterterrorism cooperation—have consistently taken higher priority. East Timor's first president and now Prime Minister Xanana Gusmao places a greater emphasis on forward-looking reconciliation, on social and economic justice, and on building a strong relationship with Indonesia than on seeking judicial accountability for the 1999 atrocities.[35] Former foreign minister and now President Jose Ramos-Horta emphasizes that "independence is a form of justice."[36] This is an important point from someone who, along with Gusmao and many others, devoted his career to East Timor's long and historic struggle. Independence for the Timorese people does provide tangible vindication for their struggle and their suffering. Given how closely East Timor's fate is tied to that of Indonesia, and taking into account the broader international unwillingness to pressure Jakarta, the path chosen by East Timor's leaders is understandable. Nevertheless, some victims and civil society organizations have been deeply disappointed about the limited accountability for the 1999 atrocities and, more broadly, for atrocities throughout the long period of Indonesian occupation—disappointment that may fester unless more is done to seek meaningful accountability.[37]

In many respects, East Timor's Commission for Reception, Truth, and Reconciliation (CAVR) probably had a more far-reaching domestic impact, particularly through its innovative community reconciliation process.[38] Under this process, lower-level offenders could acknowledge what they had done, make a public apology, and enter into a community reconciliation agreement before a community-based panel within their local communities. This process probably had a more significant impact in bringing a sense of justice processes to remote areas of East Timor, particularly because the Special Panels for Serious Crimes (unlike Sierra Leone's Special Court) engaged in very little outreach to the population.[39] Though not without flaws, the commission's reconciliation procedures helped integrate individuals back into their communities, and the commission's deliberate effort to involve women and young people alongside traditional community leaders in the community-based panels helped cultivate some potential new leaders. But, many Timorese victims supported the community-based reconciliation process in part because they expected that more serious offenders would be brought to justice before the Special Panels.[40] Yet, as mentioned earlier, many serious offenders have never even been investigated.

Today, in East Timor, public concern about impunity for the violence that wracked the country in 2006–2007 and also more recently is on the minds of many, probably even more urgently. And public concern about the ability of East Timor's domestic justice system to respond effectively to outbreaks of violence and crime remains real. More needs to be done on the "soft side" of strengthening the rule of law—that is, to educate and inform police, community leaders, and citizens alike about the law, including the seventy-two-hour detention law, East Timor's penal procedure code, and so on. The public needs to be aware of the legal mechanisms that are available to deal with the very real problems of crime and violence. If a sense of impunity grows in East Timor, it may be a substantial obstacle to building trust in the rule of law and in governmental authority more generally.

c. Cambodia's Mixed Tribunal: Challenges of Demonstrating Fair Justice

Three decades after Khmer Rouge extremism and brutality left an estimated 1.7 million Cambodians dead, the Extraordinary Chambers in the Courts of Cambodia (ECCC) began its first trial.[41]

Kaing Guek Eav ("Duch"), head of the infamous Khmer Rouge prison and torture center known as Tuol Sleng, or S-21, was the first defendant to be prosecuted before the ECCC, a mixed tribunal that combines Cambodian and international judges, prosecutors, administrators, defense counsel, and other staff. The Khmer Rouge leader, Pol Pot, died long ago. Four other defendants await trial before the ECCC: Ieng Sary, former minister of foreign affairs; Nuon Chea, who held various high-ranking positions in the Communist Party of Kampuchea; Khieu Samphan, former head of state; and Ieng Thirith, former minister of social affairs. All four were members of the Khmer Rouge Central Committee.

The Cambodia tribunal has never fully overcome the contentious issues that delayed its formation. Created pursuant to a 2003 framework agreement between Cambodia and the United Nations, the ECCC took ten years to negotiate—a process in which the Cambodian side stressed issues of sovereignty and sought maximum Cambodian control and in which the UN sought to ensure an impartial tribunal that would meet international standards of justice. The mistrust that plagued negotiations is reflected in the structure of the court itself, which consists of "two independently managed" and funded units: "a national, or Cambodian, side and an international, or UN, side."[42] The Cambodian government of Hun Sen sought and obtained a tribunal structure with a majority of Cambodian judges on the Pre-Trial, Trial, and Appeal (or Supreme Court) Chambers.[43] Co-prosecutors (one Cambodian and one international) must both agree for a case to go forward. Prime Minister Hun Sen has made very clear that he does not want to see the number of defendants increase beyond the current five. The international co-prosecutor has sought to move forward to indict six additional individuals, but the Cambodian co-prosecutor has objected on political grounds similar to those proffered by the government: that additional indictments could be destabilizing by costing too much, taking too long, and violating the spirit of the court, which, she contended, envisioned "only a small number of trials."[44] Beyond these disagreements and other tensions, unresolved allegations that some court employees on the Cambodian side were forced to pay bribes to secure their jobs—allegations denied on the Cambodian side—raised concerns about the institution's independence and caused some donors to freeze their funding of the tribunal.[45]

Still, as the Duch trial moved forward, it commanded enormous public interest in Cambodia, providing a vital opportunity to build a public record of the egregious crimes committed at S-21, where an estimated 15,000 Cambodians were killed. Duch was accused and subsequently convicted of war crimes and crimes against humanity, including murder and torture, committed while he headed the notorious prison, and former S-21 prisoners testified, in graphic detail, about the cruel torture he ordered and engaged in himself.[46] Duch's trial appears to have been cathartic for many but also at times a frustrating experience. For example, although Duch apologized and accepted responsibility at the beginning of the trial for many of the crimes of which he was accused, as the proceedings continued, the level of culpability Duch admitted to became "more and more nuanced as he distanc[ed] himself from the worst brutality of the regime and plac[ed] himself within a chain of command where disobedience often meant death."[47] Duch's French co-counsel urged the court to give him a mitigated sentence, but, in a surprising close to his defense, Duch's Cambodian defense attorney argued that he should be acquitted and released on the grounds that the tribunal has no jurisdiction over him because of his relatively low level in the Khmer Rouge power structure.[48] Duch himself apologized for the many deaths at S-21 but nevertheless asked the court to release him—a surprising turn in the case that particularly shocked and troubled victims participating as civil parties in the proceedings.[49] Ultimately, in July 2010, the ECCC Trial Chamber convicted Duch of war crimes and crimes against humanity and sentenced him to thirty-five years imprisonment, reduced to nineteen years in part for time served—a sentence that survivors criticized as far too short in light of the seriousness of his crimes.[50] Although Duch's sentence evoked controversy and anguish, his conviction is a significant milestone for Cambodia, representing the first time a significant Khmer Rouge official has been held legally accountable for the atrocities of the Khmer Rouge era in a credible court proceeding.

The Duch trial before the ECCC stimulated considerable public interest in the Court, and support for the tribunal's role in bringing

Khmer Rouge leaders to justice appears to be quite strong. According to recent survey research, significant majorities in Cambodia indicate that they support prosecution of Khmer Rouge leaders, with older Cambodians who lived through that period voicing greater desire for retributive justice than those who never experienced directly the Khmer Rouge's harsh and terrifying policies.[51] Yet, approximately a third of those surveyed expressed concerns about the court's independence, likely informed by widespread public mistrust of the domestic justice system, where political influence and bribery are common.[52] Some pro-court observers hold out the hope that the hybrid tribunal may set an example of judicial independence that could have broader implications for domestic justice. Indeed, some experts contend that Hun Sen's government, accustomed to political influence over the courts, is concerned about exactly this issue.[53]

Outreach to the Cambodian public about the ECCC's proceedings has been a mixed story thus far and has been heavily reliant upon NGOs.[54] On the positive side, an array of local NGOs is engaging in an impressive range of educational activities focused on the tribunal and the many issues of history, memory, justice, and accountability raised by its proceedings. For example, experienced local NGOs are conducting initiatives such as "train the trainer programs" that educate students, teachers, community leaders, elders, and others about the history of the Khmer Rouge and about the ECCC's jurisdiction and process and then support participants' travel to villages across Cambodia to discuss the court and justice issues with local villagers. Cambodian NGOs also hold public forums and dialogues with Cambodian citizens; these meetings often include films about the Khmer Rouge period and about the ECCC, and discussion of topics include the purpose of the court, victim participation, and healing.[55] Furthermore, the tribunal itself has a unit specifically empowered to reach out to victims, who have the opportunity to participate in the court's proceedings as civil parties. In addition, international NGOs have helped fund and support activities such as weekly video updates on the tribunal proceedings, which are broadcast on local TV, and wide-ranging radio call-in programs that discuss the ECCC, as well as broader topics relating to justice and legal issues.

Less positively, the ECCC's own outreach and public affairs office has not been as active in crafting an outreach strategy of its own as that in Sierra Leone, nor has it deployed as systematically around the country to engage in the kinds of intensive dialogue that distinguished the work of Sierra Leone's district outreach staff. Observers close to the ground also remark on the need for the ECCC's outreach office to be more responsive to public and NGO reactions to publications and other outreach tools developed by the office thus far and the need to develop a more coordinated interface with the many NGOs involved in various forms of outreach. The heavy reliance on numerous NGOs as the primary agents of outreach perhaps has led to some confusion on the part of the population, given the wide variety of activities these NGOs are undertaking; yet, this major NGO role is probably inevitable and desirable given the very real tensions between the Cambodian and the international sides of the tribunal that have marked the court from the start.

Yet despite tensions surrounding the ECCC, the court's very existence has stimulated an innovative array of activities that probably is having some empowering ripple effects within Cambodian society. When most of Cambodia's population never experienced the Khmer Rouge reign, the trials and related outreach are conveying valuable education about this historical period. And the focus on justice, education about due process, and exposure to ideals of legal accountability are potentially nurturing some demand-side capacity building among the Cambodian populace. What remains unclear is how the outcome of the Duch trial and the subsequent trials will shape public confidence in fair justice and whether the outreach surrounding the tribunal's work will have any enduring impact on public expectations and demand for better justice and accountability from Cambodia's own legal and political institutions. This brings us directly to the question of capacity building.

5. CAPACITY-BUILDING EFFECTS IN SIERRA LEONE, EAST TIMOR, AND CAMBODIA: STRENGTHENING DOMESTIC JUSTICE?

What does the record of these hybrid courts thus far suggest about their potential to contribute to domestic justice systems? On the capacity-building front, the hybrid tribunals in Sierra Leone and in

East Timor have both made some useful contributions, although much more certainly could have been done in both situations. In Cambodia, on the other hand, the prospects for positive spillover impacts on the domestic justice system are as yet uncertain.

Clearly, Sierra Leone's mixed tribunal has provided some genuine opportunities for "supply side" capacity building. The Sierra Leoneans who have worked at the Special Court as prosecutors, investigators, defense counsel, judges, administrators, outreach officers, and other staff have learned a great deal about international humanitarian law and its basic principles, about the conduct of fair trials, and about substantive issues in their specific areas of responsibility. Interactions between international and national staff have been a valuable two-way street of mutual learning—as the international investigators who have worked hand in hand with their Sierra Leonean counterparts are the first to attest. Even so, two issues have festered. The near-term challenge has been a competition for people and resources. When talented local personnel (such as court administrators) opt to work in the Special Court, they are not available for the domestic system, which is widely viewed as needing substantial reform and greater resources. And the longer-term issue is how many of the local judges, prosecutors, defense counsel, investigators, and other court staff serving at the Special Court actually will remain in Sierra Leone after the court completes its work—and consequently use their valuable skills in the national justice system.

Even in the face of these challenges, the Special Court has contributed expertise and training to Sierra Leone's domestic justice system. International investigators at the Special Court, for instance, have trained a number of Sierra Leonean police officers in witness management and protection—a critical issue given the long-term dangers that witnesses take on in coming forward to testify before the Special Court. A number of the court's judges and other legal professionals have lectured on law reform and related topics at local universities and bar associations. More generally, the Special Court has worked with the Sierra Leone Bar Association and with various organizations, both domestic and international, to identify and develop projects aimed at "helping to rebuild a devastated judiciary."[56] Through its Legacy Working Group, the

Special Court has worked to identify and carry out a number of projects designed to have a lasting effect.[57]

In East Timor, the capacity-building impact of the hybrid tribunal has been more positive than its very mixed demonstration effects. For one thing, the Special Panels for Serious Crimes were established as a part of the domestic court system in Dili. Thus, because Timorese judges who served on the hybrid trial and appellate panels were already part of the domestic justice system and (in most cases) continued to serve as judges, their experience on the Special Panels—in trial procedures, opinion drafting, and so forth—was of direct benefit to the national courts. Several conscientious Timorese judges who ably served on the trial and appellate Special Panels are continuing to make important contributions as judges in the national system today. In addition, East Timor's deputy prosecutor general in the domestic justice system learned valuable skills when he served as a prosecutor with the Serious Crimes Unit. Several Timorese who worked as translators at the Special Panels have also gone on to valuable employment with an NGO working on rule of law development in East Timor.

At the same time, the Special Panels could have done quite a bit more to facilitate mutual learning between international and national judges and lawyers working at the court and in the prosecution and defense units. On the prosecution side, few Timorese were integrated into top positions in the serious crimes prosecutorial office. On the defense side, the capacity building was even more limited. Internationals largely handled the defense in serious crimes cases, while providing some training for Timorese public defenders.[58] In short, although the hybrid arrangement enabled some very important local capacity building to occur, the potential offered by East Timor's hybrid arrangement was realized only partially.

What, then, about Cambodia? There, the challenges of supply-side capacity building are particularly acute because of issues of political control and corruption in the domestic court system. The Cambodian justice system faces problems such as government influence on judges, lack of funding, low remuneration, and limited capacity. Public confidence in the judiciary is extremely low, and Cambodians report being deterred from using the courts

because of the expense involved (82%) and because of demands
for bribes by judges (82%) or the police (77%).[59] Some outside
observers believe that the key issue is not so much lack of training
or knowledge as the government's refusal to let judges do their
jobs independently.[60] If political pressure and control continues to
pervade the domestic system, even valuable training provided to
Cambodian judges, prosecutors, and defense attorneys involved in
the work of the ECCC may not have meaningful spillover effects.
(The ECCC and particularly NGOs have provided skills training to
members of the prosecutor's office, to Cambodian lawyers working as defense counsel before the ECCC, and to tribunal judges.)
Yet, the possibility exists that if the ECCC itself functions independently and credibly in rendering its judgments, it can serve as an
example of impartial justice and accountability that provides a
more promising alternative model to domestic jurists and the public more broadly. The full verdict on the court's impact is still to be
determined.

Capacity Building through Civil Society Empowerment

Experience with *demand-side* capacity building—civil society empowerment that strengthens public demand for fair justice—has
varied considerably in different postconflict societies. In East
Timor, the Special Panels for Serious Crimes did not have a major outreach program to the country's population; rather, it was
the Commission on Reception, Truth, and Reconciliation that engaged the population around the country most directly.[61] In addition, international support helped build the Judicial System Monitoring Programme, an NGO that monitored proceedings before
East Timor's hybrid war crimes tribunal and before its truth and
reconciliation commission and that continues to play a valuable
role today by evaluating the national justice system, providing information to the wider public, and recommending reforms in the
country's legal and political system. In Cambodia, it is NGOs that
have played the most active role in demand-side capacity building,
as discussed earlier. In Sierra Leone, in contrast, the Special Court
developed its own extensive and far-reaching outreach program
—largely funded by voluntary contributions and led by a talented
Sierra Leonean, Binta Mansaray, and her capable team of local dis-

trict officers who traversed the country and engaged in lively town hall meetings in the local dialects.[62]

In addition to building public awareness about the court's work through such efforts, the Special Court for Sierra Leone engaged in active partnership and dialogue with NGOs interested in the court's work and in accountability more broadly. To this end, the tribunal established the Special Court Interactive Forum—an ongoing dialogue, approximately once a month, between civil society organizations and court personnel, who meet to discuss the work of the court and how it can be improved but who also network on related accountability and human rights issues. Also, the Special Court's outreach office helped establish "Accountability Now Clubs" across the country, which invite university-age students to discuss issues of accountability, justice, human rights, and good governance, with the expectation that club members will visit secondary and elementary schools to address these issues and communicate the critical importance of accountability—past, present, and future.[63]

In the end, whether the Special Court's capacity-building efforts will make a lasting and sustainable impact will depend on longer-term reforms within Sierra Leone. The jury is still out on this, and the challenges are immense. Still, the degree of outreach and serious public dialogue about accountability that the Special Court has inspired is impressive. But the enormous challenge of institutionalizing principles of accountability—including strengthening a weak and underresourced domestic justice system and addressing deep and long-standing problems of weak capacity and governance—ultimately will determine how sustainable these efforts prove to be.

6. The International Criminal Court and Justice on the Ground

No account of the domestic impact of international tribunals would be complete without discussion of the International Criminal Court (ICC), whose jurisdiction took effect in July 2002.[64] The ICC is already having significant implications for "justice on the ground" in a number of countries. How should we assess its impact?

The ICC shares many of the goals of previous tribunals, such as the ICTY and ICTR: seeking justice by holding major perpetrators of international crimes accountable in accordance with international standards of due process; deterring atrocities by holding out the prospect of punishment for violations; and building a truthful record of crimes, among other goals. Its ambitious overarching goal, as stated in the preamble of the Rome Statute of the ICC, is to "end impunity."

Yet, the ICC has a number of advantages over the earlier ad hoc tribunals. Its permanence and its broader temporal and geographic jurisdiction give it a potentially greater deterrent impact over time (at least as more states become parties), and it should be able to build a body of precedents over a longer time period that can serve as clear standards for the future.

The ICC also is structured in a way that should enable it to promote "justice on the ground" by encouraging responsible domestic investigations and prosecutions. In contrast to the ICTY and ICTR, the ICC is a court deliberately designed to be complementary to and to give primacy to national jurisdiction. The ICC itself has jurisdiction to prosecute genocide, crimes against humanity, and war crimes only if countries that otherwise have jurisdiction are "unwilling or unable" "genuinely" to investigate or prosecute.[65] This arrangement—called "complementarity"—gives states that are directly affected by atrocities the first opportunity to take action.[66] Meanwhile, the possibility of ICC jurisdiction can serve as a prod to domestic authorities to take credible action to investigate and prosecute international crimes, with the ICC as a backstop if domestic action falls short.

Indeed, if the ICC actually serves to encourage responsible domestic action, the court may help to combat impunity even if it ultimately tries only a limited number of cases itself. In some instances, "there are strong indications that the ICC . . . is altering incentives at the national level and catalyzing reform efforts."[67] But, the degree to which the ICC can serve as an effective prod to constructive domestic action in difficult postconflict and transitional settings is proving to be a very complicated matter. Its impact will depend, in substantial part, on the conduct of the ICC and its prosecutor, on how the complementarity principle is actually applied in practice, and, crucially, on the willingness and capacity of specific governments (potentially with direct international assistance) to fairly prosecute egregious international crimes.[68]

Complementarity, Demonstration Effects, and Capacity Building

Two factors are of particular importance to whether the complex "dance of complementarity"[69] ultimately leads to accountability proceedings that demonstrate credibly that atrocities are out of bounds, impunity is being punctured, and justice can be fair. First is the nature of the government's own commitment to combating impunity for egregious crimes. The scholars Beth Simmons and Allison Danner argue that governments in societies wracked by conflict with weak domestic judicial systems have become parties to the ICC to signal their commitment to prosecute atrocities (to adversaries, rebels, and their own population), with the availability of the ICC reinforcing the credibility of that commitment in the event domestic institutions are unable to effectively prosecute.[70] Professor Tom Ginsburg has provided an important qualification to this account, however, pointing out that a government commitment to prosecute does not necessarily mean a commitment to *be prosecuted itself*.[71] Indeed, governments have a considerable amount of control over whether their own officials or officers ultimately end up before the ICC: governments can either help or hinder ICC investigations and thus influence the possibility of effective ICC prosecutions in particular conflict situations, and a government can pursue domestic action against its own officers, invoking the complementarity principle to avoid ICC prosecution of particular cases.[72] As a result, a government may be able to encourage or assist ICC prosecution of its domestic enemies while insulating itself to some degree from prosecution. Depending on the facts of a particular conflict, this may undercut a message of fair justice.

A second key factor determining whether the complementarity dynamic yields credible "justice on the ground" is the ICC's response to domestic or "bottom-up" accountability. For instance, if a state is genuinely willing but not fully able to fairly prosecute defendants for crimes against humanity in domestic courts, should the ICC offer—or encourage others to offer—international support to strengthen domestic processes? Or, if a state is developing a comprehensive accountability process that emphasizes reconciliation over criminal prosecution in the vast majority of cases, to what extent should the ICC defer to those domestic proceedings? While it may be possible for the ICC to focus on major offenders, leaving lesser offenders to be addressed by local justice mechanisms, the question of complementarity in the face of such situations raises complex issues that already are confronting the ICC, as in Uganda.

In particular, the question of how proactive the ICC should be in promoting "justice on the ground" by assisting domestic prosecutions and trials has already sparked an intense debate. The scholar William Burke-White advocates a policy of "proactive complementarity," urging the ICC to encourage—and even to assist directly—domestic prosecutions in circumstances where a national government genuinely wishes to try defendants for international crimes before domestic courts and could, if given sufficient international help (including, potentially, from the ICC itself), do so fairly.[73] But, beyond information sharing, the ICC's chief prosecutor and its president have expressed some caution about a proactive ICC *assistance* role.[74] Practical tensions over these issues are especially likely where the ICC's Office of the Prosecutor has already invested enormous resources in investigating and preparing a case for prosecution before the ICC.

Other scholars and practitioners argue that transnational networks are in a better position to provide tangible, direct assistance to domestic accountability proceedings.[75] Organizations such as the International Bar Association, various NGOs, and individual experts can offer concrete support to domestic courts prosecuting atrocity crimes.[76] Thus, in the Democratic Republic of Congo (DRC), for example, transnational networks (including NGOs, UN staff, and foreign experts on the ground) have encouraged and assisted war crimes prosecutions before Congolese military courts.[77] In this situation, the Rome Statute of the ICC has been applied directly by domestic courts. Although such proceedings are only a drop in the bucket of the larger challenge of accountability in the DRC, the very existence of the ICC and its statute is providing a spur to domestic proceedings assisted by transnational networks—a dynamic that is likely to increase in more countries in the future.

While the very prospect of an ICC investigation or indictment can have tangible prodding effects in conflict-affected societies, the impact of an actual indictment can be particularly significant, as in Uganda, even when the government itself referred the situation to the ICC in the first place.

The ICC, Uganda, and Justice on the Ground

The ICC's catalyzing impact regarding justice on the ground is illustrated by the drama unfolding within Uganda—and between Uganda and the ICC—over bringing leaders of the infamous Lord's Resistance Army (LRA) to justice. For over two decades, the LRA has waged an insurgency campaign against the government of Uganda. Led by Joseph Kony, the LRA has raped and murdered civilians and abducted and enslaved children, forcing them to serve as child soldiers and to commit atrocities. The primary victims of this violent campaign have been the Acholi people of northern Uganda, of which Kony is a member.

How did the ICC get involved in this situation? Uganda's president, Yoweri Museveni, asked the ICC to get involved. Uganda —a party to the ICC—referred the situation in northern Uganda to the international court in 2003 for investigation and potential prosecution.[78] Two years later, the ICC indicted Kony, leader of the LRA, along with four other LRA leaders, for crimes against humanity.[79]

These indictments have had some galvanizing domestic effects. For one thing, they may well have contributed to Kony's decision to enter into peace negotiations with the Ugandan government. (Eight months after the ICC indictments were unsealed, the LRA indicated its willingness to resume a new round of peace negotiations with the government.)[80] These negotiations led to a 2007 framework peace agreement, followed by a 2008 agreement regarding accountability. Under this accountability accord, the Ugandan government and the LRA agreed that senior LRA leaders most responsible for atrocities during the long civil conflict would be prosecuted in Ugandan domestic courts, while lower-level perpetrators would be held accountable before traditional justice mechanisms that emphasize apology, reconciliation, and reintegration, rather than retributive justice.[81] But Kony failed to appear at the location on the Sudan-Congo border where the peace agreement was to be finalized. Kony has said that he will

not surrender until the ICC indictments are lifted. The Ugandan
government, in turn, has said that it would not seek a lifting of the
indictments until Kony surrendered.[82]

How this will all play out remains to be seen. Kony and the remnants of the LRA reportedly are back in the bush in a remote cor-
ner of the DRC, where they continue to terrorize local villagers.

Meanwhile, what domestic impacts have the ICC indictments
had regarding justice on the ground in Uganda? First, the ICC
indictments of LRA leaders have contributed to an ongoing and
deeply felt public debate down to the village level about justice
and accountability. On one hand, the ICC indictments have made
clear that the crimes of which the LRA leadership is accused are
universally condemned and that impunity will not be accepted.
On the other hand, the ICC—as an external agent injected into
a complex domestic situation—has also triggered strong internal
antibodies in reaction. For many Acholi leaders and citizens, the
ICC's focus on international criminal justice is contrary to their
strong preference for domestic accountability. The fact that so
many of the LRA perpetrators are also victims—Acholi children
who were forced to fight and to commit horrific acts—makes the
idea of trials for other than a very select few persons deeply problematic for many Acholi.[83] Traditional justice mechanisms with a
reparative rather than retributive focus are likely to be the preferred option in the vast majority of cases.

A second impact of the ICC indictments has been to encourage practical reforms to enable domestic prosecutions of LRA
leaders for international crimes as an alternative to the ICC. For
instance, the 2008 accountability accord provides that "a special
division of the High Court of Uganda shall be established to try
individuals who are alleged to have committed serious crimes during the conflict" with a focus on those individuals who "bear particular responsibility for the most serious crimes, especially crimes
amounting to international crimes."[84] In addition, in March 2010,
Uganda's parliament passed a domestic law on accountability for
international crimes.[85] As a result of these initiatives, Uganda may
be both willing and potentially able to prosecute some LRA leaders domestically, although a degree of international assistance may
be important to reassure domestic and international audiences
about the fairness of the proceedings. Depending on how matters

evolve, prosecution of at least some LRA leaders before the domestic War Crimes Division has the potential to satisfy the ICC's complementarity principle.[86]

Yet, whether Uganda's saga ultimately is a story about positive complementarity between international and domestic processes remains to be seen. It is possible to envision a division of labor in which the ICC prosecutes a few high-level LRA leaders but assists Uganda in domestic prosecution of others, while lower level LRA members go through traditional reparative justice processes. But, the extent of the ICC's willingness to assist domestic prosecutions is not yet clear. Furthermore, whoever ends up prosecuting LRA leaders will need to work hard to assure the communities most directly affected by the cases about the fairness of the process, providing them with good information about the proceedings and engaging in effective outreach to address their concerns.

If nothing else, the Ugandan experience shows that, although the ICC's complementarity principle may be simple in theory, it can be quite complicated in practice. This is particularly true in circumstances where a government genuinely wishes to investigate and prosecute but clearly needs some external assistance in order to do so credibly and effectively. Although the principle of complementarity argues in favor of offering international support for domestic prosecutions in such circumstances, the ICC, as a new court with a strong stake in establishing its own credibility,[87] may be extremely reluctant, once it has investigated and indicted suspects, to step aside and let domestic courts prosecute, even if they are genuinely willing to do so and could (with some international assistance) do so fairly. How this ultimately is resolved has profound implications for domestic capacity building.

Looking forward, the extent to which the ICC will be prepared to take a more proactive role in providing—or encouraging others to provide—international assistance to domestic prosecutions of international crimes will be a central issue. "Positive complementarity" was debated actively at the ICC Review Conference in Kapala, Uganda, in May-June 2010. How this matter is addressed concretely in the future could make a huge difference to justice on the ground in many situations. Even independent of the ICC itself, new, more flexible and informal hybrid arrangements—in which transnational networks of experts provide assistance to domestic justice institutions prosecuting atrocity crimes—may become more significant in the future. And scholars are producing useful research on the role and impact of such networks in international criminal law—networks that have the potential to help strengthen domestic justice systems going forward.[88] Moreover, in cases where the ICC itself tries individuals for atrocity crimes, valuable opportunities for outreach and for modest domestic capacity building may exist.[89]

7. Conclusion

So where does this all lead us? Are international and hybrid criminal courts contributing substantially to justice on the ground in the postconflict societies most directly affected by the crimes these courts are prosecuting, and how might they do better in the future? Let me make three points by way of conclusion.

First, the impact of international and hybrid trials "on the ground" in terms of their demonstration effects and capacity-building effects has been a complicated and mixed story thus far, as the experience of the past decade suggests. Furthermore, the messages about justice that international and hybrid courts impart are always going to be contested and imperfect—and this should be acknowledged with honesty and humility.

Criminal trials alone, even with ambitious outreach programs, are—at best—only part of what is needed to grapple with past atrocities. Trials focus on only a limited number of offenders, and different groups within the affected societies inevitably will have sharply differing views about the fairness or adequacy of the endeavor. Furthermore, other accountability processes—such as truth and reconciliation commissions or efforts to provide reparative justice through modest reparations to victims—may touch more people on the ground more directly. Combined approaches that include truth and reconciliation mechanisms and forms of reparative justice, as in East Timor, are more likely to produce more effective and far-reaching demonstration effects and capacity building than trials alone.

But, however the balance between trials and other measures is ultimately constructed, international or hybrid trials will send messages nonetheless. And those involved in these tribunals need to be more aware of the impact they are having in terms of local populations views of and confidence in fair justice. Indeed, if these tribunals hope to convey in any credible way that certain conduct (genocide, crimes against humanity, war crimes) is out of bounds, that impunity for such crimes is beginning to be punctured, and that justice can and should be fair, they need to work harder to engage local populations, who often will be justifiably skeptical of justice institutions based on domestic experience.

Second, with a bit more vision, effort, planning, and resources, international and hybrid courts can do much more to advance justice on the ground in the societies most affected by the atrocities they are prosecuting, even despite all the difficulties. By thoughtfully developing a domestic impact strategy that includes several key elements, these tribunals could contribute more substantially to building public confidence about fair justice and to strengthening domestic capacity in societies recovering from atrocities. These elements include the need to:

(1) Understand the local terrain more deeply and fully;
(2) Think systematically about the tribunal's demonstration effects and be creative about outreach; and
(3) Be proactive about capacity building and look for synergies.

Understanding the local terrain deeply and fully is crucial to any strategy for advancing justice on the ground. Each conflict or postconflict situation is unique in ways that profoundly shape the possibilities for advancing justice; there is no "one size fits all" approach. Countries' circumstances vary widely in crucial respects, including the condition of the domestic justice system, public attitudes and expectations about postconflict accountability, the degree of tension among different groups or factions, the commitment (or lack thereof) of domestic leaders to accountability for atrocities, and the prospects for supplementing trials with truth and reconciliation commissions, reparations, memorials, and traditional justice mechanisms that enjoy local legitimacy. Whether holding domestic or hybrid atrocity trials within the affected country is realistic at all or whether, instead, only international proceedings outside the country offer prospects for fair justice will also differ significantly across countries recovering from atrocities. All of these circumstances, especially whether domestic justice mechanisms enjoy local legitimacy (or can be strengthened to improve their credibility), will be enormously significant both in shaping the concrete possibilities for postconflict criminal justice and in influencing public attitudes and confidence in those efforts.

In light of these challenges, international and hybrid criminal tribunals should each have professional staff whose full-time job is to focus specifically on understanding the concerns of the local population and engaging with domestic audiences through outreach and capacity building. This team of people should be multidisciplinary and include not only legal experts but also country experts and anthropologists, who can work together with local leaders and civil society groups to understand the possibilities for constructive domestic outreach and capacity building as part of a tribunal's work.

To be sure, most of the people working at international or hybrid courts—as prosecutors, judges, defense counsel, administrators, investigators, and so forth—will concentrate, as they should, on the tribunals' central responsibility of bringing to justice in fair trials those accused of atrocity crimes. As a result, they may regard questions about the domestic impact of the tribunal's work in the affected country (in terms of public perceptions about the court's work or domestic capacity building) as not their responsibility or, at best, as an add-on to their already demanding jobs. But this is precisely why having dedicated staff with specific responsibility for outreach and capacity building is so important.

Also, outreach should be included explicitly in the mandate of international and hybrid tribunals, and resources for outreach— and for targeted capacity building—should be included in their budget. Otherwise, outreach will be cobbled together with only voluntary funds if they are available.

Developing outreach programs that respond appropriately and creatively to local circumstances and that use media and the arts in culturally resonant ways in engaging with local audiences should be an important priority in decades ahead.[90] Because atrocity trials place the issue of accountability and justice explicitly on the national agenda and galvanize public interest and discussion of these crucial issues, they can help create a space for citizen understanding, involvement, and mobilization for greater governmental accountability, transparency, and attention to fair justice going forward. This potential for empowering ripple effects should be nurtured in thoughtful and creative ways.

In seeking to do this, scholars and practitioners alike can help refine our understanding of the impact on the ground of different postconflict accountability processes. We are beginning to see helpful empirical work, such as the studies in East Timor of the community-based reconciliation process and the perceptions of the victims, perpetrators, and others who participated.[91] Further scholarly work examining the impact of criminal atrocity trials (and other accountability mechanisms) on public understandings and confidence about justice in affected postconflict countries could be especially useful in future efforts to develop more meaningful and effective outreach programs. Also, practitioners who have led creative outreach programs such as Sierra Leone's can offer valuable insights to those developing similar initiatives in other settings.

Also vital to advancing justice on the ground is being proactive about capacity building and looking for synergies—that is, for ways that international and hybrid tribunals can contribute concretely to domestic legal capacity while doing their own important work to advance justice. Given the resources (relatively speaking) that international and hybrid courts enjoy, they can, with a bit more effort and systematic planning, make more tangible and meaningful contributions to domestic justice systems—and to civil society empowerment—in the societies affected by the atrocities being prosecuted. Hiring dedicated staff whose full-time job is to focus on effective contributions to domestic capacity building would be a tangible way to give these issues higher priority; those involved in this work should look for synergies that will help strengthen domestic capacity for justice in enduring ways.

My final point is this: those of us involved in international criminal justice, whether as scholars or practitioners, need to be humbler and bolder at the same time. We need to be humbler about the ability of criminal trials to ever adequately address the wounds and needs of those who have suffered genocide, war crimes, or crimes against humanity or to fully provide justice after atrocities. But, at the same time, we need to be bolder in understanding that

it is possible to hold fair trials—to do justice in individual cases
—while also contributing more tangibly to justice on the ground
in postconflict societies through sensitive outreach to local communities and through capacity building aimed at both domestic
justice systems and civil society. Scholars can contribute to justice
on the ground by doing valuable empirical research on the domestic impacts of international and hybrid courts and of other accountability mechanisms. Practitioners can help by thinking more
systematically and creatively about how international and hybrid
courts can advance their fundamental goal of justice through fair
trials while also contributing more significantly to justice on the
ground. Governments and organizations can help by providing explicit funding and support for outreach and capacity building so
that funds aren't simply cobbled together on a shoestring. If we
all give more attention to the complex needs, struggles, and hopes
of the people and countries recovering from atrocities, genuine
progress in advancing justice on the ground is possible in the challenging years ahead.

NOTES

I am grateful for the excellent research assistance provided by Nicholas
Wexler and Kate Klonick.

1. Jane Stromseth, David Wippman, and Rosa Brooks, *Can Might Make
Rights? Building the Rule of Law after Military Interventions* (New York: Cambridge University Press, 2006). For a summary of the book's arguments,
see Jane Stromseth, "Post-Conflict Rule of Law Building: The Need for a
Multi-layered, Synergistic Approach," 49 *Wm. and Mary L. Rev.* 49 (2008):
1443.

2. Stromseth et al., *Can Might Make Rights?*, 78. Thus, we devote a chapter of our book to the especially difficult and important question of nurturing public support for the rule of law, highlighting the importance of
innovative programs aimed at getting to the grassroots, strengthening civil
society organizations, reaching out to the next generation, and giving ordinary people a stake in the law. Ibid., chapter 8.

3. For a discussion of the challenges of postconflict justice system reform, see ibid., chapter 6. I am grateful to my colleague David Luban for
suggesting the "spaceship" metaphor.

4. See Stromseth et al., *Can Might Make Rights?*, at 285–89 for a discussion of the work of East Timor's Commission for Reception, Truth, and Reconciliation.

5. "Chega!: Final Report of the Commission for Reception, Truth and Reconciliation in East Timor" (2005), available at http://www.etan.org/news/2006/cavr.htm (hereinafter "Chega!: Final Report of the CAVR"). "Chega!" means "Enough!" in Portuguese.

6. For a thoughtful discussion and critique of expressivism as a goal of international trial and punishment, see Mark Drumbl, *Atrocity, Punishment, and International Law* (New York: Cambridge University Press, 2007), 173–79.

7. Many Afghans, for instance, have made clear that their trust in justice and in government institutions depends on removing serious abusers from positions of power and that they view this as essential for, not contrary to, security and long-term stability. See Afghan Independent Human Rights Commission, "A Call for Justice: A National Consultation on Past Human Rights Violations in Afghanistan" (hereinafter "A Call for Justice"), 17, 41–44, available at http://www.aihrc.org.af/rep_Eng_29_01_05.htm.

8. Drumbl, *Atrocity, Punishment, and International Law*, 174. For a perceptive discussion of the importance of addressing the role of bystanders as part of "the crucial normative glue for restoring the rule of law," see Larry May, "Bystanders, the Rule of Law, and Criminal Trials," this volume.

9. Prosecutor v. Blaskic, ICTY Case No. IT-95-14A, Judgment (July 29, 2004), para. 678.

10. On the problem of impunity in Afghanistan, see Rama Mani, "Afghanistan Research and Evaluation Unit, Ending Impunity and Building Justice in Afghanistan" (2003), available at http://unpan1.un.org/intradoc/groups/public/documents/APCITY/UNPAN016655.pdf; "A Call for Justice," 17 ("Many persons who committed gross human rights violations remain in power today. This has provoked a profound disappointment in Afghans together with an almost total breakdown of trust in authority and public institutions").

11. As the ICTY explained in the Blaskic case, a key purpose considered in imposing sentence was "individual and general deterrence concerning the accused and, in particular, commanders in similar situations in the future." Para. 678.

12. See, e.g., Drumbl, *Atrocity, Punishment, and International Law*, 169–73.

13. See James Cockayne, "The Fraying Shoestring: Rethinking Hybrid War Crimes Tribunals," *Fordham Int'l L.J.* 28 (2005): 616, 674–75. And different choices about how to structure hybrids—particularly their relationship to the domestic justice system—can influence their capacity-building impact. One especially interesting hybrid arrangement, in which

international participation phases out over time, is the special hybrid War Crimes Chamber within the national State Court of Bosnia and Herzegovina. Stromseth et al., *Can Might Make Rights?*, 267.

14. For a discussion of the importance and challenges of strengthening cultural commitments to the rule of law, see Stromseth et al., *Can Might Make Rights?*, especially chapter 8.

15. Published by Cambridge University Press, 2009.

16. For a discussion of the potential benefits of hybrid tribunals, see Laura A. Dickinson, "The Promise of Hybrid Courts," *Am. J. Int'l L.* 97 (2003): 295.

17. For analysis of another hybrid court—in Bosnia and Herzegovina—see William W. Burke-White, "The Domestic Influence of International Criminal Tribunals: The International Criminal Tribunal for the Former Yugoslavia and the Creation of the State Court of Bosnia and Herzegovina," *Colum. J. Transnat'l L.* 46 (2008): 279; Refik Hodzic, "Living the Legacy of Mass Atrocities: Victim's Perspectives on War Crimes Trials," *J. Int'l Crim. Just.* 8 (2010): 113.

18. Press Release, "Office of the Prosecutor Demands Full Cooperation from Taylor," May 5, 2003, available at http://www.sc-sl.org/Press/prosecutor-051503.html; U.S. State Department, Bureau of Intelligence and Research, "Background Note on Sierra Leone," May 2006, available at http://www.state.gov/r/pa/ei/bgn/5475.

19. See, e.g., John E. Leigh, op-ed, "Bringing It All Back Home," *New York Times*, April 17, 2006, at A25. Leigh, who is Sierra Leone's former ambassador to the United States, argued that transferring Taylor to The Hague for trial "would defeat a principal purpose behind the establishment of the special court in Sierra Leone—namely, to teach Africans, firsthand and in their own countries, the fundamentals of justice and to drive home that no one is above the law." Ibid.

20. Interview with Prosecutor David Crane, Freetown, Sierra Leone, June 2004.

21. Case No. SCSL-04-14-J, Judgement of 9 October 2007, para. 85.

22. Ibid., para. 87.

23. Quote is from the stated mandate of the outreach office.

24. Interviews with Outreach officers and with Prosecutor David Crane, Freetown, Sierra Leone, June 2004.

25. See International Crisis Group, "The Special Court for Sierra Leone: Promises and Pitfalls of a 'New Model,'" 17, Africa Briefing No. 16, August 4, 2003, available at http://www.crisisgroup.org/home/index.cfm?id=1803&1=1.

26. Cockayne, "The Fraying Shoestring," 672.

27. Human Rights Watch, "Bringing Justice: The Special Court for

Sierra Leone: Accessibility and Legacy," 2004, at 2, available at http://hrw
.org/reports/2004/sierraleone0904/8.htm.

28. For research assessing the Special Court's outreach program, see
Memunatu Baby Pratt, "Nation-Wide Survey on Public Perceptions of
the Special Court for Sierra Leone" (2007); Tom Perriello and Marieke
Wierda, "The Special Court for Sierra Leone Under Scrutiny," International Center for Transitional Justice, 36–40 (March 2006); Rachel Kerr
and Jessica Lincoln, "The Special Court for Sierra Leone: Outreach, Legacy and Impact," War Crimes Research Group, Department of War Studies, King's College London, Draft Interim Report (July 2007).

29. The European Union has provided some funds to the court for survey research. Perriello and Wierda, "The Special Court for Sierra Leone
under Scrutiny," 37. Perriello and Wierda provide helpful analysis of the
court's outreach efforts, legacy, and public perceptions of the court. Ibid.,
at 35–40.

30. UN Doc. S/2005/533, "Progress Report of the Secretary-General on
the United Nations Office in Timor-Leste," August 18, 2005, para. 49.

31. As of April 2004, the Special Panels had tried fifty-two individuals,
with fifty convictions and two acquittals. Those convicted include individuals found guilty of crimes against humanity for murders, rapes, and torture
in the Lolotoe area and militia members found guilty of serious crimes
in the Los Palo case. Judicial System Monitoring Program, available at
http://www.jsmp.minihub.org/index.htm.

32. Since beginning operations in January 2001, the Serious Crimes
Unit issued more than eighty-two indictments against 369 persons. "Report of the Secretary General on the United Nations Mission of Support
in East Timor," S/2004/333 (April 29, 2004), at http://ods-dds-ny.un.org/
doc/UNDOC/GEN/N04/323/42/IMG/N0432342.pdf. Those indicted
include General Wiranto (former Defense Minister and Commander
of the Armed Forces); Major General Zacky Anwar Makarim (Security
Task Force Advisor); Major General Adam Damiri (former chief of the
Regional Military Command); Brigadier General Suhartono Suratman
(former Timor-Leste Military Commander); Colonel Mohmanned Noer
Muis (Commander of the Sub-Regional Command 164); Brigadier General Timbul Silaen (former Chief of Police for Timor-Leste); Lieutenant
Colonel Yayat Sudrajat (Commander of the Intelligence Task Force of
Sub-Regional Command 164). Amnesty International, Indonesia & Timor-
Leste, International responsibility for justice, at 8, available at http://www
.amnesty.org/en/library/info/ASA03/001/2003/en.

33. Evelyn Rusli, "Indonesia Court Voids 4 Convictions in 1999 East
Timor Strife," *New York Times*, August 7, 2004, at A2.

34. In the end, all those tried before Indonesia's Ad Hoc Human Rights

Court "were acquitted either at trial or on appeal except for one, Eurico
Guterres." S/2005/458, "Report to the Secretary-General of the Commission of Experts to Review the Prosecution of Serious Violations of Human
Rights in Timor-Leste (then East Timor) in 1999," May 26, 2005 (hereinafter "Commission of Experts Report"), at para.171. Guterres, a former Timorese pro-Indonesian militia leader, began serving a ten-year sentence in
May 2006. "Shawn Donnan, Pro-Jakarta Militia Leader Begins Sentence,"
Financial Times, May 4, 2006, available at http://www.etan.org/et2006/
may/01/04pro-j.htm. The August 2004 acquittals triggered sharply diver-
gent reactions. They caused an outcry among human rights NGOs, both
domestic and international, and provoked strong statements by a number
of governments. But many Timorese officials took a very different view.
Foreign Minister Ramos-Horta expressed support for an international
truth commission but opposed an international criminal tribunal. Prosecution of Indonesian officials, he argued, could be destabilizing within
Indonesia and would undermine East Timor's efforts to improve its relations with Indonesia. Dan Eaton, "East Timor Urges End to Push for UN
Tribunal," *Reuters*, August 9, 2004; "East Timor's Foreign Minister Opposes
Rights Tribunal," *Associated Press*, September 8, 2004. For a discussion and
critique of the Indonesian prosecutions before the Ad Hoc Human Rights
Court, see "Commission of Experts Report," 38–80.

35. President Gusmao was elected overwhelmingly as East Timor's first
president, and he placed a strong emphasis on looking forward. Gusmao
focused on pursuing economic development and "social justice" in East
Timor—and on achieving reconciliation and reintegrating resistance
fighters and remaining remnants of opposing militias into Timorese
society. See Rachel S. Taylor, "Justice and Reconciliation in East Timor,
Interview: East Timorese President Xanana Gusmao," *World Press Review*,
October 1, 2002, available at http://www.worldpress.org/Asia/743.cfm.
Gusmao also sought to establish constructive relations with Indonesia, East
Timor's powerful neighbor and key trading partner.

36. Interview with Foreign Minister Jose Ramos-Horta in Dili, Timor-
Leste, November 2003.

37. Many Timorese participating in the community-based reconciliation proceedings have expressed strong disappointment that many of
those who committed serious crimes have not been prosecuted at all.
"See Chega!: Final Report of the CAVR," Part 9: Community Reconciliation, at 48 (para. 170); Spencer Zifcak, The Asia Foundation, "Restorative Justice in East Timor: An Evaluation of the Community Reconciliation Process of the CAVR," (2004), 41, available at http://pdf.usaid.gov/
pdf_docs/PNADO632.pdf; Piers Pigou, United Nations Development Programme, "The Community Reconciliation Process of the Commission for

Reception, Truth and Reconciliation" (2004), 100–1, available at http://www.cavr-imorleste.org/Analysis/Laporan%20Piers%20tentang%20CRP .pdf; Commission of Experts Report, at 89 (para.381) (citing 2004 opinion poll in which "52 per cent of the population responded that justice must be sought even if it slows down reconciliation with Indonesia, while 39 per cent favoured reconciliation even if that meant significantly reducing efforts to seek justice").

38. See Stromseth et al., *Can Might Make Rights?*, 285–88. The innovative truth and reconciliation commission also played a crucial role in addressing the larger factors that led to atrocities, reaching out to victims, and recommending systemic reforms.

39. Particularly in postconflict societies in which formal justice systems have limited geographic reach, community-based accountability proceedings that both enjoy local legitimacy and respect human rights can have an important immediate impact and also contribute to the longer-term goal of strengthening the rule of law. East Timor's Commission for Reception, Truth and Reconciliation, in particular, has made a difference in rural areas with limited access to formal justice.

40. In fact, the response of victims to the community-based reconciliation process has been more mixed than the generally positive response of the 'deponents" who confessed wrongdoing and found that the process helped them integrate back into their communities. For some victims, the confessions of the deponents were not as forthright as hoped for, and the community agreements were not very demanding. Victims hoping for more information about the fate of their loved ones were sometimes disappointed. Some victims found the proceedings and the public apology before the community to be constructive and affirming, but others felt a sense of pressure or community expection to reconcile with perpetrators. For helpful studies, see Zifcak, "Restorative Justice in East Timor: An Evaluation of the Community Reconciliation Process of the CAVR"; Pigou, "The Community Reconciliation Process of the Commission for Reception, Truth and Reconciliation." The CAVR itself acknowledged that clearer guidelines regarding the role of victims in the proceedings and a greater focus on their needs would have been beneficial. "Chega!: Final Report of the CAVR," pt. 9, para. 133, at 39.

41. The Duch trial began in March 2009, and the trial proceedings concluded in November 2009. The verdict from the ECCC Trial Chamber was handed down in July 2010, and arguments on the appeals filed by both the defense and the prosecution commenced in March 2011. James O'Toole and Cheang Sokha, "Duch appeal hearings set for March," *Phnom Penh Post*, Dec. 23, 2010.

42 Norman Henry Pentelovich, "Seeing Justice Done: The Importance

of Prioritizing Outreach Efforts at International Criminal Courts," *Geo. J. Int'l L.* 39 (2008): 445, 464.

43. Furthermore, if the judges cannot reach unanimous agreement, a decision requires a "supermajority" in which four of five Trial Chamber judges, and five of seven Supreme Court Chamber judges vote affirmatively.

44. Seth Mydans, "Efforts to Limit Khmer Rouge Trials Decried," *New York Times,* February 1, 2009, at A8.

45. Seth Mydans, "Corruption Allegations Affect Khmer Rouge Trials," *New York Times,* April 9, 2009, available at http://www.nytimes.com/2009/04/10/world/asia/10cambo.html.

46. Former prisoners recounted the various forms of torture commonly practiced at S-21 under Duch's orders, including "beatings, whippings, electric shocks and removal of toenails." Such torture sessions usually ended in execution. Seth Mydans, "Survivors Shed Light on Dark Days of Khmer Rouge,"*New York Times,* May 17, 2009, at A14.

47. Seth Mydans, "Legal Strategy Fails to Hide Pride a Khmer Rouge Torturer Took in His Job," *New York Times,* June 21, 2009, at A12.

48. Thierry Cruvellier, "Duch Trial Ends with a Twist," *Int'l Justice Tribune,* December 9, 2009.

49. Robbie Corey Boulet, "Duch Defense Split on Verdict," *The Phnom Penh Post,* November 27, 2009.

50. Seth Mydans, "Prison Term for Khmer Rouge Jailer Leaves Many Dissatisfied," *New York Times,* July 27, 2010, at A4.

51. Phuong Pham et al., *So We Will Never Forget: A Population-Based Survey on Attitudes about Social Reconstruction and the Extraordinary Chambers in the Courts of Cambodia* 3 (2009) [hereinafter Berkeley Study], at 3, 20, 29–30.

52. Ibid., 4, 15–16, 39.

53. Mydans, "Efforts to Limit Khmer Rouge Trials Decried," A8.

54. This paragraph relies on the helpful article by my former student Norman Pentelovich, who has spent a number of months on the ground in Cambodia working for a local NGO. See Pentelovich, "Seeing Justice Done," 463–80.

55. Ibid., 470–75.

56. David Crane, "Dancing with the Devil: Prosecuting West Africa's Warlords, Current Lessons Learned and Challenges," in *Colloquium of Prosecutors of International Criminal Tribunals, Arusha* (2004) at 6–7, available at http://65/18/216/88/ENGLISH/colloquim04/04.

57. Vincent O. Nmehielle and Charles Chernor Jalloh, "International Criminal Justice: The Legacy of the Special Court for Sierra Leone," *Fletcher F. World Aff.* 30 (2006): 107. A joint UNDP/ICTJ report recommended that, as part of its "legacy" efforts, the Special Court focus additional attention on substantive law reform in Sierra Leone, on professional

developrent for domestic justice personnel, and on programs to raise greater awareness in the provinces of the Special Court as an example of fair, effective legal process. ICTJ and UNDP, "The "Legacy" of the Special Court for Sierra Leone," at 1–2 (Sept. 2002).

58. Suzanne Katzenstein, "Note: Hybrid Tribunals: Searching for Justice in East Timor," *Harv. Hum. Rts. J.* 16 (2003): 263, 267. See also Commission of Experts Report, at 36–37.

59. Berkeley Study, 4. Only about a third of Cambodians surveyed trust the national criminal justice system (36%) or Cambodian judges (37%). Ibid. Instead, Cambodians often turn to local alternatives such as "a third party, or conciliator, as mediator," particularly in rural areas. Ibid., 15.

60. Steve Heder, "The Senior Leaders and Those Most Responsible," *Justice Initiative*, April 2006, at 53 (Heder, of the Open Society Institute, notes that, on the basis of his conversations with various jurists and lawyers dating back to 1989 "there is every reason to believe that, left to do their jobs in peace, many Cambodian judges and lawyers are perfectly capable of weighing up evidence and of exercising independence, and indeed some are eager to do so, given the chance"); see also Kate Gibson, "An Uneasy Coexistence: The Relationship between the Internationalised Courts and Their Domestic Counterparts," *J. Int'l Crim. Just.* 9 (2009): 294 ("key political players prevent training and knowledge from being put to use against their political interests."); Berkeley Study, 15 ("[t]he Ministry of Justice often provides instructions to judges on how to interpret the laws; the Executive pressures the court to overturn their rulings.").

61. See Stromseth et al., *Can Might Make Rights?*, 285.

62. Ibid., 295–96.

63. See http://www.sc-sl.org/outreach.html.

64. Created by states through a multilateral treaty known as the "Rome Statute," 114 countries are parties to the ICC as of October 2010. See http://www.icc-cpi.int/Menus/ASP/states+parties/.

65. Rome Statute of the International Criminal Court, Art. 17, July 17, 1998, 2187 U.N.T.S. 90. Under the complementarity provisions of the ICC, a case is inadmissible if a state with jurisdiction has genuinely investigated the matter and prosecuted or made a good-faith determination not to prosecute. States wishing to avoid ICC jurisdiction under the Rome Statute thus can take steps to ensure that they are able and willing to investigate and, if appropriate, to prosecute individuals domestically for ICC crimes. So, ideally, the impulses of sovereignty should combine with the prospect of international action to produce more effective national accountability efforts. For discussions of complementarity, see Michael A. Newton, "Comparative Complementarity: Domestic Jurisdiction Consistent with the Rome Statute of the International Criminal Court," *Mil. L. Rev.* 167

(2001): 20; David J. Scheffer, "Fourteenth Waldemar A. Solf Lecture in International Law: A Negotiator's Perspective on the International Criminal Court," *Mil. L. Rev.* 167 (2001): 10–11.

66. Many states already have adapted their domestic criminal law to provide for national prosecution of genocide, crimes against humanity, and war crimes. This may be the ICC's most significant impact to date on strengthening domestic rule of law.

67. William W. Burke-White, "Complementarity in Practice: The International Criminal Court as Part of a System of Multi-Level Global Governance in the Democratic Republic of Congo," *Leiden J. Int'l L.* 18 (2005): 557, 574.

68. Gaps exist, in any event, in the ICC's ability to serve as a lever to prod and encourage responsible domestic accountability processes. Many of the worst atrocities in recent memory occurred during internal conflicts. When perpetrators of atrocities come from the state on whose territory the crimes occurred, the ICC will be in a position to assert jurisdiction only if that state is a party to the ICC statute or otherwise consents or if the UN Security Council refers the matter to the court. Rome Statute of the International Criminal Court, Art. 12, July 17, 1998, 2187 U.N.T.S. 90. Thus, many situations of internal conflict in which atrocities occur may not be amenable to the ICC's prodding function. In addition, atrocities committed before the ICC's jurisdiction took effect on July 1, 2002, are not subject to prosecution before the court.

69. Laura A. Dickinson, "The Dance of Complementarity: Relationships among Domestic, International, and Transnational Accountability Mechanisms in East Timor and Indonesia," in *Accountability For Atrocities: National and International Responses*, ed. Jane E. Stromseth (Ardsley, NY: Transnational, 2003).

70. Beth Simmons and Allison Danner, "Credible Commitments and the International Criminal Court," *Int'l Org.* 64 (2010): 225.

71. Tom Ginsburg, "The Clash of Commitments at the International Criminal Court," Public Law and Legal Theory Working Paper No. 251, University of Chicago Law School, November 2008, available at http://www.law.uchicago.edu/academics/publiclaw/index.html.

72. Ibid. The fact that the ICC statute, in Article 14, requires referrals to be of "situations" rather than of particular cases or individuals helps somewhat but not completely to avoid self-dealing.

73. William Burke-White, "Proactive Complementarity: The International Criminal Court and National Courts in the Rome System of Justice," *Harv. Int'l L. J.* 49 (2008): 53.

74. See, e.g., the discussion of complementarity at the ICC review conference in June 2010, "Review Conference: ICC President and Prosecutor

Participate in Panels on Complementarity and Co-operation," available at http://www.icc-cpi.int.

75. Elena Baylis, "Reassessing the Role of International Criminal Law: Rebuilding National Courts through Transnational Networks," *Boston College L. Rev.* 50 (2009): 1.

76. Mark S. Ellis, "International Justice and the Rule of Law: Strengthening the ICC through Domestic Prosecutions," *Hague J. on the Rule of Law* 1 (2009): 79.

77. Baylis, "Reassessing the Role of International Criminal Law"; Drumbl, *Atrocity, Punishment, and International Law*, 145 and n. 127.

78. For an analysis of the self-referral, see William W. Burke-White and Scott Kaplan, "Shaping the Contours of Domestic Justice: The International Criminal Court and an Admissibility Challenge in the Uganda Situation," University of Pennsylvania Law School Public Law and Legal Theory Research Paper Series, Research Paper No. 08-13. A significant and unexpected twist on the role of the ICC has been the significant number of so-called self-referrals. These occur when a country that has jurisdiction to try a case decides instead to refer the situation to the ICC. A state may "self-refer" to the ICC for any number of reasons: it lacks sufficient capacity to try the case; it faces domestic political difficulties in prosecuting a situation; it needs assistance because perpetrators are in another country beyond the ability of the domestic state to assert enforcement jurisdiction; or it seeks to put international pressure on rebel forces to name a few. Indeed, a substantial portion of the situations that the ICC is currently investigating are self-referrals, including the situation in northern Uganda.

79. Ibid.

80. Ibid.

81. Scott Worden, "The Justice Dilemma in Uganda," USIP Briefing, February 2008.

82. Jeffrey Gettleman and Alexis Okeowo, "Warlord's Absence Derails Peace Efforts in Uganda," *New York Times*, April 12, 2008. The government also is keenly aware, however, of the strong preference of many Ugandan tribal elders and citizens for domestic justice rather than for international justice at The Hague. BBC, "Museveni Rejects Hague LRA Trial," March 12, 2008, available at http://news.bbc.co.uk/2/hi/africa/7291274.stm; Jeffrey Gettleman and Alexi Okeowo, "Ugandan Rebels Delay Peace Deal," *New York Times*, April 11, 2008, available at http://www.nytimes.com/2008/04/11/world/africa/11uganda.html.

83. Worden, "The Justice Dilemma in Uganda," 7.

84. Ibid.

85. In May 2010, Uganda's President Museveni signed the bill into

law. Uganda, Implementing Legislation, http://www.iccnow.org/?mod=
country&iduct=181.

86. If the government ultimately wishes to prosecute LRA leaders already indicted by the ICC, the government presumably would seek to challenge the admissibility of those cases before the ICC. Whether, on the basis
of the principle of complementarity, the ICC Pre-Trial Chamber would
rule the matter inadmissible before the international court would depend
on issues such as the nature of the charges, proceedings, and potential
penalty facing Kony and other LRA leaders in Ugandan domestic court.
For a thoughtful analysis, see Burke-White and Kaplan, "Shaping the Contours of Domestic Justice."

87. See Tom Ginsburg's helpful discussion on this point in "The Clash
of Commitments at the International Criminal Court."

88. For discussion of different modes of international assistance to domestic trials, see Ellis, "International Justice and the Rule of Law"; Baylis,
"Reassessing the Role of International Criminal Law"; Burke-White, "Proactive Complementarity"; Jenia Iontcheva Turner, "Transnational Networks and International Criminal Justice," *Mich. L. Rev.* 105 (2007): 985.

89. On the supply side, for instance, the ICC can contribute to domestic capacity building through workshops, discussions, and training sessions
aimed at domestic jurists and others involved in domestic justice systems.
On the demand side, the ICC can engage in outreach—through interactive
face-to-face meetings and radio and in other ways—with a wide range of
civil society groups, including students and educators, human rights NGOs,
women's organizations, community leaders, and others, to explain the ICC's
proceedings and the principles underlying them, to address questions and
concerns, to understand public perceptions, and to engage the population
on crucial issues of justice and accountability. Currently, the ICC is engaging in a number of outreach activities in the societies affected by its work,
including the DRC, the Central African Republic, and Uganda. See, e.g.,
ICC Newsletter No. 20 (March 2008), available at http://www.icc-cpi.int/
NR/rdonlyres/C5C7252B-8D2E-49A5-8BB8-90C56CD71B60/278442/
ICCNL20200803_En.pdf; ICC Newsletter No. 19 (February 2008), available at http://www.icc-cpi.int/NR/rdonlyres/6FDDE5D6-A46B-4059-8748
-751C2F60704D/278444/ICCNL19200802_En.pdf. Nongovernmental organizations can supplement such efforts in creative and empowering ways.
For example, in the DRC, an innovative NGO initiative, Interactive Radio
for Justice, led by Wanda Hall, is building on public interest in the ICC
and in justice issues by broadcasting dialogues with ICC officials, domestic
officials, and others on a wide range of legal issues, providing both valuable public education and a space for civic dialogue on vital questions of

accountability and fair justice. See the organization's Web site, Interactive Radio for Justice, http://www.irfj.org.

90. For an innovative example of radio-based outreach, see the work of Interactive Radio for Justice at http://www.irfj.org.

91. See Zifcak, "Restorative Justice in East Timor"; Pigou, "The Community Reconciliation Process of the Commission for Reception, Truth, and Reconciliation." For a helpful study on the impact of the ICTY, see Diane Orentlicher, "Shrinking the Space for Denial: The Impact of the ICTY in Serbia," Open Society Institute Report, May 2008.

10

IN DEFENSE OF IMPERIALISM? THE RULE OF LAW AND THE STATE-BUILDING PROJECT

TOM GINSBURG

The rule of law is not only a philosopher's concept but a multi-billion-dollar industry and the dominant ideal of our time. As a concept, its success is in part a result of its vagueness, as it is broad enough to incorporate an overlapping consensus among free marketers, human rights activists, and promoters of the regulatory state. Countries as diverse as China, Chad, and the Czech Republic agree on its virtue. At the same time, the idea of the rule of law has captured the policy-making imagination of the West and has become our modern *mission civilisatrice*.[1]

The burst of activity associated with promoting the rule of law abroad has been commented on but rarely studied systematically. A notable exception was Stromseth et al.,[2] a major contribution to the literatures on postconflict societies and on the role of law and development that is further advanced in the chapter for this volume. Stromseth's distinctive move is to link issues of reconstructing basic order to the broader project of international criminal justice for perpetrators of severe human rights violations.[3]

Over the years, there have been many critiques of postconflict intervention, of legal development work, and of international criminal justice.[4] Stromseth's approach to all of these issues is one of clear-eyed optimism. She recognizes many of the critiques, and her writing is full of intelligent considerations of pitfalls, tensions, and tradeoffs. Notwithstanding the critiques, she is committed to the idea that, with more resources, better knowledge, and improved coordination, we can do a better job in postconflict intervention and institutional construction.[5] In this sense, her project is ultimately technocratic in character. We can do better if we just develop the right approaches to assessment, planning, implementation, and evaluation.

In this brief comment, I want to express some skepticism. It is not a position I have come to lightly, as a long-time advocate of a position of cautious optimism. But, for the difficult situations of contemporary postconflict reconstruction, I have come to conclude that only intervention on a far more intrusive scale, of a type no longer politically acceptable, has the potential to truly transform the societies and to enable them to achieve anything approaching the "rule of law." Hence the reference to imperialism in my title. Basic order may be more achievable but, ironically, is easier to impose with a more authoritarian model than is politically acceptable in the "intervening" societies. Without a truly massive effort of a type that is unlikely to be sustainable, our piecemeal interventions around the edges are not only likely to be ineffective but will in some cases be counterproductive. We are insufficiently imperialistic to carry out social transformation from abroad. And our intervention often undermines social transformation from within.

I begin by considering the important literature on self-enforcing institutions and then consider the effect of introducing an external enforcer. The argument is that external intervention can in some conditions crowd out domestic efforts to produce social order. I then examine the record of successful postconflict intervention and find it to be a null set with regard to the rule of law. In this section I take a brief detour to modern Japanese legal history, noting its misuses in recent debates. Japanese experience, in my view, shows not that postconflict interventions can deliver the rule of law but rather that effective state building can be done only from within. The final section concludes with some thoughts on international criminal justice. The idea that intervention to promote justice will provide a demonstration effect is attractive but not empirically verified and subject to the concerns about crowding out identified in Part I.

Throughout, my theme is that we need to consider the politics of conflict intervention in a rigorous way, thinking in terms of incentives. A hallmark of technocratic politics is its denial of politics, and this view must be overcome to make progress on the problem of building the rule of law. To be sure, it is a commonplace in discussions of the issues under consideration here that politics are important. Too often, however, the need for "political will" to effectuate reform receives lip service without serious analysis. Political will is often viewed as an essential but exogenous factor that leaders can generate autonomously. But there are deeper structural factors at play that may limit the efficacy of well-intentioned reforms.

1. DEMOCRACY AND THE RULE OF LAW:
THE PARADOXES OF EXTERNAL ENFORCEMENT

Democratic governance involves the selection of agents to govern on behalf of the people. Once selected, however, agency problems arise. How can we ensure that government agents behave on behalf of their principal, the *demos*? The rule of law provides one apparent solution: by ensuring that agents announce the rules in advance, follow proper procedures, and are subjected to punishment by independent courts when they misbehave, the rule of law helps to minimize agency problems of democratic governance. But this solution is illusory, for it raises second-order problems about why the courts will act as faithful agents and why the government will obey the courts.

To understand how democracy and the rule of law are sustainable, political scientists draw on Weingast's[6] important model, in which he elaborates the conditions for self-enforcing democracy. Self-enforcement refers to the idea that, in most cases, there is no external guarantor of constitutional or democratic order.[7] Only when it is in the interest of all major power-holders in society will democracy and the rule of law be sustained. Courts can sanction government agents, but decisions will be effectively obeyed only when the agents have an interest in compliance because they anticipate costs from attempts to violate the rules. Democracy and the rule of law, in this view, represent equilibrium outcomes, sustained when the principal (the demos) can credibly commit to enforcing the rules. But these desirable outcomes are not the only equilibria. If social groups cannot coordinate their understanding of the rules of the game and coordinate their efforts to enforce those rules, the government agent will be able to benefit some groups at the expense of others. Weingast's model thus emphasizes coordination and enforcement as key elements in developing democracy and the rule of law.

The model has many implications for postconflict societies. It helps to understand the divide-and-conquer strategies that lead to violent conflict in the first place: an autocrat seeks to disrupt social coordination by suppressing information and providing selective benefits to key groups. The model also suggests that a key element of establishing democracy and the rule of law is that the people know the rules so as to be able to enforce them; public information and education about the law and rights are important in this regard. Independent courts and other actors can help to monitor government agents, and, when they observe violations of the rules, they can provide focal points for the people to coordinate their enforcement behavior. Though the model does not say much about postconflict transitional justice, one can view such efforts as a type of enforcement behavior, helping to generate focal points for future enforcement activity. The demonstration effect might plausibly signal that future enforcement is possible, thus deterring violations of the rules down the road.

Self-enforcement is an attractive idea that accords with many of our intuitions about the bases of social order. In the real world, however, democracy is not always self-enforcing, but international and foreign actors play a legitimate role.[8] Only in the richest countries can self-enforcement be said to be a primary mechanism of democratic stability. In most societies, external actors *do* play a role in enforcing democracy in some sense, for example through supplemental monitoring of government behavior, publicizing violations of the rules, and disincentivizing regressions to autocracy. For example, a mandatory cutoff of aid after a military coup disincentivizes coups and thus can be said to be, in part, an enforcement mechanism that sustains democracy. More extreme cases include invasions to restore or protect democracy, as have repeatedly been undertaken by the international community in places like Haiti and the Dominican Republic. Some of the cases Stromseth is concerned with are such efforts to restore democracy. And all of them involve an element of external enforcement.

The problem with external enforcement is that it can, in some circumstances, "crowd out" local enforcement efforts. "Crowding out" refers to the idea that, under market circumstances, prices can disincentivize altruistic behavior. Paying people for blood donations, for example, may actually reduce the amount of blood donated as people's intrinsic motivation is reduced.[9] External enforcement is the society-wide equivalent of extrinsic motivation, while internal enforcement is loosely analogous to intrinsic motivation. Just as intrinsic and extrinsic motivation can substitute for each other, external enforcement may sometimes rival internal enforcement.[10]

The alternative conception is that external enforcement is complementary with local efforts. This position is normatively attractive but not necessarily accurate. Enforcement activity has the quality of a public good—everyone benefits from a restrained state, even those who do not participate in enforcement efforts. In addition, enforcement activity is costly and risky. As Weingast points out, coordination of enforcement efforts involves trust that other actors in the society will join in the effort—otherwise, the government agent can use the divide and conquer strategy. Why should local groups take the risk of enforcing democracy when an external actor is willing to bear those costs? Creating self-enforcing democracy in ordinary circumstances is difficult; with the possibility of external enforcement, it may become impossible.

One might think about the consequences in terms of moral hazard. Knowing that external actors will monitor the behavior of government, local actors can pay less attention to that behavior. Because there will be external costs imposed on government agents who violate the rules, local actors will not themselves have to bear the risk. Indeed, it might incentivize holdout behavior in which local actors make reckless demands, knowing that government cannot punish them too severely without risking international opprobrium. All this may in fact invite the very violence that we seek to prevent.

There are hints of the problem in *Can Might Make Rights?* The story about East Timor inviting Australia, Malaysia, and New Zealand to enforce the peace in 2006 is one illustration.[11] Another example concerns the impact of intervention on local bargaining. In the discussion of Bosnia, the short-term solution to an ethnically divided polity was to create a mutual veto at the national level, mediated by the use of the so-called Bonn powers vested in the High Commissioner. These powers arguably make it *more* difficult for the substate entities to reach agreement, and indeed at this writing there are significant internal tensions. Why should the Bosnian representatives engage in hard bargaining? There are no costs to holding out if the ultimate decision gets made by the High Commissioner. Indeed, there are benefits with one's own constituents from signaling resolve in such a situation. This seems to be exactly what has occurred in Bosnia.

To be sure, it is not *always* the case that external enforcement crowds out the local. In many cases, external enforcement can complement local efforts by providing a relatively neutral enforcer, by supplementing gaps in definitions of the rules of the game, and by supplementing local monitors.[12] But, where locals have potentially high costs and are subject to major dilemmas of collective action, external enforcers may indeed undermine incentives for internal enforcement.

The technocratic response to such dynamics is to try some new or deeper intervention. In 1997, the international community strengthened the power of the High Commissioner in Bosnia, resolving a short-term deadlock but undermining future agreement. Stromseth and co-authors point out that "had interveners been willing to run the risks of a significant military engagement in Bosnia, they could have insisted on a more workable blueprint at the outset."[13] The remedy for intervention is thus more intervention.

Weakness can become addictive on the part of local interlocutors: be small and weak enough and your coalition will get the benefits of significant international aid. Stand on your own, and your country may be better off in some sense but risks a cutoff in aid as funds get shifted to other hot spots in worse condition. In any case, even if a country would be better off without support, the ruling coalition will almost certainly not be. There is little political incentive to "graduate." (Nationalism, to be sure, is one important factor that can overcome this incentive structure and has done so in important cases like that of South Korea.)

There is another level of moral hazard problem induced by the possibility of external enforcement of democracy, namely moral hazard on the part of potential secessionist state builders. Today we are talking about creating state entities that are not in any real sense viable without significant international aid on a permanent basis. There are certain fixed costs to state building, and, without a certain size and administrative apparatus, one cannot provide for basic public goods.[14] To be sure, these fixed costs are less than they used to be, and a more benevolent international environment has led to a secular increase in the number of small states. Free trade means that the size of one's domestic market is of less importance, making smallness less costly.[15] Furthermore, the post–World War II security regime has lowered the costs of national defense, in part because of external enforcement of norms of territorial integrity. But it does not follow from all this that Kosovo is a viable proposition.

In short, external enforcement can crowd out local enforcement, encouraging the creation of inherently dependent entities. This analysis suggests that the law of unintended consequences is alive and well. It implies that some consideration ought to be given not to fine-tuning ever-deeper interventions but to the virtues of doing nothing.

At the more micro-level of legal assistance, consider another unintended consequence that has not received sufficient attention: the effect of intervention on the local labor market. When Rule of Law builders show up, they need local staff conversant in English and able to function in the local legal system. Such people are often the most talented on the local scene, and these people are certainly more likely to be familiar with international norms than the rump judiciary left over from the preconflict days. The interveners hire the local talent at a significant wage premium, justifying it to themselves by arguing that the local system will be better off with the intervention. But the collective result of this is that all the human capital is on the intervention side, and none is left on the local side. No wonder the local legal system always seems pathologically weak. And pity the poor chief justice or minister of justice in such a country; his life is a parade of meetings with donors and diplomats, eager to gather information and negotiate the terms of cooperation. Every minute spent with the interveners is a minute *not* deciding cases or managing the courts.[16]

Hence, I take some issue with the notion that the answer lies in devoting more resources to developing the rule of law. It is not clear that Rule of Law efforts are "underresourced." Without evidence that funds can be used effectively, why should we spend more funds? We are now deep enough into the effort that more empirical evidence ought to be required before we double down on the rule of law.

2. Democracy from Scratch? The Misuses of Japan

Here is the problem: we have no real examples of anything approaching the rule of law in recent postconflict intervention. Externally building democracy from scratch is not merely a daunting challenge: it has *never* been done. Never. The frequently cited cases of the post–World War II occupations of Germany and Japan, sometimes invoked by members of the Bush II administration as models for the interventions in Iraq and Afghanistan, are widely misunderstood (though not by Stromseth et al.). These were cases of authoritarian legality, in which an advanced state structure was produced before the rule of law and democracy were introduced. We turn to a brief discussion of the Japanese case in this section.

As Stromseth et al. recognize, both postwar Germany and Japan were already industrialized before they needed reconstruction, and each had substantial if unsustained prewar experience with democratic governance. Perhaps more important for our discussion, each country had experience with a culture of authoritarian legality: nineteenth-century Prussia and Meiji Japan *did* have the "rule of law" of a sort, in which legality structured and limited the behavior of most state agents even if it did not constrain those at the core of the system. It is this experience, and not the postwar occupations, that has the most relevance for contemporary practice.

I use the term "rule of law," but, more precisely, both countries were imbued with the idea of the *rechtstaat*, which is of far more relevance for today's world than the Diceyan notion of the rule of law. As used in contemporary practice, the rule of law is really shorthand for the rule of lawyers, though of course the two projects can overlap. But the *rechtstaat* idea focuses much less on technical lawyering and courts and much more on the bureaucratic legality of a predictable, organized state operating according to rules.

Japan and Prussia adopted the *rechtstaat* idea not as a result of external assistance but *in reaction to* external pressure. Prussia felt constrained by its location, bounded by powerful states in Russia, Britain, and France; Japan was under direct threat of Western colonialism. In response to these security threats, nineteenth-century Japan and Germany created nationalist programs of developmentalist modernization in order to *retain* autonomy. State building in each case was internally directed under external constraint. In contrast, today's postconflict interventions might be thought of as cases of external direction under internal constraint—the local operating environment is seen as the chief limitation on building the rule of law.

Let us focus for a moment on the Japanese case, and in particular the somewhat distinct dynamics of creating the rule of law in authoritarian Meiji Japan. The Western nations that arrived in East Asia in the mid-nineteenth century borrowed an element of Chinese statecraft to impose "unequal treaties" on the East Asian monarchies. These treaties involved exclusive extraterritorial jurisdiction over the activities of foreign nationals on East Asian soil, justified by the view of local criminal justice as barbaric. The treaties were a grave insult to the sovereign pride of these ancient nations.[17]

What followed in Japan (and with less success in China) was an effort to build a legal system from scratch. It followed an internal revolution, the Meiji Restoration, in which the proto-totalitarian Tokugawa shogunate was replaced with direct imperial rule. Hiring foreign advisers from France and Germany, the Meiji leaders set out to build the legal system so as to undercut the claim of legal barbarity. Their central goal was revision of the unequal treaties. And, within three decades, the newly formed legal institutions were sufficiently autonomous that a version of the *rechtstaat* was arguably in place.

The sequence is important and of some interest to contemporary efforts. We have a good overall statement of goals and conception at the outset of the period in the form of the quasi-constitutional Charter Oath of the Emperor, promulgated in 1868: this promised to base policy on public opinion, expand administration, and, particularly relevant to the international context, "abolish the uncivilized customs of antiquity and administer justice and

impartiality in accordance with universally recognized principles."
In the immediate aftermath of the Meiji Restoration, in 1868,
some law was needed, but Tokugawa law was considered insufficiently legitimate. Local custom played a gap-filling role, even as
the institutions of authoritarian rule were replaced. There was a
brief flirtation with Chinese models, but thereafter all legal knowledge came from France, Germany, and other Western nations.

Public order was threatened in these early years. The new leaders had to contend with removing the privileges of the samurai,
a class of potential "spoilers" who were heavily armed. Two rebel-
lions, including one led by a major legal reformer (Etō Shimpei),
were effectively quashed.[18] In terms of transitional justice, the last
shogun was stripped of titles and land but allowed to live in quiet
retirement for the remaining several decades of his life.

In building a legal system, the Japanese focused on institutions
before rules. In the first decade after the Restoration, courts were
initially set up under the Ministry of Justice. Soon, however, they
were broken off into a distinct court structure, then as now one
of the central requirements of Western models. Prosecutors were
also set up as a distinct profession. Lawyers followed (but were less
emphasized). Legal training was established under the Ministry of
Justice at a school which later became Tokyo Imperial University.

Only in the second decade of reform did constitution making
occur, and then as a rearguard action to protect *against* rising demands from liberals for democracy. The constitution was not democratic—it was formally a gift from the emperor to the people,
drafted by a small group around one of the oligarchic advisers to
the emperor. It is interesting that the constitution *followed* institutional reform. In modern intervention efforts, we often proceed
in an implicitly Kelsenian sequence. Because the constitution has
the highest order in the legal system, it must—as a matter of legal
logic—come first. But, as a matter of social if not legal reality, this
seems exactly backwards. A constitution can purport to create institutions, but it can be effective only if the underpinnings of those
institutions are already in place.

The constitution preceded the codes of law. Modern codes of
law and procedure were being drafted well before the constitution
but were not adopted until vigorous internal debate occurred on
which model to follow, pitting the so-called English school against

the French school. The choice of the German Bürgerliches Gesetz-
buch (BGB) as a model—four years before it came into force in
Germany—reflected a sense that German law was the most modern law and institutionally most similar to Japan. Crucially, all this
was an internal choice, in which foreign models were chosen and
not imposed, which certainly explains part of the success.[19]

By the 1890s, Japanese legal institutions were sufficiently independent that the courts could rule against a position advocated
by the executive in a high-profile case.[20] Law schools were now
fully functioning, including important private universities. And
the country was an industrial and military powerhouse, by then engaged in colonial adventures of its own.

This nineteenth-century experience of building a legal system
from scratch occurred under a developmentalist authoritarian
leadership in which democracy was postponed. The key analytic
point from this tale is that state building, including legal modernization, was defensive in character. It was driven by security imperatives above all: there was no external enforcement but only
external threat. This not only provides a very different context
from contemporary Afghanistan but in some sense provides a
counterexample. Only out of fear of being colonized did the Japanese state transform. Had foreigners been administering justice in
Japan directly, the local institutions would simply not have developed the way they did. They would likely have been crowded out.

This prewar history is important because it means that the postwar occupation was not working on an empty slate. The story of
the adoption of the 1946 constitution is a fascinating one that involved, even in its apparent imposition, important points of nego-
tiation and collusion with Japanese actors.[21] And the institutional
structures that made the Japanese postwar state so effective were
largely continuous with prewar versions. The crude version of the
rule of law associated with authoritarian legality was already in
place. The allied forces did not build the rule of law; rather, they
were successful precisely because it already existed.[22]

It is at least possible that authoritarian legality may be a helpful
stage for societies undergoing such dramatic transformations. One
surely does not want to generalize to all cases, but the experiences
of some developmental authoritarian states suggest that in some
circumstances it might be a viable trajectory to the rule of law. It

is surely not the case that authoritarianism is a desirable end in and of itself. But, as Mill reminds us in *Considerations on Representative Government,* the long-run capacity for self-government might sometimes be advanced through nondemocratic means. It is surely an empirical question whether societies starting from a situation of major conflict can get to the desirable end of the rule of law within a reasonable historical period and what the fastest and best pathway might be. An authoritarian state-building stage might be helpful in many circumstances as a path toward democracy and the rule of law. Indeed, surveying members of the OECD as the most successful exemplars of democracy and the rule of law, one sees only a handful (Switzerland, along with settler societies such as the United States, Australia, and Israel) that did not experience a long stage of authoritarian state building before developing the rule of law. Leap-frogging such a stage might be possible, but we ought to at least acknowledge the historical record.

3. MOTIVES OF INTERVENERS

As suggested in the first part of this chapter, order is a public good whose provision is costly. In the absence of a world hegemon, too little order will be produced globally. In the absence of effective government incentives, too little order will be produced domestically. Nationalism seems to be a helpful condition at the level of the nation-state to incentivize local enforcement.[23]

We ought to consider, then, the motives of interveners to produce the rule of law. Why do interveners seek to do so? The answers are as varied as the situations in which intervention arises. Sometimes, as in Afghanistan, an intervention is designed to replace a hostile regime; other times, as in Haiti, it is undertaken to prevent a refugee crisis; in rare instances, it may even be intended to prevent humanitarian catastrophe. For all of these outcomes, the intervening country need not build a full-fledged democracy with the rule of law. It simply needs a local actor capable of providing a basic level of order.

To externally produce something approaching the rule of law in developing societies, we would need to incentivize intervention more than we do. Colonialism, in which an external actor takes charge of the society to extract wealth, might under some circum-

stances leave an institutional legacy that could contribute to the
rule of law. To be sure, it did not always do so. But many societies do attribute a positive legacy to colonial legal structures—take
Hong Kong, Singapore, or Malaysia, to name a few former British
colonies. Taiwan probably benefited in this regard from Japanese
colonialism. Fortunately, we live in an era in which colonialism is
not only illegal as a matter of international law; it is undesirable
from the point of view of "interventionist" state populations. Who
wants to take responsibility for a loss operation like Kosovo, which
will surely need external assistance if not outright occupation for
many years to come?

Without more vigorous interventions, outcomes may be worse,
and compromises with brutal forces will have to be made. Stromseth et al.'s[24] story of Sierra Leone is illustrative. The1999 RUF invasion of Sierra Leone "galvanized the international community"
but did not motivate it to provide the proverbial boots on the
ground. Nigeria, which had already played a role, had no incentive
to stay. In the absence of external enforcement, all that was left was
for Sierra Leone's nascent leadership to compromise with Foday
Sankoh, extending and to some degree rewarding his horrific record, until Britain took it upon itself to provide the public good of
intervention.

A final footnote on the Japanese experience is relevant to the
argument advanced in Stromseth's chapter in this volume.[25] As
in postwar Germany, the allied authorities sought to try the military leadership for various international crimes. They drew on the
Nuremberg Charter, though the standards of evidence were significantly relaxed: unlike the Germans, the Japanese had kept less
meticulous records of their wartime abuses, and many of the records had been destroyed. Many of the Japanese war crimes were
committed in the chaos of war rather than as part of a specific
exterminationist plan and in this sense were closer to many contemporary situations than were those of the well-documented Nazi
regime. As elucidated in the famous dissenting opinion of Justice
Radhabinod Pal of India, the trial failed to meet basic standards of
legitimacy. It is speculative, but I think it safe to say that the Tokyo
War Crimes trials had little if any demonstration effect.[26] The Japanese already knew what a trial was. But, at the time, the war crimes

trials were seen as unadulterated victor's justice. To some degree, this view of the trials persists today.[27]

In my view, the notorious problems of the Tokyo war crimes trials have more continuing relevance than we might hope. Certainly, by any objective standard of the rule of law, our contemporary efforts fare much better. In contemporary postconflict justice, procedural fairness is sometimes pursued to excess (see Slobodan Milosevic). The view is that external criminal enforcement is complementary with local criminal enforcement, through a demonstration effect. But we have little evidence of the actual existence of any demonstration effect. We must, necessarily, proceed by counterfactuals. We have to ask whether Romania would be better off if Nicolau Ceasescu had been tried rather than shot; whether Cambodians would have more faith in law had the initial trials of the Khmer Rouge in the early 1980s followed the standards of Western justice rather than Vietnamese, or whether it would have been better had the current hybrid tribunal been established a decade or two earlier. These points can be argued, but the answers are not obviously yes in each case.

4. CONCLUSION

All these questions are technocratic and empirical in character. I want to close with a more reflexive perspective. In my view, international criminal law is not (only) about the perpetrators and victims, about punishment and reconciliation. The international criminal law project from the beginning has been as much about the interveners as about the target societies. Nuremberg and Tokyo were self-conscious attempts to demonstrate that allied justice was of a higher quality than that of the Axis powers. This demonstration was as much for the home audience as for the target society. *We* are different from them; *we* follow procedures, whereas *they* pursue summary justice.

Similarly, the contemporary zeal for the rule of law says more about us than them. If intervention, however, is partly for our own benefit, then we ought to consider the potential externalities for the target populations. If our enforcement efforts crowd out the local, then they may in fact cause harm to those we seek to benefit.

A central theme of this short, and perhaps overly skeptical, essay has been that we need to understand the politics of postconflict intervention. We ought not assume a target population governed by primal politics and a set of neutral interveners guided by law. Interveners have to have the *motive* to intervene. How could it be otherwise? The expressive function of distinguishing a civilized us from a genocidal other is such a motive. But we ought at least to recognize that we are intervening partly for ourselves.

External intervention in the name of the rule of law and democracy has promised a good deal. It has delivered very little. Basic order, to be sure, has been restored in each case. But basic order is perfectly compatible with a form of developmentalist authoritarianism that is quite different from the international models on offer. Many of the same ends sought by democratic interveners—basic order, effective constraints on state agents, and some role for legal institutions—can be achieved equally well or better in a version of authoritarian legality that might be called *Rule by Law*.[28] For East Timor or Kosovo, Singaporean institutions would be more desirable than American ones—and possibly easier to produce.

The possibility of authoritarian legality exposes the inherent tensions among democracy, order, and independence.[29] Perhaps postconflict societies can have only two of the three goods: they can be democratic and independent of foreign support but likely will be wracked by conflict; they can be democratic and have order safeguarded from outside, or they can have independence and authoritarian order. We have not yet, alas, figured out a technocratic way to produce independent, democratic states with high levels of public order.

NOTES

Many thanks to Allen Buchanan, Jeremy Waldron, and other participants at the Nomos Meeting, January 2010, for helpful comments. Special thanks to James Fleming for his invitation to think about these issues.

1. Roland Paris, "International Peacekeeping and the Mission Civilisatrice," *Review of International Studies* 28 (2002): 637.

2. Jane Stromseth, David Wippman, and Rosa Brooks, *Can Might Make Rights? Building the Rule of Law after Military Interventions* (New York: Cambridge University Press, 2006).

3. For a thoughtful approach to these issues, see Brad R. Roth, "Peaceful Transition and Retrospective Justice: Some Reservations," *Ethics and International Affairs* 15 (2001): 45.

4. For example, the 1970s law and development movement ended with a mea culpa decrying the effort as legal imperialism. James A. Gardner, *Legal Imperialism* (Madison: University of Wisconsin Press, 1980). On international criminal law, see Mark Drumbl, *Atrocity, Punishment, and International Law* (New York: Cambridge University Press, 2007).

5. Stromseth et al., *Can Might Make Rights?*, chapter 9.

6. Barry Weingast, "The Political Foundation of Democracy and the Rule of Law," *American Political Science Review* 91 (1997): 245.

7. See also Russell Hardin, "Why a Constitution?," in *The Federalist Papers and the New Institutionalism*, ed. Bernard Grofman and Donald Wittman (New York: Agathon Press, 1989), 100.

8. Alan Buchanan and Robert Keohane, "Reciprocal Legitimation: Reframing the Problem of International Legitimacy," paper on file with author.

9. Richard Titmuss, *The Gift Relationship* (London: Allen and Unwin, 1970) Bruno S. Frey and Felix Oberholzer-Gee, "The Cost of Price Incentives: An Empirical Analysis of Motivation Crowding Out," *American Economic Review* 87 (1997): 746.

10. On rivalrous enforcement, see Robert Scott and Paul Stephan, *The Limits of Leviathan* (New York: Cambridge University Press, 2006), 101–3.

11. Stromseth et al., *Can Might Make Rights?*, 192.

12. Stephen Gardbaum, "Human Rights as International Constitutional Rights," *European Journal of International Law* 19 (2008): 749.

13. Stromseth et al., *Can Might Make Rights?*, 111.

14 Alberto Alesina and Enrico Spolaore, *The Size of Nations* (Cambridge, MA: MIT Press, 2003); Philip Roeder, *Where Nation-States Come From* (Princeton: Princeton University Press, 2006).

15. David Lake and Angela O'Mahoney, "The Incredible Shrinking State: Explaining the Territorial Size of Countries," *Journal of Conflict Resolution* 48 (2004): 699.

16. Stromseth discusses this briefly in the context of the hybrid court of Sierra Leone. Jane Stromseth, "Justice on the Ground? International Criminal Courts and Domestic Rule of Law Building in Conflict-Affected Societies," this volume, 185–90. I raise it to identify it as a broader point, beyond the criminal justice capacity.

17. The East Asian countries can be considered as more or less natural

nation-states in the modern sense, a further point of dis-analogy from, say, contemporary Kosovo.

18. Donald Keene, *Emperor of Japan* (New York: Columbia University Press, 2002).

19. Daniel Berkowitz, Katharina Pistor, and Francois Richard, "Economic Development, Legality and the Transplant Effect," *European Economic Review* 47 (2003): 165.

20. The Otsu incident. For a brief discussion see Tom Ginsburg, "Studying Japanese Law Because It's There," *American Journal of Comparative Law* 58 (2010): 15.

21. Ray Moore and Donald Robinson, *Partners for Democracy: Crafting the New Japanese State under MacArthur* (New York: Oxford University Press, 2002); Zachary Elkins, Tom Ginsburg, and James Melton, "Baghdad, Tokyo, Kabul: Constitution-Making in Occupied States," *William and Mary Law Review* 49 (2008): 1139.

22. It is important to note that Japanese courts in World War II were largely autonomous and were not subject to the same ideological pressures that characterized Nazi law. The legal system both during *and* after the war had a relatively small scope. But it was effective in the domains in which it operated.

23. Liah Greenfeld, *Nationalism: Five Roads to Modernity* (Cambridge, MA: Harvard University Press, 1992).

24. Stromseth et al., *Can Might Make Rights?*, 158.

25. Stromseth, "Justice on the Ground."

26. Timothy Brook, "The Tokyo Judgement and the Rape of Nanking," *Journal of Asian Studies* 60 (2001): 673.

27. See the films *Puraido—Unmei no Toki* (Pride: The Fateful Moment; dir. Toshiya Ito, 1998); *Ashita E No Yuigon* (Best Wishes for Tomorrow, dir. Takashi Koizumi, 2008).

28. *Rule by Law? The Politics of Courts in Authoritarian Regimes*, ed. Tom Ginsburg and Tamir Moustafa (New York: Cambridge University Press, 2009).

29. I should be clear that these tensions are recognized by Stromseth.

11

BYSTANDERS, THE RULE OF LAW, AND CRIMINAL TRIALS

LARRY MAY

In discussions about the rule of law in transitional justice, whether in domestic or international contexts, the focus is normally on those who are perpetrators. The puzzle is to figure out how to get those who have been perpetrators or those who might become so instead to conform to the rule of law so that a lasting peace can be restored. But there should also be a strong focus on those who have been or who might become mere bystanders to atrocities. In building or restoring the rule of law, it is the bystanders who are often overlooked, and yet it is they who play a significant role in the rule of law. Most significant, bystanders form the bulk of a society, and the rule of law can exist only where the bulk of the society has respect for law and does not acquiesce in the face of violence. For it is the bulk of the society, rather than the few who are perpetrators or might become so, whose conformity to law is what glues a peaceful society together.

In this essay, I will argue that it is society's respect for procedures and its belief that such procedures are fair, especially among current and potential bystanders to atrocities, that are the crucial normative glue for restoring the rule of law. I will draw on the just-war tradition, as well as on recent work concerning the rule of law in transitional societies, especially by Jane Stromseth, and I will also discuss the Rwandan transitional justice process known as gacaca.

Whether the rule of law has been disrupted by mass atrocities such as genocide or by aggression, similar normative issues arise about how best to restore respect for law and end cycles of violence.

1. JANE STROMSETH ON REBUILDING THE RULE OF LAW

Jane Stromseth has raised a set of questions and challenges to the idea that "accountability processes" have fully positive effects on the "domestic rule of law."[1] In this section I will summarize some of her views and indicate how I will later respond to some of her concerns, while admitting that I am generally sympathetic to her position. In later sections of this chapter, I will discuss one of the most important issues in much more detail, namely how such "accountability processes" might be able to counter the problem of bystanders who are complicit in large-scale atrocities. As I will explain, the issues that Stromseth has addressed are hugely important in understanding the rule of law "on the ground."

One of Stromseth's worries concerns "demonstration effects." She begins her discussion of these effects by citing their overall positive contributions:

> accountability proceedings can contribute to strengthening the rule of law in postconflict societies through demonstration effects. Most tangibly and directly by removing perpetrators of atrocities from positions in which they can control and abuse others, criminal trials (and processes such as rigorous vetting) can have a cathartic impact by assuring the population that old patterns of impunity and exploitation are no longer tolerable. . . . They aim to substantiate concretely, and to demonstrate, a norm of accountability.[2]

And she argues that "pursuing accountability fairly and credibly can have empowering ripple effects in a postconflict society."[3]

I agree with Stromseth here and will, in later sections, add additional reasons especially to support the idea of the importance of these empowering ripple effects on bystanders to atrocities. The ripple effects that I will focus on are those that have a direct bearing on bystanders. In particular, I am interested in how the building or rebuilding of a fair and credible system of procedural accountability, one that treats all members of society as equal before the law, can have the profound ripple effect of instilling equal respect within a society. The rule of law is not rebuilt merely by having an accountability system in place. Rather, it seems to me, specific groups in the population must see the accountability in some sense instilling respect for their fellow citizens or fulfilling some other normative goal that would make folks more prone to reconciliation than they were before.

Stromseth rightly points out that in some cases trials have actually increased tensions in the society.

> With a few notable exceptions, a disturbing pattern has emerged with members of each of the three ethnic groups [in Bosnia] engaged in attempts to arrest, prosecute, and punish for war crimes members of their rival ethnic groups, who often are still viewed as heroes by their respective communities. . . . Rather than promoting healing and confidence-building among the parties, trials often end up exacerbating divisions and mutual suspicion.[4]

In addition, she argues that in places like Rwanda, the high-profile trials in Arusha have not had consistently positive effects. "For many Rwandans, moreover, the individuals who directly committed atrocities in front of their own eyes matter as much as the distant architects of the genocide."[5] When only the leaders are prosecuted in Arusha by the International Criminal Tribunal for Rwanda (ICTR), the "demonstration effects" are diminished. As a result, Rwandans are generally displeased with the ICTR's criminal trials in Arusha.

Stromseth has put her finger on several important worries about the uses of criminal trials as vehicles of public accountability. But, in addition, we need an analysis of how such failings made the reinstatement of the rule of law more difficult. What interests me is not just the abuses we have seen in various international trials but also what ideally trials can become. It is curious that Stromseth looks primarily at the high-profile trials in Arusha and The Hague, on one hand, and truth and reconciliation processes, on the other, but does not spend much time on mixed models of localized trials such as the gacaca in Rwanda. I will spend time doing just this, but in doing so I am as interested in the actual functioning and abuses of these courts as I am in their potential.

The other way that trials can have a positive effect, according to Stromseth, is in their "capacity-building effects."

Accountability proceedings cannot simply be an "aside"—standing totally apart from ordinary and ongoing processes of reform. Instead, over time, accountability norms—the condemnation of brutal atrocities, the importance of fair proceedings for determining responsibility, and the need for effective and impartial procedures for resolving future disputes more generally—must become embedded in domestic practices.[6]

The idea of locally embedding accountability proceedings is indeed crucial to Rule of Law issues, but we need a framework for us to see what these conceptual connections are.

Stromseth talks of outreach programs and other efforts to disseminate the results of the high-profile trials to people living far away from the site of these trials in The Hague. Sometimes high-profile international criminal trials can have a positive effect on rebuilding domestic criminal processes devastated by war and atrocity, especially when the local judiciary has been targeted or dismantled by invading armies or by insurgent movements bent on creating havoc in these societies. But the analysis of the failures she discusses is hard to assess since we lack a conceptual framework for understanding the rule of law and its relationship to such failures at the local level.

Stromseth argues that international criminal proceedings are sometimes so expensive that they drain resources from domestic judicial proceedings and hence retard rather than advance the likelihood of "capacity-building effects." She argues that local and hybrid proceedings stand a much better chance of advancing the goal of capacity building but that, too often, the international tribunals hold their proceedings far away from the site of the atrocities and that the proceedings are conducted in a way that does not address the root of the local problems or even speak to the local populations in their own languages. And in this I am in complete agreement with Stromseth, although she focuses almost exclusively on public outreach campaigns by those who are running the high-profile trials. But it seems to me that it is primarily localized trials, not mere public relations campaigns for the high-profile trials, that promote the building of capacity on the ground.

Stromseth does say that "criminal trials, alone, even with ambitious outreach programs, are—at best—only part of what is needed to grapple with past atrocities or to build local capacity for justice."[7] Indeed, this is the view that has been taken by several important figures in the just-war tradition, as we will see in the next section. What Stromseth needs is a normative framework that would allow us to determine what else is needed. In what follows, I will build on her analysis and concerns, as well as go back to theoretical considerations in a way that begins to indicate how trials can be reformed so that they can have a causal impact on diminishing the likelihood of atrocities happening in the future and increasing the likelihood that the society can heal, specifically in terms of restoring respect for the rule of law.

2. Historical Origins of the Idea of Due Process

An interesting historical source is Magna Carta, which was an agreement extracted from King John of England by feudal barons. In the England of 1215, the rule of law was in disarray. Magna Carta was the result of negotiations to establish the rule of law out of a patchwork quilt of feudal rules and abuse at the hands of the king's sheriffs.[8] In my other writings on this topic, I have argued that Magna Carta can serve as a very interesting model for the development of procedural justice at the international level. Here I will highlight several aspects of Magna Carta for thinking about the restoration of the rule of law.[9]

Chapter 39 of Magna Carta (normally referred to as Chapter 29, in the 1225 revised version of King Henry III) says:

> No freeman shall be taken or imprisoned or desseised or exiled or outlawed or in any way destroyed, nor will we go upon him nor send upon him, except by the lawful judgment of his peers or by the law of the land.

Due process of law is often associated with habeas corpus and other procedural rights. The phrase "due process" is thought to have been used in one of the early restatements of the Magna Carta rights.[10] Indeed, the phrase "by the law of the land" came to be understood as "due process of law" as early as the fourteenth century. So, from a fairly early point, the Magna Carta provisions, especially its guarantee of no arbitrary imprisonment, were associated with the idea that arbitrary treatment was to be understood in terms of not following the procedures of the "law of the land."

And, as it developed, Magna Carta was actually changed to reflect this fact by the inclusion of the words "in due manner, or by process."

It is hard to overstress the importance of procedural rights and especially equal treatment before the law in the development of the rule of law in England from the thirteenth century on. William Blackstone argued that Magna Carta rights were the basis of fundamental law in England,[11] and it also seems to me that these procedural rights were crucial in establishing, over a lengthy period of time, respect for national law that was grounded in respect for all people under the law. It is this idea that I will develop as the essay proceeds and that helps fill in the story that Jane Stromseth tells about the rebuilding of the rule of law in places like Sierra Leone and Cambodia today.

Several centuries after Magna Carta, Hugo Grotius argued that we should understand law as a "body of rights." One of the rights that is crucial for law is the "right to one's own," especially the right "over oneself."[12] Grotius and many who followed after him spoke of these rights as substantive rights to freedom. The rights to freedom or liberty were crucial for marking a society ruled by law from one that was not. Respect for the rights of subjects was crucial for providing law with its moral core—one based in natural or human rights. Hugo Grotius was well known for his espousal of a secular version of natural law theory.

Writing in 1625, Grotius proposed that there is an "association which binds together the human race, or binds many nations together" and that such an association "has need of law."[13] Grotius then famously defended the idea "that there is a common law among nations, which is valid alike for war and in war."[14] Grotius spoke explicitly of such a society bound together "by good faith" and "tempered with humanity."[15] Grotius recognized that "law fails of its outward effect unless it has a sanction behind it." Even when there is no sanction, law "is not entirely void of effect" as long as "justice is approved, and injustice condemned, by the common agreement of good men."[16] The conscience of humanity can be affected even without sanctions, but the international society is yet better served if the condemnations of injustice can be backed by sanctions against those states and individuals that act unjustly. Whatever the sanctions of law, even the sanctions of war, these should be governed by the singular task of "the enforcement of rights."[17]

There is also part of the natural law tradition that saw rights over oneself in terms of the procedural right to be treated before the law in the same way as everyone else and for the individual's rights not to be unduly restricted before the law. William Blackstone, writing in 1765, argues that the rights of "personal security, personal liberty, and private property" cannot be secured without what he calls "auxiliary subordinate rights of the subject, which serve principally as barriers to protect and maintain inviolate the great primary rights." And one of the most important is the right of every citizen "of applying to the courts of justice for redress of injuries." According to Blackstone, the "courts of justice must at all times be open to the subject, and the law must be duly administered therein."[18] This is the guiding normative insight behind the idea of due process of law.

As the term indicates, "due process of law" concerns the requirement that laws must follow a certain process and that that process must be what is due to the people in question. Here there are two components: that there is a process that governs how law is administered and that the process in some sense must be what is due to the people who are subject to the law. The difficult question is how to understand what process is due to the subjects or citizens of a particular state. Perhaps the simplest idea is that all subjects or citizens stand equally before the law and that the process that is due them is that process that treats them equally before the law and perhaps that guarantees and safeguards their equal standing before the law. Societies should not distinguish between second-class citizens and the rest of citizens. What is initially due is that people not be demoted to second-class standing by the way the process of law is constructed.

What else is due is that the process in question be one that involves at least a minimum amount of fairness and accountability for the officials who are supposed to administer the law. This is a matter of equity, which is different from equality before the law. One of the main reasons for accountability is to curtail or deter abuse by these officials. Mere threat of publicity can do quite a lot, but it is sometimes also necessary to have procedures in place that hold officials to account in a more formal way, by having hearings

to which individuals can appeal to bring the officials to answer and
where the appeals process can result in penalties for gross misconduct on the part of officials who are supposed to be fairly administering the law.

3. Procedural Justice and the Rule of Law

Taking my cue from the development of English law from Magna
Carta onward, as well as from the writings of Grotius already mentioned, I will focus on procedural justice as a gap-filling and norm-
strengthening basis for the eventual establishment of a robust system of international rule of law. It is very difficult to create a system
of law merely by compiling a set of substantive or primary rules,
as is seemingly the way international law is proceeding at the moment. Such a set of rules will have gaps in terms of both the reach
of its rules and the protection it offers to those who are subject to
its rules. It is also difficult to restore respect for the rule of law in
war-torn societies merely by holding high-profile trials. As Stromseth reminds us, people often care more about what happens to
those who were perpetrators or bystanders than about what happens to the political or military leaders who orchestrate atrocities.

Procedural justice can be understood as Rawls saw it, in terms of
fair procedures that all or nearly all would consent to from behind
a veil of ignorance.[19] The basic structure of a social order is primarily a matter of understanding what would be acceptable if people
did not know their positions in society and yet nonetheless had to
design the rules for that society. I find the Rawlsian approach quite
helpful on the ideal level, as an attempt to make sense of the idea
of fairness to which any system of law must aspire. The Rawlsian
ideal is a powerful one, but it is hard to see whether perpetrators,
victims, and bystanders could agree to anything other than the
most general of principles at the ideal level.

In my view, nonideal procedural justice is better captured by
the idea that all are subject to the same rules and that these rules
act to provide a minimally fair basis for treating all people with respect in terms of the protection of their human rights. Rawls and
his followers, at least some of them, have seen international justice
as being a matter of the relations of peoples or of states.[20] Some
others, including some who follow Rawls, have seen global justice

as a matter of how individuals act toward each other and so have called themselves cosmopolitans.[21] My own position falls somewhere in between a state-centric and a completely person-centric conception of global justice in general and global procedural justice in particular. We can think of this position, as Simon Caney has said, as a society of states,[22] much as Grotius did, but one that is aimed at eventually providing a rough equality for all individuals regardless of which states they reside in. Nonetheless, I do not support either the elimination of states or the current strong state-centric approach.

A Grotian society of states approach sees states as instrumentally valuable insofar as they provide protection for the rights of their subjects or citizens and do not jeopardize the rights of nonsubjects or noncitizens. The Grotian approach I favor looks to the existing states as often being aids to the development of adequate protection of basic human rights. But, at the same time, when a state does not provide or actively undermines such protection, then the state loses any claim to the benefit of the doubt. I have made a similar argument concerning an account of international justice.[23] And, in the aftermath of atrocity, what is most important is that states be rebuilt in such a way that they are protectors of the human rights of their members.

Procedural justice is primarily about equal protection of the law, where this idea has two important components. First, and foremost, procedural justice provides people with protection of their rights. In the international arena, this means that procedural justice must provide a framework for the protection of human rights, especially basic human rights. Second, and nearly as important, procedural justice conveys the idea that everyone will be subject to and protected by the same rules. Each person is to be seen as equal before the law. In international law, this means that each person must be afforded the same level of protection of his or her basic human rights, regardless of where in the world that person resides. It is this latter condition of procedural justice that makes it constitutive of the international rule of law but also so difficult to instantiate over the objections of strong states that do not want to be subject to anyone else's rule.

There is thus a minimal substantive component to the very idea of global procedural justice, namely that each person will have at least minimal protection of his or her basic human rights. But the substantive part here is quite thin. The emphasis is on the framework for the protection of these rights and especially on the way that dignity and respect for persons are protected through the concept of equality before the law. There must be some rights that people have universally for the idea of equality before the law to make sense at all; the substance of this equality need not be extensive, as long as minimal human dignity is maintained. And, similarly, when such minimal human dignity and respect are afforded, then people will find it easier to support the rule of law, both domestically and internationally.

Here I follow certain aspects of the writings of H. L. A. Hart and Lon L. Fuller about procedural natural law in thinking that there is "minimal content of natural law" that any system of law must seek to promote and preserve. While still controversial, this kind of idea can be seen to draw support from very different schools of thought. But, as Hart recognized, there is still room for great iniquity in such a system of law,[24] but perhaps not quite as much as Hart seemed to think was likely to result. In this sense, I follow Fuller more than Hart in thinking that procedural justice and the rule of law will lead to at least minimal respect for people and will rule out some of the worst abuses against persons.[25]

4. BYSTANDERS AND SHARED RESPONSIBILITY

One of the key problems often identified in criminal trials for atrocities like genocide is that trials seemingly cannot deal with the crucial role that bystanders play in these atrocities and that therefore these trials do not advance reconciliation. Criminal trials might be bifurcated, with a sizable portion devoted to the circumstances of the larger event, rather than just those that the defendant contributed to. If trials can be set up in this way without significant loss of rights of the defendant, there can be some discussion at trial of the role of bystanders. Bystanders may be morally guilty, but it is very hard to show that they are legally guilty, and therefore they are rarely indicted in mass-atrocity cases. It seems that criminal trials are simply not good vehicles for addressing the role of bystanders in a way that would lead to the kind of self-understanding on the part of members of the society where an atrocity has occurred that would decrease the likelihood of atrocities in the future.

The term "bystander" admits of several meanings, at least three of which are initially obvious. Bystanders are those who do not directly cause the harm in question. But they may be those who indirectly cause such harm by facilitating it. Or they may allow the harm to occur by not stopping it. Bystanders also may be those who do not indirectly cause harm or those who could have prevented it but merely those on the sidelines who are present when the harms occur. Bystanders rarely are mentioned by prosecutors in international criminal trials. Even those bystanders who are straightforwardly complicit in that they facilitate those crimes are not normally charged unless they are high-ranking members of the armed services or high-profile members of the society. Those who played lesser roles but were crucial for the perpetration of the crimes are not considered to be indictable.

Laurel Fletcher has recently written on the role and responsibility of bystanders. She has identified several problems that need to be addressed, the most important of which is this:

> international criminal convictions single out and stigmatize the accused, normalizing the behavior of bystanders and potentially creating a false moral innocence for the unindicted and their bystander supporters . . . [and] international criminal law constrains the doctrinal ability of international justice mechanisms to address more directly the role of bystanders in atrocities.[26]

Fletcher is right to think that courts cannot do a good job of "examining the [defendant's] behavior against that of the non-accused—whether bystanders or other perpetrators."[27] But judges and prosecutors are not the only players in trials.

While the prosecutor often cannot be successful and focus attention on perpetrators other than those in the dock, this has historically been one of the main strategies of good defense attorneys. I agree with Fletcher that what is needed is for someone to discuss openly and in an aggressive way the "false moral innocence" of bystanders. Defense attorneys are sometimes well placed to do this. The legal guilt of the bystanders does not need to be established for either defense or, ultimately, reconciliation. What needs to be established is that the defendant is not alone responsible and hence cannot be a mere "scapegoat" for the larger atrocity, even if he or she did participate in the atrocity.

There are other problems with international tribunals that are perhaps not so easy to address. Fletcher is right to note that the complicated and highly differentiated roles that bystanders play cannot easily be addressed at trial, and I would add that this is true even if we focus on defense counsel, rather than prosecutors and judges. This is especially true in international trials if we continue to focus, as we should, on the big fish, rather than the small fry. It remains a strong possibility that convicting the big fish will make it seem as if others, especially bystanders, didn't really do anything wrong after all. I want to say two things about this point. First, it may be possible, as I'll indicate in the final sections of this essay, to have lesser localized trials that focus on the small fish, perhaps very many small fish, and thus begin to address the roles of bystanders, at least those who were complicit. Second, the point of focusing on bystanders in terms of moral responsibility has to do not with justice or with reconciliation directly but with an intermediate idea, namely shared responsibility.

In some of my earlier writings, I focused on the idea that, in mass violence, what is crucial for change is that members of a community come to see how they shared responsibility for those atrocities.[28] Here, legal complicity is not the issue, since a large basis of shared responsibility for atrocities comes from one's attitudes and omissions, rather than from any direct harm that one caused. Yet, it is still true that those who held attitudes similar to those of the direct perpetrators or whose omissions played a causal role can be viewed as having facilitated the atrocity. It may be that moral blame is not appropriate, even as it still might be said that moral shame or moral taint is assigned to all those who were complicit. Legally, of course, there are no clear parallels to moral taint and moral shame, but reconciliation may be advanced by recognition of such categories.

The idea of bystander complicity certainly blurs the line between moral and legal responsibility. At least in part, this is because of the idea that people who do not seem to play a major role, indeed, people who may appear to play no role at all in a harm are nonetheless stained with taint as if they had played a major role in the harm. This idea surely goes back in time at least to Oedipus and calls forth a very ancient idea of the stain of taint.[29] Bystanders do not necessarily have dirty hands, but they are nonetheless often tainted by association with the harms and wrongs that they could have prevented or mitigated on their own or where the harms and wrongs could have been prevented if only these bystanders had organized. Those who are bystanders on a beach when someone is drowning in very choppy waters may not be able individually to swim out and save the drowning swimmer, but they may be able to save the swimmer by collective action. They are at the very least tainted by not having done so.

Mass atrocities normally take place in populous regions, and the victims are to a certain extent like the drowning swimmer—if only someone had stepped forward and acted, or organized other bystanders to take collective action, or refused to facilitate the actions of the perpetrators, the harm might have been averted. As Mark Drumbl has said, "Part of the riddle of purposively responding to mass atrocity, and preventing it, is to assess how law can implicate the complicit and acquiescent masses who are responsible even if not formally guilty."[30] And, in figuring out what kind of response will be efficacious, responding to bystander complicity is a key. Drumbl says, "The deep complicity cascade plays a much more dynamic role in the commission of mass atrocity than it does in isolated, ordinary common crimes. Ignoring or denying the uniqueness of the criminality of mass atrocity stunts the development of effective methods to promote accountability for mass criminals."[31] Punishment can play a role here, but it is complicated by the different type of psychology that is involved in mass killing as opposed to isolated killing.[32]

5. The Moral Psychology of Bystanders

Ervin Straub argues that bystanders have the potential to stop or diminish mass atrocity but are often so beaten down that they lack the psychological resources to act. He lists several ingredients in the psychological incapacity of bystanders. Straub points to the fact that "Severe, persistent difficulties of life" frustrate people and make them turn against one another.[33] In addition, he says that studies show that "Devaluation of individuals and groups, whatever its source, makes it easier to harm them."[34] And, most significant

for bystanders, "Scapegoating protects a positive identity by reducing the feeling of responsibility for problems. . . . It can unite
people against the scapegoated other, thereby fulfilling the need
for positive connection and support in difficult times."[35] Socializa-
tion toward obedience also plays a role.[36] As a result of these psychological factors, Straub concludes, "In the face of suffering of a
subgroup of society, bystanders frequently remain silent, passive."[37]
Indeed, Straub links these factors to why it is that external bystanders, including nations, become passive bystanders: "Rwanda presents a recent, disturbing, example of international passivity."[38]

Yet, Straub is hopeful that bystanders can be motivated not to
remain passive in the face of mass atrocity, despite the fact that
bystanders' complicity "is likely to encourage perpetrators even
more."[39] Bystanders can exert both negative and positive influences on those who perpetrate atrocity.

> By speaking out and taking action, bystanders can elevate values
> prohibiting violence, which over time perpetrators had come to ig-
> nore in their treatment of the victim group. Most groups, but es-
> pecially ideologically committed ones, have difficulty seeing them-
> selves, having a perspective on their own actions and evolution.
> They need others as mirrors.[40]

Once some bystanders start to act, they tend to encourage others
to act, as well. "The research on rescuers of Jews and other information suggests that over time the range of concern for engaged
helpers usually expands."[41] Straub offers this insight into how to
get bystanders to act: "This will only happen if people—children,
adults, whole societies—develop an awareness of their common
humanity with other people, as well as of the psychological processes in themselves that turn them against others."[42] This is very
similar to the insight from Grotius that I cited earlier and that was
expressed 350 years earlier.

In my view, mass killing cannot normally take place in a region
where people have the disposition to act to protect one another.
And such dispositions are made more likely when population
groups do not divide themselves up into "us and them" opposi-
tions. Reconciliation involves the confrontation of conditions that
foster such dispositions. Part of this task is to see oneself as tainted

or shamed when one fails to act to prevent atrocities. As Marina Oshana has argued, "the extent to which each of these persons remains tainted and their moral record darkened is a function of the person's refusal to repudiate the wrong that has been done and to repair the circumstances" that could cause such harms.[43]

Let me mention another way that morality and legality can partially merge as a way to motivate bystanders. Thomas Hill has talked of second-order moral responsibilities most appropriate for bystanders. The responsibility that seems most apt is what Hill calls the "duty of moral self-scrutiny." Hill argues that bystanders generally have not cognitive failings but rather motivational failings. In particular, bystanders let their baser inclinations rule them "through self-deception, special pleading, and other ways of representing our motivations to ourselves as better than they are." And one of the most serious of these motivational problems is that bystanders often see themselves as acting for bad reasons because they see them as good reasons, assuming that their motives are good whatever those motives are.[44] If we combine this idea with the idea of moral taint, we get the idea that bystanders need to see themselves as tainted by their passivity and to see their passivity, even in the light of widespread commonality of behavior by others, as a failure of responsibility. Once again, this is also the underlying idea behind the "responsibility to protect" movement that was spawned by the 2005 conference sponsored by the United Nations General Assembly.[45]

Paying attention to bystanders allows us to see how large-scale harm can occur in societies where there were so many people "standing around." And one way to prevent such atrocities is for people to see themselves as empowered and capable of acting and as motivated to do so. As we will next see, the recognition of the fact of widespread complicity, and one's role in it, is crucial for self-understanding and also for providing impetus for change in those societies. But there is no magic here—individual cases will differ, and pointing a finger at those who were complicit may further entrench mutual resentments. I have been speaking of only some of the factors that can advance reconciliation and that are not inconsistent with criminal trials. It is beyond the scope of this chapter to address the other factors in the detail they deserve.

6. THE GACACA PROCESS IN RWANDA

In Rwanda, there has been a serious attempt to deal with the desire for justice after genocide and the sometimes-conflicting need to have reconciliation after such a horrific experience in a society. One of the main difficulties faced is that many members of Rwandan society either participated in the killings, directly or indirectly, or were passive bystanders who could have stopped the horror. Reconciliation is not merely a matter of getting the Tutsis and the Hutus to stop harming each other. Reconciliation will also involve the population's coming to terms with the widespread complicity in the genocide, where the two ethnic group affiliations did not match up with victim and perpetrator groups in the society, for this is important to prevent future atrocities. And here is where criminal trials could, in my view, help in that reconciliation endeavor.

Earlier, I discussed the point often made by critics of international criminal trials that such trials can further inflame the passions of two sides to an ethnic or religious group dispute. Passions have been inflamed in the Balkans, where the trials in The Hague have often made ethnic Serbs even more suspicious and resentful of the other ethnic groups in the former Yugoslavia. But in Rwanda the trials of those responsible for the genocide have taken two forms: a small set of trials by the International Criminal Tribunal for Rwanda (the ICTR) in Arusha, aimed at the main perpetrators, and a large set of local trials, the gacaca (literally, "justice in the grass" in the Kinyarwanda language), that have looked at a wide array of those who were potentially complicit in the genocide. In these cases, despite their difficulties, both types of trial have aided in making it clear how extensive was the complicity in the genocide and how much shared responsibility there was for the atrocity, although members of only one ethnic group have been subject to these proceedings.[46]

The gacaca have been trials rather than truth and reconciliation–style proceedings, although there is a bit of a mixture of both. The gacaca are "trials" in that proceedings are held and judges pass sentences. There is then an appellate level, where judges all apply the same substantive criminal law. But the local-level trials are presided over by elected elders, rather than by trained lawyers, and the rules of evidence are partially relaxed in these proceedings, with the judges having more discretion than would be true in normal trials but with an attempt to protect the rights of the defendants nonetheless. The decentralized trials of the gacaca have been credited with helping the communities repair themselves by bringing community and perpetrator together, although it is also true that the communities are not the same as they were before the genocide, since so many people have become dislocated or have relocated.[47]

Mark Drumbl raises the worry that the ICTR, sitting in Arusha, has put pressure on the gacaca process in the local regions of Rwanda, perhaps to the gacaca's detriment.[48] Pressure from the ICTR trickles down to the gacaca urging them to focus on retributive and deterrent goals in meting out punishments, rather than on the traditional restorative goals of the older versions of gacaca. And, indeed, other critics contend that deterrence and retribution, the traditional normative goals of criminal law, are largely inconsistent with reconciliation.[49] This is one of the reasons that the South African Truth and Reconciliation Commission (TRC) did not allow for criminal trials for atrocities at the same time that the TRC was operating, much to the dismay of many families of victims who sought something other than reconciliation, namely justice.[50]

At the societal level, reconciliation is not primarily about individuals, and for this reason the normative goal of retribution can indeed conflict with reconciliation. Retribution is, in effect, one sided, not two sided or multi-sided, as is reconciliation. The idea that there can be reconciliation where only one of two parties is satisfied with the result runs contrary to what the term "reconciliation" means. And retribution is about not two parties feeling satisfied but only one, the party that has been aggrieved. Retribution, especially when it is the focus of a criminal trial, is concerned with the society and the victim. The perpetrator is a subject of the trial not as someone who is to achieve satisfaction but as someone generally who is about to become greatly dissatisfied if found guilty. For the victim and the society to achieve retribution, there must be some suffering on the part of the perpetrator, either monetary loss or incarceration. But the suffering need not involve long prison terms, especially if the participation by the defendant was not major.

The gacaca process in Rwanda has attempted to provide a mod-
icum of retribution for the victims and their families, through meting out some punishments, as it has also sought to foster reconciliation among previously antagonistic social groups in the society,
by involving the community in the proceedings. In my view, this is
best carried out when the community members look inside themselves and ask about their complicity, not when they merely look
to those who are marked as perpetrators. It is true that achieving
both retribution and reconciliation is a delicate balance, and, if
pressure is exerted to move the gacaca process more in line with .
standard trials, retribution tends to become dominant over reconciliation. But this is not to say that the balance between the two
goals cannot be maintained—only that the delicacy of the balance
needs to be protected from outside pressure that could disrupt
that balance.

Those who take a defendant-oriented approach, as I do, will put
pressure on international criminal trials not to focus exclusively
on the victims but also to respect the accused perpetrators, as well
as other possible perpetrators within the larger population. Such
considerations make trials focus on goals that are not necessarily
opposed to reconciliation. Take the trial of Saddam Hussein. If
more consideration had been given to preserving the dignity and
rights of that defendant in the trial and to those who still cared
about Saddam, the trial and execution would not have worsened
the chance of reconciliation in Iraq. The pressure that should
have been placed on those conducting the trial to treat the defendant humanely could have aided in reconciling Shiites and Sun-
nis in Iraq, that ravaged country. The pressure to have retribution
but to achieve it in a fair trial is not inconsistent with the goals of
reconciliation.[51]

So, the worries that some critics, such as Mark Drumbl, have
expressed about having trials that put pressure on other methods
of reconciliation that are taking place at the same time as the trials is not an insurmountable problem. The problem does become
acute if international criminal trials are seen as providing satisfaction only for the victims and their families. Indeed, this trivi-
alizes the retributive justice dimension of trials. But, in my view,
international criminal trials should pay as much attention to the
rights and treatment of the alleged perpetrators, both those in the

dock and those outside it, as to the victims and their families. If so, then international criminal trials will not necessarily work at cross-purposes to the goals of reconciliation.

There is one other problem that I wish briefly to discuss in this section of the chapter. For some members of society in Rwanda, the gacaca have reinforced the government's attempt to blame "outsiders for creating divisions in Rwanda society."[52] This is an unfortunate result of the gacaca process but not one that is necessarily linked to the process itself. It may very well be that the gacaca process could play quite a different role. By showing how many members of the Rwandan society were complicit in the atrocities, the gacaca can show that the problem was also very much one of what "insiders" did, including those who used the machetes to kill their neighbors, those who sold the machetes, and those who looked the other way. Most of those who were complicit in the Rwandan genocide were not mere "outsiders." In general, there are reasons to think that some criminal trials could positively advance reconciliation in a society that has experienced genocide.

One of the problems discussed earlier is that focusing on just a few individuals makes it very hard indeed to understand what caused and who is responsible for the genocide. The more trials there are, the more pieces of the puzzle are exposed to the light of day. But if trials do indeed sweep to capture very low-ranking people whose role was minor, localized trials that stress healing as much as retribution may be the best proceedings. It is for this reason that I endorse the gacaca process in Rwanda, even as I remain worried about keeping these trials fair to the defendants.[53]

7. Instilling Respect for Persons and Law

When people have respect for their fellow members of society and see that they will in turn receive respect from others, a society is well situated to conform to the rule of law, rather than to fall into violence and political struggle. Here bystanders play two very important roles in building or rebuilding the rule of law. First, bystanders signal that members of a society are respected when they come to the aid of their compatriots when they are in danger. Second, when bystanders who do not aid their compatriots are criticized, morally or legally, for their failures, the rule of law is also strengthened by this additional show of respect for those who were in danger. The rule of law is built, or rebuilt, on the backs of such demonstration that all members of the society are respected and are in this sense equal before the law and that, if individuals are singled out for adverse treatment, their compatriots will come to their aid, rather than allow them to be subject to disparate and prejudicial treatment.

The rule of law is built on the basis of equality before the law and also on the basis of considerations of equity. For both equality and equity, respect for each person who is a member of society is the key. Equality before the law is premised on the idea that legally no one, and especially no minority group, will be treated as second-class citizens and, most especially, that no one will be subject to danger and risk of harm merely for being a member of a minority group within a society. To ensure that the rule of law is maintained, bystanders must speak up or take action to confront those who show disrespect for members of minority groups and other disaffected members of society.

Equity means that minimal justice must be secured for each person in the society. It is not enough that all are treated equally if that means that all are treated badly. Arbitrary and capricious treatment, especially being subject to undeserved harm or the risk of such harm, must not be part of what it means to follow the rule of law. This is in part what Fuller meant by procedural natural law and also in part what Hart alluded to as the minimal content of natural law.[54] And, again, bystanders can play a very important role in not acquiescing in a regime that fails to provide for minimal justice within a society. One of the most important ways that this can be accomplished is by supporting legal institutions, judges, and lawyers that act as a check against arbitrary and capricious actions by those in the executive branch of government.

When there is equality before the law and minimal justice in a society, then respect for people, as well as respect for law, is secured in that society. The rule of law cannot be built or sustained merely by having procedures and institutions, although this is very important for the rule of law. In addition, the bulk of the people must support the guiding ideas of the rule of law. Jane Stromseth has shown that there must be capacity building, as well. And I have similarly stressed that if the bulk of the society merely stands by and lets the government or majority groups trample on the rights of minorities in a way that undermines equality or equity considerations, merely having good procedures in place will not guarantee the rule of law. But having procedures in place may work to inspire bystanders not to acquiesce in this manner. And, thus, there is a sense in which having good procedures that are recognized as fair supports the rule of law not only directly but also indirectly by encouraging bystanders to respect people and laws in their society.

Some have argued that the gacaca courts have failed or are likely to fail precisely because they have not provided fair proceedings. There have been reports that both bribing of gacaca judges and intimidation or even killing of witnesses have occurred.[55] Insofar as this is true, my tentative support for the actual gacaca process would have to be withdrawn. But the idea of having localized trials that respect all parties and try to bridge the gap between justice and reconciliation is still worth pursuing and may be one of the only ways to rekindle the rule of law in such societies as that of Rwanda.

I have argued in this chapter that the rule of law can be built or rebuilt with the institution of fair procedures and when bystanders in the society see these procedures as deserving of their respect. Merely having domestic or international trials for the perpetrators of atrocities who have destroyed or waylaid the rule of law is not sufficient, but it is often a necessary ingredient in a return to the rule of law. From the time of Magna Carta through the seminal writings of Hugo Grotius and William Blackstone, fair procedures have been seen as the key ingredient in instilling respect for law. Today, we have seen that instilling this respect for law is also dependent on fair procedures. But we have, in addition, seen that bystanders must see the legal procedures as deserving of respect and must then not acquiesce in their abridgement. Criminal trials, at both the domestic and the international level, can play a significant role in building or rebuilding the rule of law in war-torn or atrocity-ravaged societies. Bystanders must come to see that they are empowered to make such a difference in their societies, especially by going to the aid of their compatriots who are in need, so that respect for persons can breed respect for law.

NOTES

1. See Jane Stromseth, David Wippman, and Rosa Brooks, *Can Might Make Rights? Building the Rule of Law after Military Interventions* (New York: Cambridge University Press, 2006), 307.

2. Ibid., 258–59.

3. Ibid., 260.

4. Ibid., 267.

5. Ibid., 271.

6. Ibid., 261.

7. Ibid., 308.

8. See my essay "Magna Carta, Guantanamo, and the Interstices of Procedure," *Case Western Reserve Journal of International Law* 42 (2009): 1.

9. See my book *Global Justice and Due Process* (New York: Cambridge University Press, 2011).

10. See Mark Freeman's intriguing discussion of the relevance of Magna Carta and due process to the operation of truth commissions. *Truth Commissions and Procedural Fairness* (New York: Cambridge University Press, 2006), especially 109–13.

11. William Blackstone, *Commentaries on the Laws of England* (n.p., 1765; reprint, Chicago: University of Chicago Press, 1979), vol. I.

12. Hugo Grotius, *De Jure Belli Ac Pacis* (On the Law of War and Peace), translated by Francis W. Kelsey (n.p., 1625; reprint, Oxford: Clarendon Press, 1925), 35.

13. Ibid., 17.

14. Ibid., 20.

15. Ibid., 860–61.

16. Ibid., 16–17.

17. Ibid., 18.

18. Blackstone, *Commentaries on the Laws of England*, vol. I, 136–37.

19. See John Rawls, *A Theory of Justice* (Cambridge, MA: Harvard University Press, 1971).

20. See David Reidy and Rex Martin, eds., *Rawls's Law of Peoples: A Realistic Utopia?* (Malden, MA: Blackwell, 2006).

21. See Thomas Pogge, *World Poverty and Human Rights* (Cambridge: Polity Press, 2002).

22. See Simon Caney, *Justice Beyond Borders* (Oxford: Oxford University Press, 2005).

23. See my book *Crimes against Humanity: A Normative Account* (New York: Cambridge University Press, 2005), chapter 1.

24. H. L. A. Hart, *The Concept of Law* (Oxford: Clarendon Press, 1961).

25. Lon L. Fuller, *The Morality of Law* (New Haven: Yale University

Press, 1969). Also see my essay "International Law and the Inner Morality of Law," *The Hart-Fuller Debate in the Twenty-First Century*, ed. Peter Cane (Oxford: Hart, 2010), 79.

26. Laurel E. Fletcher, "From Indifference to Engagement: Bystanders and International Criminal Justice," *Michigan Journal of International Law* 26 (2005): 1076–77.

27. Ibid., 1078.

28. See my book *Sharing Responsibility* (Chicago: University of Chicago Press, 1992).

29. See my "Metaphysical Guilt and Moral Taint," chapter 8 of my book *Sharing Responsibility*. Also see Marina Oshana, "Moral Taint," in *Genocide's Aftermath*, ed. Claudia Card and Armen T. Marsoobian (Oxford: Blackwell, 2007), 71–93.

30. Mark Drumbl, *Atrocity, Punishment, and International Law* (New York: Cambridge University Press, 2007), 26.

31. Ibid., 32.

32. See James Waller, *Becoming Evil: How Ordinary People Commit Genocide and Mass Killing* (New York: Oxford University Press, 2002). Also see Ervin Straub, "The Psychology of Bystanders, Perpetrators, and Heroic Helpers," in *Understanding Genocide*, ed. Leonard S. Newman and Ralph Erber (New York: Oxford University Press, 2002), 11–42.

33. Straub, "The Psychology of Bystanders," 13.

34. Ibid., 15.

35. Ibid., 19.

36. Ibid., 21.

37. Ibid., 24.

38. Ibid., 27.

39. Ibid.

40. Ibid., 29.

41. Ibid., 35.

42. Ibid.

43. Oshana, "Moral Taint," 85.

44. Thomas Hill, "Moral Responsibilities of Bystanders," *Journal of Social Philosophy* 41 (2010): 28–39, at 35.

45. See UN General Assembly World Outcome Document (2005), paras. 138 and 139.

46. See Phil Clark, "When the Killers Come Home," *Dissent* (Summer 2005): 14–21.

47. See Mark Drumbl's discussion of gacaca in his book *Atrocity, Punishment, and International Law*, chapter 4.

48. Ibid.

49. See Michael Scharf, "Swapping Amnesty for Peace: Was There a

Duty to Prosecute International Crimes in Haiti?," *Texas International Law Journal* 31 (1996): 1–38; and Leila Sadat, "Exile, Amnesty, and International Law," *Notre Dame Law Review* 81 (2006): 955–1036.

50. See the case of Steve Biko, discussed in the final chapter of my book *Crimes against Humanity.*

51. See Michael Newton and Michael Scharf, *Enemy of the State* (New York: St. Martin's Press, 2008).

52. Phil Clark, "Hybridity, Holism and 'Traditional' Justice: The Case of the Gacaca Courts in Post-Genocide Rwanda," *George Washington University Law Review* 39 (2007): 48.

53. Some of the ideas in the middle sections of this chapter appear, in somewhat different form, in my book *Genocide: A Normative Account* (New York: Cambridge University Press, 2010).

54. See my paper "International Law and the Inner Morality of Law."

55. See Christopher J. Le Mon, "Rwanda's Troubled Gacaca Courts," *Human Rights Briefs* 14, no. 2 (Winter 2007): 16–20.

12

MIGHT STILL DISTORTS RIGHT:
PERILS OF THE RULE OF LAW PROJECT

RICHARD W. MILLER

These days, when intervening governments, separately or in coalition, take over a country and reshape its governance, they say that their goal is the establishment of the rule of law. In this project, they are helped by cadres of civil servants, lawyers, academics, think-tankers, and members of NGOs, often under UN sponsorship, who constitute an international network of planners and implementers seeking to advance a goal that they, too, characterize as the rule of law.

Perhaps the choices actually made in the projects so described do not track the weight of evidence as to what would advance the rule of law and its underlying values. Still, clarifying that moral and political goal will help to assess those choices and proposals to improve that practice. In light of an appropriate construal, one can pose the following questions, among many others. As a general rule, would more frequent institution of criminal trials to punish those who violated human rights in the order or disorder that has been supplanted advance the values that make the rule of law important? Would substantial strengthening of the Rule of Law Network (i.e., the international network of planners and implementers who regard the establishment of the rule of law as their goal) advance those values? Would those values be advanced if broadly anti-imperialist sentiments opposed to great power intervention were weakened, so that there was more frequent intervention to spread the rule of law by the Rule of Law Imposers (i.e., the governments that exercise or sponsor military force to change foreign governance and say that their postconflict goals include the rule of law)? Would citizens of Imposers advance the values underlying the rule of law by supporting a general precept of great perseverance in shaping governance postintervention? After offering a construal of the rule of law and the values behind it, I will argue that the right response to these proposals to strengthen impositions in the name of the rule of law is "Probably not." Because of, not despite, the importance of the rule of law, the rule of law project should be anxiously scrutinized and cautiously contained.

1. THE RULE OF LAW AND ITS VALUE

One familiar construal of the rule of law might be called "justice as regularity"—as John Rawls does in recommending it.[1] People are to be governed by imposing general, publicly proclaimed rules, precise enough that they can be reasonably sure of what is proscribed. These rules are to be reliably applied by judges who show no bias and strive for reasoned interpretations making the system of rules as a whole as coherent as possible and giving weight to precedent. Prosecutors and police are to act in ways that serve the same purpose of reliable, impartial enforcement. Rules that people cannot take into account in making choices, above all, ex post facto prohibitions, are to be avoided. Those who obey these rules are in the clear so far as political coercion is concerned: *nullum crimen sine lege*. The public authority established by law effectively monopolizes permission to use force and grants it under strict, law-governed supervision.

In their richly informed, thoughtful inquiry into the rule of law after military interventions, *Can Might Make Rights?* Jane Stromseth, David Wippman, and Rosa Brooks label this conception of the rule of law "formal" and "minimalist," noting that a regime meeting this test could impose laws that are unjust in fundamental ways and suggesting that partisans of more substantive accounts "insist that injustice is incompatible with true rule of law."[2] But if this is the whole critique of the regularity account, minimalism should triumph. The alternative would be to make "the rule of law" mean the same as "just governance," losing a means of characterizing one specific feature of just governance.

A better strategy (consistent with the main thrust of Stromseth et al.'s discussion) is to note that the rule of law, in the narrow sense of regularity, is important because of a moral value of autonomy which can be traduced, not just by irregularity but by regular laws of certain kinds with certain origins. Rather than expressing a pedantic obsession with generality, precision, and clarity, the rule of law in the narrow sense is morally important because it is necessary for people to be able peacefully to go about their business, forming constructive life goals with which they intelligently identify, and devoting their energies and attention to these projects with reasonable assurance that their choices will have point and value. Under the rule of law as regularity, Leviathan will not unpredictably intervene to deprive their choices of point and value, but rather will protect them from private intrusion. Deprived of the impartiality of the rule of law in the narrow sense, people will have to live lives of anxious deference to those who call the shots or invest important resources, energy, and attention in defense against their incursions.

Still, what is necessary for adequate protection may not be sufficient. Those profoundly important values of autonomy can also be violated through the regular rule of sufficiently bad laws. People deprived of means to peacefully, enjoyably pursue a life plan with which they can identify because of legal religious persecution, people who must devote themselves to deference or self-defense in the face of domination by racially discriminatory laws, and people doomed to devote their energies to mere survival because the laws take insufficient account of the needs of the poor suffer the same deprivation of autonomy as those subjected to the depredations of a tyrant's arbitrariness or a judge's corruption. So it would be unreasonable to support the rule of law in the narrow sense without supporting protection against these forms of discrimination and neglect.

Similarly, if the basic mechanisms of legislation have no tendency to promote the common good, one can be routinely victimized by the passage of laws tailored to others' interests, as serious an intrusion on secure pursuit of one's life plan as a bill of attainder or a corrupt legal judgment. So support for the rule of law in the narrow sense ought to be accompanied by support for legislative arrangements tending to promote the common good. This arrangement might, in principle, involve the decrees of a high-minded monarch or aristocracy. But, in modern circumstances, democracy is a better bet.

In sum, the interests making the rule of law in the narrow sense important make basic civil liberties, political concern for urgent needs, and basic constitutional arrangements tending to promote the common good important, as well. So, one might include these features of governance under the rubric "the rule of law." In contrast, even more ambitious political goals will rely, for their justification, on other moral interests, on further, controversial construals of values of autonomy, or both. By refusing further expansion, one keeps "the rule of law" useful as a label of one specific feature of just governance. In assessing Rule of Law Imposers, this modesty has a further, moral and pragmatic advantage. More ambitious measures to shape a foreign country's governance raise the question of whether these measures are properly imposed from outside or properly left to the people who will live with them. When the Imposers declare that their favored resolution of these further issues—for example, of the role of religion in the state or the role of the state in the economy—is part of an effort to establish the rule of law, they short-circuit the needed discussion, by associating their measure with arrangements whose effective establishment serves fundamental interests in individual autonomy that are not properly overridden by respect for local collective autonomy. This is such a tempting maneuver that Imposers will inevitably help themselves to it. All the more reason to uphold a narrower usage, encouraging scrutiny of whether they make proper use of their power.

In addition to permitting an alternative, somewhat more ambitious construal, attention to the interests that make the rule of law as regularity important is a basis for principled assessment of what strengthens and weakens the rule of law as a whole. In unfavorable circumstances, all aspects of the rule of law as regularity, much less the somewhat more ambitious alternative, cannot be fully realized. The set of measures that do the most to strengthen the rule of law is the set that best serves the interests that make the rule of law important.

Suppose, for example, that a reduction in uniform application of the law, involving non-prosecution of human rights abusers in the deposed regime, would increase a government's capacity to keep the peace. The proposal to trade the defect for the gain should not be treated lightly. Tyrants love to abuse such justifications. Still, the rule of law is actual rule by laws, not just a matter of their content and adjudication. The less effective a government is in maintaining an effective monopoly of permission to use force and protecting people against illegal intrusion, the weaker the rule of law, all else being equal. If efforts to punish human rights abuses by leading figures in the deposed regime would keep defiant militias in the field, encourage threatened local elites to maintain their access to means of violent defense and intimidation, keep a vast supply of small arms in circulation, and ensure that policing is a fearsome and corrupt occupation, it weakens the rule of law. Any other assessment ignores the interest in effective individual autonomy that makes the rule of law important.

Finally, reflection on the underlying interest in autonomy is required by a vital question of transition: whether conduct weakening the rule of law for a while honors the values underlying the rule of law because it strengthens the rule of law later. Consider Iraq. In the decade before the invasion that overthrew Saddam Hussein, there was a dictatorial mockery of the rule of law. It featured brutal, utterly partial, sometimes arbitrary attacks to maintain the power of Saddam and his clique, with citizens having no recourse to due process. The attacks directly targeted relatively few but created a political life in which profoundly dangerous resistance was the only alternative to deference. Otherwise, there was order, with a low level of civil crime. The sequel to the invasion showed that such mockery is not the abyss, so far as the values underlying the rule of law are concerned. Within four years, the disorder of invasion, insurgency, counterinsurgency, sectarian violence, and crime produced more than half a million deaths in excess of those to be expected from the death rate before the invasion, including hundreds of thousands of violent deaths.[3] In a survey in March 2008, 24 percent of respondents said that they had personally seen or experienced a murder of a family member or relative since the invasion and 12 percent a murder of a friend or colleague, while the corresponding reports of kidnappings were, respectively, 11 percent and 7 percent.[4] When the conflagration died down, justice as regularity, civil liberties, and democracy, though imperfectly established, were much more effective than before the invasion.

Do the very great values that make the rule of law important entail approval or condemnation of the whole process? The proper valuing of the rule of law depends on the denial that the lives of people innocently going about their business are to be intruded on for use as means to advance other's ends. So the ultimate improvement does not, in itself, justify the process. Given the valuing of autonomy that invests the rule of law with its importance, the right assessment of the whole process of dangerous intrusion depends on the judgment of those put at risk. In March 2008, five years after the invasion that overthrew Saddam Hussein, a poll asked Iraqis whether the invasion would turn out to be in the best interests of Iraq in the long run. The "Nos" outnumbered the "Yeses" by two to one.[5] Asked to judge the rightness or wrongness of the invasion in late February 2009, 56 percent of a large representative sample of Iraqis judged it to have been wrong, indicating condemnation by about two thirds of those living outside of the northern Kurdish protectorate that had been shielded from Saddam before the invasion.[6] Evidently, the whole process of overthrowing and supplanting Saddam ought to be condemned to honor very great values underlying the rule of law.

2. CRIME AND PUNISHMENT

Now, we can meaningfully ask whether the values of autonomy that make the rule of law important, even in the narrow construal, are generally advanced by punishing perpetrators of serious violations of human rights, when the Rule of Law Imposers shape governance. Such reliable punishment is part of the rule of law, even in the narrow sense (to which I will adhere from now on, for reasons of clarity. Adopting the broader conception would not affect my conclusions.) Such punishment should certainly be pursued by a government when effective, enduring authority in conditions of basic civil order is secure. The value of the lives and liberties of the victims will be honored. The government's evenhanded respect for its citizens' autonomy will be affirmed. Those who might prey on others despite the basic order may be dissuaded.

However, that security is very different from the situation of governments seeking to establish their authority after military intervention. Virtually by definition, a supplanted failed state has been the scene of a vicious competition in organized violence on the part of entrenched armed groups taking advantage of regional, ethnic, sectarian, or social differences. A triumphant secessionist insurgency whose victory depended on outside intervention will confront clients, beneficiaries, and co-ethnics of the old regime in conditions of animosity drawing on an abundant reservoir of arms. A dictatorship whose overthrow requires outside intervention will have made ingenious use of local splits, relied on the support of some significant local groups or elites, and created a client network of people used to violent authority who now have much to fear and much to lose. The violent intrusion of the outside power will inspire some nationalist or sectarian outrage, threatening a spiral of armed resistance, violent suppression, and further outrage and resistance.

Efforts to establish the rule of law after military intervention are few and are works-in-progress. These efforts have not produced self-sustaining regimes of basic justice. So there is not much success to learn from.[7] Still, those assessing the proper role of trials for past human rights violations postintervention can learn from the extensive experience of countries that have made the transition from grave injustice to basic justice on their own.

These countries have sometimes subjected human rights abusers of the old regime to trial and punishment, but sometimes they have not. There is little reason to believe that the interests that make the rule of law important would have been served by resort to the stricter regularity of trial and punishment across the board. In South Africa, the African National Congress on coming to power might have resorted to trials, rather than a truth and reconciliation process. Would the consequent flight of people and capital and severe alienation of the Afrikaner minority, well entrenched in the countryside, military and police, have been part of a rule of law project that better served the interests of people in the Black majority in peacefully pursuing life goals with which they identified? In Brazil, there was no punishment for human rights abuses during or after the process in which the military gradually instituted civilian rule, culminating in direct elections in a period of 1,800 percent inflation accompanied by massive human rights abuses by police and by plantation owners who had been at the core of the social base for military rule. Would it have helped consolidate the new framework for autonomous self-advancement if the civilian regime had turned around and put people in the old military regime and their leading supporters on trial?

The leaders of new regimes supplanting tyranny who have not taken the path of trial and punishment of human rights abusers had local knowledge and the access to local affiliations and loyalties needed to establish an enduring regime. Quite apart from moral commitments, they also had powerful personal incentives to use their political resources to achieve the enduring stability on which their compatriots' enjoyment of autonomy depended. The basic success of their own life projects and even their personal survival were at risk if the civic project failed. That people with these capabilities and interests made their choice is, in itself, evidence that their choice advanced the autonomy-respecting order that gives the rule of law its moral importance.

Granted, in the most intensively studied cases, transitions from repression to basic justice in Latin America, trials were correlated with subsequent reductions in human rights abuses such as torture, summary execution, disappearance, and political imprisonment, over the next ten years.[8] But would the interests underlying the rule of law in nonprosecuting countries have been best served by following the lead of prosecuting countries? Inevitably, the search for answers through statistical analyses must rely on measures of relevant local social factors that are poor proxies for local knowledge. Using such measures, Hunjoon Kim and Kathryn Sikkink, the leading partisan of a "justice cascade" based on the expansion of prosecutions, have investigated the average independent effect of criminal prosecutions on the reduction of human rights abuses through regressions on a large database of transitional countries. On this basis, truth commissions appear to be substantially more effective than trials in reducing subsequent incidence of such abuses, in general and in civil conflict situations.[9]

No doubt, a local government's support for impunity can reflect a desire to maintain power that also leads to too much tolerance of corruption and arbitrariness. Still, craven interests in self-preservation of powerful people can advance the legitimate interests that give point to the rule of law. In saving himself, Afghan president Hamid Karzai can help the vast majority of people outside of the Pashtun countryside to evade the terrible choice between continual civil war and submission to a political order that they hate, imposed by the Taliban. Indeed, when the local post-intervention leadership is overly responsive to special interests, this is in itself a reason not to press for trials, which are apt to be the sort of victors' justice that rightly infuriates those who identify with the losing side. Pashtuns will not forget the atrocities of Rashid Dostum, a leading figure in the 2001 invasion whose forces massacred many captured Taliban (3,000 or more on a plausible estimate), often by tossing them into the cargo containers that litter the sides of Afghan highways, machine gunning the containers, and leaving those contained to suffocate and bleed to death.[10] Shoring up an essential component of his support, Karzai ended his 2009 presidential campaign by barnstorming the Uzbek north with Dostum. Those who press for trials for human rights abuses in Afghanistan do Afghans no favors if they do not take account of the likely outcome: the punishment of criminals whose support Karzai no longer needs or could never expect, while Dostum enjoys comfortable self-chosen exile.

There is no reason to believe that a general increase in resort to criminal prosecutions for human rights abuse in supplanted regimes would advance the interests underlying the rule of law. To the contrary, it might well endanger the values that make justice as regularity an important goal.

3. Strengthening the Network?

The possibility that nonprosecution of human rights abusers might sometimes strengthen the rule of law, even in the narrow sense of justice as regularity, is one example of a larger distinction, between justice as regularity and legal uniformity. The rule of law in the narrow sense is sometimes characterized as a formal goal, in contrast to more ambitious alternatives. This suggests that its presence can be read off of laws and judicial proceedings: if a country has a single corpus of general, precise laws that apply to all and judgments are rendered through impartial findings, justice as regularity is sustained. But a corpus meeting these requirements of

uniformity administered by incorruptible impartial judges might
utterly fail to rule.[11] Both the need for effective protection of individual autonomy and the possibility that jurisdictional differences
(for example, between states in the United States) are benign are
reasons to distinguish justice as regularity from legal uniformity.
The practical importance of this distinction helps to support a
negative answer to the next question: should the Rule of Law Network be significantly strengthened?

Participants in this Network help the governments supported
by external powers to plan and implement legal processes and
institutions that may ultimately be self-sustaining, pursuing these
tasks with humane commitment and, often, remarkable courage.
Typically, they are lawyers, or hold law degrees, are civil servants
in the bureaucracies of multinational organizations or the Rule of
Law Imposers, or have long experience in NGOs dependent on
these external sources of support or on foundations in developed
countries. While deeply concerned with outreach, those who are
citizens of the postintervention country are typically members of
educated urban elites. These are the right resources, in current
circumstances, for clear, constructive advice and effective coordination in the daunting task of transforming national institutions
degraded by dictatorship, civil disorder, or domination overthrown by secessionist insurrection. But, inevitably, they dispose
practitioners to favor legal uniformity.

This inclination is strengthened by the postintervention division
of labor. Ultimately, the local branch of the Network is a servant of
the intervening power. This subordination tends to associate planning for the rule of law with establishment of national authority on
modern models of basic legal uniformity, the most desirable final
outcome for the Imposers. The mission of the local branch of the
Network does not and should not emphasize the use of departures
from this model to promote stability. Assessment and implementation of these tactics is best left to politicians and proconsuls—who
will, in any case, jealously keep these prerogatives to themselves.

The Rule of Law Network already has substantial resources to
advise, plan, and implement governance, in ways that ultimately
depend on acceptance and empowerment by the Rule of Law
Imposers and affiliated local governments. Should their independent role be substantially augmented—say, by giving them a much

larger share of foreign aid or more vigorous support by Imposers in case of conflict with the new regime? The previous assessment of regular criminal prosecution for human rights abuses suggests, "Probably not." In the postintervention division of labor, the supplanting political leadership and the local branch of the Rule of Law Network tend to respond differently to the benefits and dangers of legal uniformity. Since the dangers can be serious and local political leaders are distinctly responsive to them, the current balance seems about right.

The treatment of pre-intervention human rights abusers is far from the only area in which the interests that make the rule of law important can conflict with the legal uniformity toward which the Rule of Law Network is inclined. The sites of actual or likely intervention are, nearly all, developing countries with sharp divides between the rich and the poor, cities and the countryside and, often, different regions. If what has worked is an indicator of what will work, then strong pressure to comply with a comprehensive, precise, and general national legal code, impartially judicially applied, will sometimes hurt, not help, in liberating people from the bonds of abject poverty. The great event in development, the liberation of hundreds of millions from abject poverty in China, was accomplished with utterly obscure property rights, government initiatives that were relatively unrestrained by law and often unpublicized, and wide variations in permitted practices and subsidized practices from region to region. While certainly a recipe for abuse and corruption, this irregularity was also a basis for fluent sequencing of entry of sectors into world markets, adjustment to foreign investors' preferences, and balancing of current needs with long-term development goals. South Korea, Japan, and Indonesia have also combined rapid growth with a combination of crony capitalism and unrestrained policymaking by a ruling clique or entrenched bureaucracy.

Would efforts to impose greater legal uniformity postintervention enhance or inhibit escapes from destitution when all effects are taken into account? The right answers are likely to depend on variations in local circumstances to which the Rule of Law Network is insensitive. Applying an influential World Bank index of quality of governance in which legal uniformity plays a substantial role, M. G. Quibria found that in Asia, from 1999 through 2003, developing countries that were below the global average rating for countries with their per capita income had growth performance far superior to developing countries above their respective income-based governance expectation.[12] This hardly suggests that kleptocracy in oil-cursed African countries (admittedly, unthreatened by great power military intervention) is benign.

Other open questions about legal uniformity are internal to ordinary citizens' experiences of the legal process in developing countries. Among the poor majority in most developing countries, peacefully getting ahead typically involves self-advancement in an informal economy in which commercial laws are ignored and the legal prerogatives of established firms and agencies are frequently violated (for example, by tapping into electric power lines). Enforcement of a uniform legal code would often impose crippling financial costs of compliance, litigation, and legal defense and burdens of inferiority in knowledge, contacts, and cultural or linguistic skills as the poor are forced to defend their interests in bureaucracies and courts.

In developing countries, economic, cultural, and regional differences have often given rise to a great multiplicity of systems of law and adjudication—for example, the combination of a national legal corpus and judiciary familiar from developed countries with village justice with diverse local norms and practices, the judgment of clergy relying on a variety of traditions of interpretation, adjudication by tribal elders, and adjudication by large landowners. The regulation by the national legal corpus that the Rule of Law Network tends to favor may be distrusted by the vast majority for excellent reasons, reflecting disadvantages that the Network is ill equipped to overcome.[13]

Heightened efforts to impose a legally uniform order postintervention would probably help Imposers subject the economy to the discipline of the world market and keep future local governments out of the commanding heights of the economy. But, like the Washington Consensus in general, these efforts probably will not, on the whole, advance people's interest in peacefully pursuing worthwhile goals with which they identify. Certainly, the equation of the rule of law with virtue on the one hand, and legal uniformity on the other, would obscure, not illuminate, urgent choices for the poor majority in countries that might be targets of intervention.

Granted, the local branch of the Rule of Law Network can be an independent source of initiatives that are neglected or opposed by local national political leaderships who are not guided by the judgment of the citizenry as a whole. The reasonably well-informed verdict of the vast majority of the citizenry should have great independent weight, normally decisive, in steering their governance. This lends considerable importance to a report cited six times in *Can Might Make Rights?*[14] as well as in Stromseth's contribution to this volume, as indicating broad popular support for punishment of past human rights abuses. In Afghanistan, the site of the most vigorous and dangerous rule of law project now, the Afghanistan Independent Human Rights Commission has reported that 76 percent of respondents in a national survey said that "bringing war criminals to justice in the near future would" "increase the stability of the peace and bring stability to Afghanistan."[15] In focus groups conducted at the same time, 41 percent mentioned security as their most serious concern, 10 percent an end to disappearances, and 10 percent disarmament (as opposed to only 4 percent who mentioned the rule of law, far behind "electric power," the first concern of 14 percent).[16]

This finding about Afghan views seems crucial evidence of a demand for increased prosecution, promoting uniformity to advance security, in sharp contrast to the Karzai regime's practice. It is presented as such by the Commission. In fact, the survey is important for a very different reason. At the site of the most vigorous and deadly current rule of law project, it establishes a diverse array of views, sophisticated, flexible, and ruefully informed, among those whose lives will be deeply affected by the project, an array providing strong evidence that efforts to shape their governance should not be regimented by the legal uniformity to which the Rule of Law Network are inclined.

The AIHRC virtually all have backgrounds such as I have described. The Commission was established under the Bonn Accord, was appointed by Karzai, but has displayed incisive independence in reporting harms to civilians by Afghan and US/NATO forces. By 2003, they had taken a firm stand in favor of systematic punishment for those who had violated human rights, especially through war crimes. The survey was conducted in 2004, before the resurgence of the Taliban.

Asked whether they had "confidence in Afghanistan's legal system to be able to bring about accountability for human rights abuses," 58 percent of those polled said "No."[17] It is by no means clear that respondents took enhanced stability to be the likely outcome of increased prosecutions by their actual government, as opposed to the government they wished they had. On the role of prosecutions and punishment in postconflict justice, the respondents often strayed from the stringent uniformity of punishment for crimes duly ascertained. Asked "What does justice mean to you?" 40 percent chose "Criminal justice," but 26 percent chose either "Reconciliation" (15 percent), "Compensation" (6 percent) or "Publication of truth" (5 percent), and 26 percent chose "All of the above." Asked "Would you support amnesties or pardons for anyone who confessed their crimes before an institution created for transitional justice?," 39 percent answered "Yes," a proportion rising to "two thirds of the northeastern region of the country."[18] Without support from the northeastern region, the Kabul government would collapse. For example, 56 percent of the officers of the Afghan Army are Tajiks, the ethnic group based in the northeast.[19] Would respondents who took account of these opinions about amnesties and the accompanying political realities generally have taken punishment of war crimes to be the sort of justice that contributes to security? The answer is not explicit in the reports of the focus groups, but this response would be surprising among people so open-minded and resourceful concerning the appalling abuses that they had suffered and so desperate for security. Read carefully, the survey is evidence of the caution and flexibility with which Afghans approach questions of justice which the Rule of Law Network tends to associate with the punishment due for appalling crimes when justice as regularity is fully realized.[20]

4. MORE MIGHT MAKES MORE RIGHT?

The topics so far have been something of a sideshow. Where the Rule of Law Network is active after military intervention, what it does and whether its advice actually shapes governance is basically determined by the Rule of Law Imposers. So the central questions concern their conduct.

Would it advance the interests underlying the rule of law if current sentiments of opposition to intrusion, broadly anti-imperialist in tenor, were weakened and the Imposers were encouraged to intervene more often? Some think that this shift would be the right response to terrible problems, since millions suffer gravely from the absence of the rule of law, and self-sustaining rule of law is very hard to achieve. Current repugnance at great power takeovers of unruly countries is, in their view, a barrier to needed remedies. For example, Paul Collier proposes, in a widely read book, that beneficent military intervention would be a vital source of benefit in the poorest countries, lamenting the tendency of events in Iraq to deprive this stance of deserved popularity.[21] Niall Ferguson has argued that the establishment of "strong institutional foundations of law and order" should be a goal of the de facto American empire, in a project that is dangerously inhibited by current reluctance to frankly embrace imperial ambitions: "[t]he proper role of an imperial America is to establish these institutions where they are lacking, if necessary, . . . by military force."[22]

In judging these proposals to revive alleged virtues of empire to promote the rule of law, it is important to distinguish among different departures from the rule of law that are to be remedied. It is also important to assess interventionist proposals in light of an accurate appraisal of the underlying tendencies of the Imposers, with emphasis on the most important Imposer, the United States.

One category of plight is now epitomized by Rwanda. Widespread, ongoing large-scale massacres ought to be forcibly stopped, unless there are strong reasons to believe that intervention will lead to greater carnage. The importance of speed and effectiveness favors rescue by strong powers. There is no question, here, as to whether the intended beneficiaries will welcome rescue despite its costs. The rarity of this atrocious cause for intervention and its special offense to the conscience of humanity make it less likely than other kinds of intervention to inspire militarization, heightened tensions, and instability due to the fears of rival powers. While this humane service of rescue has been performed effectively by regional powers (for example, India in East Pakistan, Vietnam in Cambodia), greater willingness to intervene by great powers, including the United States, would be a humane resource, as well.

However, in these cases, assertions of sovereignty are already
held in contempt. There is no major obstacle of anti-imperialist
repugnance to be overcome. To the contrary, the obstacle seems
to be the preference of great powers to husband their military resources for more advantageous goals. Certainly, in the crucial UN
Security Council deliberations over Rwanda, namely the nonpublic
ones, whose records were subsequently leaked by Secretariat staff,
there is no indication whatever of concern for the violation of
Rwandan sovereignty. The permanent members were simply concerned that they would have to invest large resources to achieve a
successful rescue. Despite the pleas for reinforcements on the part
of UN personnel in Rwanda as genocide by machetes took shape
and then engulfed half a million victims, "not once was there any
debate at all about what these people [the remaining peacekeep-
ers and medical workers] were managing to achieve to alleviate
the suffering, nor any discussion about how reinforcements might
help them."[23]

The mayhem of failed states, in which no one is in charge and
armed bands inflict murderous disorder, has important similarities
to the abyss of widespread massacre: the disorder is very deadly,
and worries about sovereignty are dramatically reduced, sometimes eliminated, by the absence of effective sovereignty. Still,
there are reasons for concern about military intervention by the
United States to reverse these lethal failures of the rule of law.
When the United States moves in, protection of its forces by awe-
some firepower takes its own toll. Charles Maynes, when he was
editor of *Foreign Policy*, reported, "CIA officials privately concede
that the U.S. military may have killed from 7,000 to 10,000 Somalis
during its engagement [in a brief attempt to end state failure in
Somalia]. America lost only 34 soldiers."[24] In the primary site of
state failure, Africa, more frequent U.S. takeovers of failed states
will challenge China in a growing competition for resource-rich al-
lies, stimulating militarization and increasing prospects of conflict
in the long run. Interventions by peacekeeping forces of the UN
or of African governments, coalitions, and organizations can avoid
these dangers and, in the latter case, mobilize some useful local
knowledge. A general embrace of more frequent great power intervention seems an insufficiently discriminating prescription for
failed states.

In contrast to rescue from widespread, ongoing massacres and state failure, military rescue from stable dictatorship does violate widely recognized norms of sovereignty. If more intervention to improve such governance ought to be promoted, the sole super-power would properly take the lead. Security Council sponsorship is not remotely realistic, powerful armed forces are needed, and a general license encouraging invasion of dictatorial countries by any would-be improver of governance would be a dangerous rec-ipe for war. Would greater openness to this imperial turn promote or undermine the values of individual autonomy that make the rule of law important?

I have already argued that the answer depends on whether the Imposer only invades to overthrow when there is a well-warranted expectation that the victims of tyranny, on the whole, give their informed consent to the deadly operation, despite its perils. The bases of support that an entrenched tyranny relies on, the divi-sions it exploits, and the nationalist outrage that great power in-tervention creates are normally sources of grave danger. Iraq is the bloody exemplar of the possibility that people may take the re-moval of a hated dictator not to be worth its costs in disastrous in-trusions on their individual autonomy. No warrant for confidence in their informed consent was established before the invasion. In light of the sequel, warrant will be even harder to achieve.

Seeking greater openness, nonetheless, to U.S. invasion to re-place dictatorship by the rule of law, someone might insist that the lack of due restraint by legitimate fears of Iraqis, in the inva-sion and in its sequel, was an anomaly, or in any case, a defect that people supporting more intrusion can expect to be repaired. But encouragement of interventions based on this hope would be a bad bet, staking the lives of those who already have much to bear. Choices made by U.S. presidents of both parties and diverse strate-gic temperaments provide strong reasons for concern that Ameri-can uses of military force to change the political trajectories of de-veloping countries will be shaped by U.S. interests in geopolitical power without significant restraint by prospects of destruction.

The many indicative episodes include these, just within the two current major sites of U.S. military intervention:[25] the provi-sion of U.S. aid to opponents of a new pro-Soviet regime in Kabul "in order to draw the Russians into the Afghan trap," as Zbigniew

Brezinzski later boasted,[26] a trap in which over a million, mostly civilians died, in a conflict fueled by massive U.S. aid to Islamicist insurgents; continued funneling of arms and subsidies to favored warlords after the Soviet withdrawal, to restrict the influence of Iran, as the warlords subjected the country to a reign of lawless terror in which, for example, 25,000 people, mostly civilians, died in factional fighting over control of Kabul in 1994;[27] U.S. efforts to prevent a decisive victory of either side in the Iraq-Iran War, including the sharing of "deliberately distorted or inaccurate intelligence data . . . to prevent either Iraq or Iran from prevailing,"[28] prolonging the agony of the longest conventional war of the century, in which half a million died; the use of precision-guided weapons in the first Gulf War to destroy the power stations on which refrigeration, water supply, and sewage treatment depend, in attacks intended to strike "against 'all those things that allow a nation to sustain itself,' . . . to let people know, 'Get rid of this guy and we'll be more than happy to assist in rebuilding' ";[29] the combination of U.S. initiatives in and soon after the first Gulf War, including sanctions blocking reconstruction, that produced over 150,000 Iraqi deaths within a year after the start of military operations, the vast majority of whom were not soldiers killed in combat;[30] vigorous defense of the sanctions by the Clinton administration, blocking imports needed to restore sanitation and health care in Iraq in a public health crisis that ultimately led to 100,000 or more excess deaths among Iraqi children under five.[31]

In general, as one moves from circumstances in which broadly anti-imperialist sentiment presents no barrier to intervention to cases in which the barrier is now high, encouragement of more frequent intervention becomes more and more likely to undermine the values that make the rule of law important. Conserving its resources for the pursuit of geopolitical interests and zealously protecting abusive client-regimes, an American empire that is less inhibited by anti-imperial sentiment would threaten, not sustain, those values.

5. Is Perseverance a Virtue?

Support for greater endurance in imposing the rule of law after intervention—the last position that I will examine—can accompany doubts about the wisdom and humanity of more frequent intervention above the abyss of widespread massacre. The stakes are especially high in those countries in which the Imposer's perseverance requires widespread killing and maiming of insurgents in forceful imposition that also causes much death and destruction among noncombatants, both as collateral damage in the Imposers' attacks and in consequence of insurgent violence due to the Imposers' persistence. At critical junctures in these foci of the question of perseverance, the Imposer makes a choice among the available options, including these: to leave soon, promoting a national settlement among competing local forces that may afford a reasonable level of security but is unlikely to provide a reasonably close approximation of legal uniformity and the rule of law, or to stay and to continue to shape the local polity with an aspiration to that higher goal. There is no reason for confidence that the momentous turn onto the latter path will advance the interests underlying the rule of law, any more than it did when the United States took up Kipling's advice to persevere after its triumphant intervention in the Philippines and to "Take up the White Man's burden—In patience to abide, to veil the threat of terror and check the show of pride."[32]

Support for American perseverance after intervention is, inevitably, support for American efforts to impose a version of the rule of law that advances American power, in a steadfast initiative in which the reduction of carnage is not the first priority. In Iraq, the overthrow of Saddam Hussein might soon have been followed by elections. This was the expectation of the first head of the occupation, the hapless Jay Garner, who was fired after a month.[33] This might have spared Iraqis agonies of disorder, giving rise to a viable compromise between remnants of the Baathist regime and Shiite parties. But the likely revival of a defiant OPEC power would hardly have served American interests. The dissolution of the Iraqi army and the extensive purge of Baath party members from government positions gave major impetus to the Sunni insurgency, which soon consumed much of Iraq as counterinsurgency by occupation forces further inflamed anti-American fury. However, the same counterinsurgency measures also broke the power of well-organized groups that might have led a reversion to anti-American nationalism in a successor regime. The high point of armed opposition to the American presence, the combination, in 2004, of a Sunni insurgent center in Falluja and a Shiite uprising in Najaf, was a moment of hope for most Iraqis concerned to avoid sectarian conflict. In a Coalition Provisional Authority poll including the Kurdish north, 64 percent had said that "recent events in Fallujah and the acts of Moqtada al-Sadr [the leader of the Najaf uprising] made Iraq more unified" (as opposed to 14 percent "more divided."). Small wonder, since opposition to Coalition forces as occupiers was already the great unifying stance, the position of 92 percent.[34] But the cementing of a national settlement among anti-American forces was not fit for the agenda of the Imposer.

Repeatedly, even at the height of sectarian violence and during the subsequent Surge, the majority of Iraqis have said in polls that American withdrawal, not perseverance, would promote reconciliation and security.[35] Perhaps they have been wrong. But it is hardly clear that a less enduring commitment to implement the American agenda would have done worse than the actual outcome of forceful American endurance—hundreds of thousands of excess deaths. In any case, confidence that forceful perseverance in the American rule of law project was worthy of the informed consent of Iraqis has a future cost. Such unwarranted confidence illegitimately reduces anxieties that ought to stand in the way of future interventions. Support for perseverance based on speculations about what the United States could do if geopolitical interests were put to one side is even worse. It sacrifices vulnerable people on an altar of wishful thinking.

Currently, a question of endurance in a rule of law project is the leading question of war in the world: in Afghanistan, should the United States persevere in the project of destroying or marginalizing the Taliban in its base in the Pashtun countryside while endeavoring to severely reduce the Karzai government's reliance on ties of corruption and cronyism to warlords and other arbitrary local authorities in the rest of the country? This project would generate great violence for a long time. For years, a Kabul government's influence in most of the country will require tainted ties to local power brokers.[36] The Taliban have deep roots that will not be cut without long-lasting widespread violence. Returning from a trip in August 2009, Gilles Dorronsoro, now at the Carnegie Endowment, a deep investigator of Afghanistan for over twenty years, reported that "there is no state structure" and "no practical way to separate the insurgency and the population" in the Pashtun countryside[37] —the site of the "dominant influence in 11 of Afghanistan's 34 provinces" that the Chairman of the Joint Chiefs of Staff ascribed to the Taliban in December.[38] The Taliban are often strongly supported by local clergy, who exercise leadership in village courts that impose draconian justice based on a rigid interpretation of sharia law that has broad acceptance in this region, in the communal adjudication that most Afghans strongly favor as more trustworthy and more effective than state courts. As the Senior U.S. Civilian Representative in Zabul Province noted in his letter of resignation in September 2009, the forays meant to defeat this movement are a powerful source of recruitment: "The Pashtun insurgency . . . is fed by what is perceived by the Pashtun people as a continued and sustained assault, going back centuries, on Pashtun land, culture and religion by external and internal enemies."[39]

At President Obama's announced decision point, in June 2011, the United States could, in principle, reverse its military surge, de-escalating to a small residual force to help defend the North and the cities, on the basis of widespread anti-Taliban sentiment there and to launch antiterrorist strikes. Meanwhile the United States could encourage an Afghan compromise which would probably include Taliban domination of the Pashtun countryside. Or, the United States could persevere, battling the Taliban as long as it takes to marginalize them, or, in any case, until a reasonably noncorrupt Kabul government, providing security by impartially enforcing laws, has earned the confidence of the whole country.

There is no good reason to suppose that the majority of Afghans, much less the Pashtuns at the center of the firestorm, support the second path, of patient, abiding violent imposition.[40] However, nothing less would establish anything like the nonoppressive and uniform rule of law in Afghanistan. Perhaps this turn would be justified by considerations that are labeled "regional stability" in foreign-policy-making circles in the United States, "reasons of U.S. power" outside of those circles.[41] Perhaps, after thirty years of war, the prospects of peace in Afghanistan are so grim in all scenarios that persistent killing, maiming, and intrusion by the United States will not make matters worse. But perhaps the path of perseverance would give rise to carnage that is morally unjustified by foreseeable gains. Scrutiny of these hypotheses, on which many Afghan lives depend, is discouraged by the un-self-critical commitment to achieving legal uniformity and the self-sustaining rule of law that the Rule of Law Network tends to promote. Withdrawal when those goals have not been remotely achieved, rather than perseverance, might honor and promote the values that make the rule of law important.

6. PERILOUS GLOBAL INITIATIVES

Toward the end of the twentieth century, at the high tide of structural adjustment, development in most poor countries was steered according to directions toward market-based prosperity largely devised in the United States. The great global initiative enhanced profitable opportunities for the United States and other developed countries, but produced widespread disruption in developing countries and seems to have typically reduced their growth.[42] Deeper skepticism about the global fit of a single set of directions and the global beneficence of American interests and deeper appreciation of local knowledge might have reduced the damage while preserving what was right in the Washington Consensus. As the luster of structural adjustment has faded, the allure of the rule of law project has grown. Imposition of its directions for governance also promises urgent relief from terrible suffering, while posing the same perils of bold global initiatives backed by the global elite. Once (really, many times) bitten, twice shy. The cause of the rule of law, like the cause of market-based prosperity, is best advanced anxiously, with deep suspicion of the perils of externally imposed liberation.

NOTES

1. See *A Theory of Justice* (Cambridge: Harvard University Press, 1971), 235.

2. Jane Stromseth, David Wippman, and Rosa Brooks, *Can Might Make Rights? Building the Rule of Law after Military Interventions* (New York: Cambridge University Press, 2006), 71.

3. See Gilbert Burnham, Riyadh Lafta, Shannon Doocy, and Les Rob-

erts, "Mortality after the 2003 invasion of Iraq," *The Lancet* 368 (2006): 1421–28 (midpoint estimate of 654,965 excess deaths in the forty months after the invasion, 601,027 of them violent); Amir Alkhuzai et al., "Violence-Related Mortality in Iraq from 2002 to 2006," *New England Journal of Medicine* 358 (2008): 484–93 (entailing about 400,000 excess deaths in the same period, with an estimate of 151,000 violent deaths, after attempted compensation for the omission of 10 percent of the initial sample because of inadequate local security); Opinion Research Business, "New Analysis 'Confirms' 1 Million+ Iraq Casualties," www.opinion.co.uk, January 28, 2008 (based on a poll shortly after the fourth and most violent postinvasion year, asking Iraqis how many members of their household had died as a result of violence in the conflict since 2003, yielding an estimate of about a million such deaths).

4. Opinion Research Business, "Iraqis Confident in Security but Concerned with Economy," www.opinion.co.uk, March 14, 2008, Table 20.

5. Opinion Research Business, "Iraqis Confident in Security," Table 48; 46 percent responded "No," 23 percent "Yes," 19 percent "Impossible to tell," 11 percent "Don't know," and 2 percent did not answer.

6. ABC News, "Dramatic Advances Sweep Iraq, Boosting Support for Democracy," abcnews.go.com/PollingUnit, 20, and "Iraq Poll: Methodology," March 16, 2009, 2. Overwhelming majorities approving the invasion have, from the start, been an exceptional feature of the Kurdish north.

7. Here, as elsewhere, I follow the usual distinction between military intervention and defense against foreign aggression. In any case, the good political outcomes of the occupations of Germany and Japan hold few lessons here. The shaping of enduring terms of governance in those two countries relied on well-established, recently interrupted traditions and well-positioned elites, as Tom Ginsburg notes in this volume and has cogently documented in the case of Japan. See Zachary Elkins, Tom Ginsburg, and James Melton, "Baghdad, Tokyo, Kabul: Constitution Making in Occupied States," *William and Mary Law Review* 49 (2007): 1139–76. No one attached to the values underlying the rule of law would want to clear the ground for its construction through the devastation that destroyed German and Japanese commitments to the deposed order and produced widespread receptivity to the imposition of a new one, devastation including a death toll of about 6 million (about 8 percent of the total population) in Germany and nearly 2.7 million (nearly 4 percent of the population) in Japan.

8. See Kathryn Sikkink and Carrie Booth Walling, "The Impact of Human Rights Trials in Latin America," *Journal of Peace Research* 44 (2007): 427–45.

9. See Hunjoon Kim and Kathryn Sikkink, "Explaining the Deterrence

Effect of Human Rights Prosecutions for Transitional Countries," *International Studies Quarterly* 54 (2010): 939–63, Tables 1 through 4

10. See Rafaele Rivais, "Ce documentaire qui accuse les vainqueurs
de crimes de guerre en Afghanistan," *Le Monde,* June 13, 2002, http://
www.acftv.com/news/article.asp?news_id=4&news_page=7; Carlotta Gall,
"Witnesses Say Many Taliban Died in Custody," *New York Times,* December 11, 2001, http://query.nytimes.com/gst/fullpage.html?res=9903E1D
CDC173FF932A25751C1A9679C8B63; Carlotta Gall with Mark Landler,
"Prison Packed with Taliban Raises Concern," *New York Times,* January
5, 2002, http://nytimes.com/2002/01/05/world/a-nation-challenged-the
-captives-prison[packed-with-taliban-raises-concern.html.

11. Even Joseph Raz, in his incisive defense of a version of the justice-as-
regularity interpretation, at one point says that his conception of the rule
of law is "formal." But, in fact, he is only characterizing the second of the
two phenomena that he has just identified with the rule of law: "(1) that
people should be ruled by the law and obey it, and (2) that the law should
be such that people will be able to be guided by it." In the wake of military
intervention, the first aspect cannot be taken for granted. See Raz, "The
Rule of Law and Its Virtue," in his *The Authority of Law* (Oxford: Oxford
University Press, 2009), 213f.

12. See M. G. Quibria, "Does Governance Matter? Yes, No or Maybe:
Some Evidence from Developing Asia," *Kyklos* 59 (2006): 99–114. The average inferior-governance advantage in the rate of growth varied, from
year to year, from 2.4 percent to 6.8 percent.

13. For example, local processes of adjudication, independent of the
state, are distinctly preferred in Afghanistan. See Center for Policy and
Human Development and UN Development Program, *Afghanistan Human
Development Report 2007* (Kabul: University of Kabul, 2007), 96; Sanayee
Development Organization, *Linking Formal and Informal Conflict Resolution
Mechanisms in Afghanistan* (Kabul: Friedrich Ebert Stiftung, 2008), library
.fes.de/pdf-files/bueros/kabul/05655.pdf.

14. See 252, 258, 259, 260, 304.

15. Afghanistan Independent Human Rights Commission, *A Call for Justice,* www.aihrc.org.af (2005), 17, 70.

16. Ibid., 16.

17. Ibid., 22, 70.

18. Ibid., 21, 70.

19. See Antonio Giustozzi, *Koran, Kalashnikov and Laptop* (New York: Columbia University Press, 2008), 187.

20. It should be noted that the survey was not, and was not presented as,
reasonably rigorous social science. Random sampling was pursued by having "researchers . . . walk around and select participants who they thought

would meet the criteria of random selection" (*A Call for Justice*, 55). No breakdown by education, employment, income, ethnicity, or urban-rural residence is supplied. The provincial survey chart shows significant over-representation of non-Pashtun provinces in the center of the country. Ibid., 72.

21. See Paul Collier, *The Bottom Billion* (Oxford: Oxford University Press, 2007), chapter 8.

22. Niall Ferguson, *Colossus* (New York: Penguin, 2004), 301, presenting a passage from his earlier book *The Cash Nexus* (London: Penguin, 2001).

23. Linda Melvern, "The Security Council: Behind the Scenes," *International Affairs* 77 (2001): 110. See, in addition, Nicholas Wheeler, *Saving Strangers* (Oxford: Oxford University Press, 2000), 241.

24. Charles W. Maynes, "Relearning Intervention," *Foreign Policy* 98 (1995): 96, at 98.

25. For a much fuller account of relevant episodes, see Richard W. Miller, *Globalizing Justice* (Oxford: Oxford University Press, 2010), 166–90.

26. In an interview appearing in in *Le Nouvel Observateur*, January 15–21, 1998, 76, but not in the shorter edition sent to the United States. For the whole interview, see "How Jimmy Carter and I Started the Mujahideen," *Counterpunch*, October 8, 2001, www.counterpunch.org/brzezinski/html. John Cooley presents some excerpts in *Unholy Wars* (London: Pluto, 2000), 19f.

27. See Human Rights Watch, "Military Assistance to the Afghan Opposition," October 2001, www.hrw.org/backgrounder/asia/afghan-bck1005.htm, 4.

28. Stephen Engelberg, "Iran and Iraq Got 'Doctored' Data, U.S. Officials Say," *New York Times*, January 12, 1987, A1.

29. Descriptions of the objective by a senior airforce officer "who played a central role in the air campaign but declined to be named" and an un-named "Air Force planner," reported in Barton Gellman, "Allied Air War Struck Broadly in Iraq," *Washington Post*, June 23, 1991, A1. Gellman attributes similar characterizations of this goal of "long-term leverage," in less pithy formulations, to Colonel John A. Warden III, deputy director of strategy, doctrine, and plans for the Air Force.

30. 158,00 Iraqi deaths, of whom 40,000 were soldiers killed in combat and 32,000 were children, was the estimate of the most extensive U.S. assessment of the human costs of the war to Iraqis, by a demographer at the U.S Census Bureau, Beth Osbourne Daponte, who was forced out after a leak of her report. See Thomas Ginsberg, "War's Toll: 158,000 Iraqis and a Researcher's Position," *Philadelphia Inquirer*, January 5, 2003, A05. The toll includes those who lost their lives after President Bush's repeated appeals to 'the Iraqi military and the Iraqi people to take matters into their own

hands—to force Saddam Hussein the dictator to step aside." When the
call produced a popular uprising rather than the desired military coup,
the United States abandoned tens of thousands of rebellious Iraqis to a
bloodbath for fear that they were too sympathetic to Iran or apt to provoke
Turkey through excessive Kurdish independence. In the south, Iraqi heli-
copters organized the carnage, with American aircraft flying above them,
as U.S. troops stopped rebels from taking abandoned arms and ammuni-
tion. See Andrew Cockburn and Patrick Cockburn, *Out of the Ashes* (New
York: HarperCollins, 1999), 23, 38, 39; Nora Boustany, "Violence Reported
Spreading in Iraq; Army Units Clash," *Washington Post*, March 6, 1991, A26;
Nora Boustany, "U.S. Troops Witness Iraqi Attack on Town in Horror, Frustration," *Washington Post*, March 31, 1991, A20.

    31. In a widely cited analysis, "Morbidity and Mortality among Iraqi
Children from 1990 through 1998," www.casi.org.uk, 1999, Richard Gar-
field defends 227,000 as the most likely estimate for those years, reviewing studies proposing higher estimates such as "Iraq—Under-Five Mortality" (1999), www.unicef.org/reseval/pdfs/irqu5est/pdf (500,000 excess
deaths, assuming that prewar trends would have resumed without the sanctions) and Mohamed Ali, John Blacker, and Gareth Jones, "Annual Mortality Rates and Excess Deaths of Children under Five in Iraq, 1991–98,"
Population Studies 57 (2003): 217–26 (estimating 400,000 excess deaths,
assuming prewar under-five mortality rates would have otherwise stayed
the same). In an analysis of records leaked by appalled UN staff of the deliberations of the committee controlling Iraqi imports, Joy Gordon found
that the United States had exercised its veto to block "most purchases of
materials necessary to generate electricity. . . . For example, Iraq was allowed to purchase a sewage-treatment plant but was blocked from buy-
ing the generator necessary to run it. . . . In September 2001, nearly one
third of water and sanitation contracts were on hold. . . . In early 2001,
the United States had placed holds on $280 million in medical supplies,
including vaccines to treat infant hepatitis, tetanus and diphtheria, as well
as incubators and cardiac equipment." See "Cool War," *Harper's Magazine*,
November 2002, 4, 2, 8.

    32. Rudyard Kipling, "The White Man's Burden: The United States and
the Philippine Islands," *McClure's Magazine* (1899).

    33. See BBC News, Newsnight interview, "General Jay Garner," newsvote
.bbc.co.uk, March 22, 2004.

    34. 86 percent said that Coalition forces should leave soon, either im-
mediately (41 percent) or after a permanent government was elected (45
percent). 55 percent said that immediate departure would make them
"feel more safe" (32 percent "less safe"). Coalition Provisional Authority,

"Public Opinion in Iraq" (June 15, 2004), wid.ap.org/documents/iraq/ cpa_files, slides 28, 35, 36, 37.

35. See, e.g., Sean Rayment, "Secret MoD poll: Iraqis Support Attacks on British Troops," *Daily Telegraph*, October 23, 2005; Oxford Research Institute, "National Survey of Iraq November 2005," www.oxfordresearch. com, 24f.; Program on International Policy Attitudes, University of Maryland, "What the Iraqi Public Wants" (from data collected January 2–5, 2006) and "The Iraq Public on the US Presence and the Future of Iraq" (September 1–4, 2006), www.worldpublicopinion.org; ABC, BBC, ARD, NHK, "Iraq Five Years Later," ABC.news.com/pollingunit, March 17, 2008, Question 23, with tabulations of responses from February 20, 2008; August 24, 2007; and March 5, 2007.

36. See, e.g., Giustozzi, *Koran, Kalashnikov and Laptop,* 167–71; Gilles Dorronsoro, *The Taliban's Winning Strategy in Afghanistan* (Washington, DC: Carnegie Endowment for International Peace, 2009), 18.

37. "Afghanization" (Washington, DC: Carnegie Endowment for International Peace, 2009), 2.

38. U.S. Senate Armed Services Committee, "Hearing to Receive Testimony on Afghanistan," December 2, 2009, 13, http://armed-services. senate.gov/Transcripts/2009/12%20December/09-65%20-2012-2-09.pdf.

39. Matthew Hoh, "Letter of Resignation," 2, http://www.washingtonpost .com/wp-srv/hp/ssi/spc/ResignationLetter.pdf?sid=ST2009102603447, attachment to Karen DeYoung, "U.S. Official Resigns over Afghan War," *Washington Post,* October 27, 2009, http://www.washingtonpost.com/ wp-dyn/content/article/2009/10/26/AR2009102603394.html.

40. In the ABC/BBC poll of January 2009, before Obama's additions to U.S. forces and in the midst of Taliban successes, many more supported a decrease (44 percent) than supported an increase (18 percent) of U.S. and NATO forces, and 51 percent supported withdrawal within four years. Like all Afghan polls, this was strongly biased toward the better off, the urban, and the better educated. For example, 6 percent of respondents were unemployed, in a country in which the government puts unemployment at 33 percent of the labor force; 37 percent were farmers or farm laborers, in contrast to the government's estimate of 56 percent employed in the agricultural sector; half of the respondents were literate in a country in which one-quarter of adults are literate. See ABC News/BBC/ARD Poll, "Support for U.S. Efforts Plummets amid Afghanistan's Ongoing Strife," February 9, 2009, www.cmi.no/pdf/?file=/afghanistan/doc/1083a1Afghanistan2009 .pdf, 24, 36, 38, 39; CPHD and UNDP, *Afghanistan Human Development Report 2007,* 23 (adult literacy rate of 23.5 percent); Giustozzi, *Koran, Kalashnikov and Laptop,* 36 (unemployment, agricultural sector).

41. The day after President Obama announced the Afghan surge, Secretary of Defense Gates explained that "failure in Afghanistan" ("a Taliban takeover of much, if not most of the country . . . Taliban-ruled areas once again sanctuary for al Qaeda") was unacceptable because of the "narrative" it would strengthen: "what makes the border area between Afghanistan and Pakistan uniquely different . . . is that this part represents the historic place where native and foreign Muslims defeated one superpower. . . . For them to be seen to defeat the sole remaining superpower in the same place would have severe consequences for the United States and for the world" (Senate Armed Services Committee, "Hearing on Afghanistan," 6f.)

42. See Adam Przeworski and James Raymond Vreeland, "The Effect of IMF Programs on Economic Growth," *Journal of Development Economics* 62 (2000), 297 (estimating a reduction in growth rate of 1.53 percent on average); Axel Dreher, "IMF and Economic Growth," *World Development* 34 (2006), 779 (estimating that the reduction would be 1.5 percent under full compliance).

INDEX